Lecture Notes
in Business Information Processing 144

Series Editors

Wil van der Aalst
  Eindhoven Technical University, The Netherlands
John Mylopoulos
  University of Trento, Italy
Michael Rosemann
  Queensland University of Technology, Brisbane, Qld, Australia
Michael J. Shaw
  University of Illinois, Urbana-Champaign, IL, USA
Clemens Szyperski
  Microsoft Research, Redmond, WA, USA

Marten van Sinderen   Paul Oude Luttighuis
Erwin Folmer   Steven Bosems (Eds.)

Enterprise Interoperability

5th International IFIP Working Conference, IWEI 2013
Enschede, The Netherlands, March 27-28, 2013
Proceedings

 Springer

Volume Editors

Marten van Sinderen
Steven Bosems
University of Twente, Enschede, The Netherlands
E-mail: {m.j.vansinderen, s.bosems}@utwente.nl

Paul Oude Luttighuis
Novay, Enschede, The Netherlands
E-mail: paul.oudeluttighuis@novay.nl

Erwin Folmer
University of Twente, Enschede, The Netherlands
E-mail: erwin.folmer@gmail.com

ISSN 1865-1348 e-ISSN 1865-1356
ISBN 978-3-642-36795-3 e-ISBN 978-3-642-36796-0
DOI 10.1007/978-3-642-36796-0
Springer Heidelberg Dordrecht London New York

Library of Congress Control Number: 2013932716

ACM Computing Classification (1998): J.1, H.3.5, H.4, D.2.12

© IFIP International Federation for Information Processing 2013
This work is subject to copyright. All rights are reserved, whether the whole or part of the material is concerned, specifically the rights of translation, reprinting, re-use of illustrations, recitation, broadcasting, reproduction on microfilms or in any other way, and storage in data banks. Duplication of this publication or parts thereof is permitted only under the provisions of the German Copyright Law of September 9, 1965, in ist current version, and permission for use must always be obtained from Springer. Violations are liable to prosecution under the German Copyright Law.
The use of general descriptive names, registered names, trademarks, etc. in this publication does not imply, even in the absence of a specific statement, that such names are exempt from the relevant protective laws and regulations and therefore free for general use.

Typesetting: Camera-ready by author, data conversion by Scientific Publishing Services, Chennai, India

Printed on acid-free paper

Springer is part of Springer Science+Business Media (www.springer.com)

Preface

Several developments are expected to change the nature and affect the operation of enterprises in the near future. These developments are not new, and their influence when considered in isolation may not be decisive, but combined they represent important challenges as well as opportunities. Globalization, as one of the most important drivers of modern times, continues to influence enterprises and makes the boundaries for enterprise operation increasingly disappear. Constant and rapid change in technological capabilities, consumer demands, and legal/regulatory constraints push enterprises to become more agile and adaptive. The ability to create and offer value-added services by anyone to anyone has blurred the distinction between the consumer role and producer role, and between the employee role and employer role. One conclusion to be drawn from these developments is that the success of an enterprise more and more depends on its ability to interoperate with other enterprises, of any size and in any place. Enterprises have to function in dynamic networks, with value being created in both directions, in order to stay competitive and achieve their business goals.

The design of information, services, and processes is of key importance for enterprises in an increasingly interoperation-demanding economy and society. Information that is exchanged needs to be correctly understood at the recipient end; processes that receive, process, and send information need to do this in a way that realizes the interoperation goals; and services need to properly represent such interoperation goals to customers as well as to remote processes. This poses important challenges, including achieving societal acceptance, embedding in real-world practices, overcoming differences between collaboration partners, exploiting opportunities, adapting to change, and providing open solutions on top of various technologies.

IWEI is the International IFIP Working Conference covering all aspects of enterprise interoperabilitywith the purpose of achieving flexible cross-organizational collaboration through integrated support at business and technical levels. It provides a forum for discussing ideas and results among both researchers and practitioners. Contributions to the following areas are highlighted: scientific foundations for specifying, analyzing, and validating interoperability solutions; architectural frameworks for addressing interoperability challenges from different viewpoints and at different levels of abstraction; maturity models to evaluate and rank interoperability solutions with respect to distinguished quality criteria; and practical solutions and tools that can be applied to interoperability problems to date.

This year's IWEI – IWEI 2013 – was held during March 27–28, 2013, in Enschede, The Netherlands, following previous events in Stockholm, Sweden (2011), Valencia, Spain (2009), Munich, Germany (2008), and Harbin, China (2012). The theme of IWEI 2013 was "Information, Services and Processes for the Interoperable Economy and Society," thus especially soliciting submissions and discussions related to the three previously mentioned interrelated areas for enterprise interoperability.

IWEI 2013 was organized by the IFIP Working Group 5.8 on Enterprise Interoperability in co-operation with INTEROP-VLab. The objective of IFIP WG5.8 is to advance and disseminate research and development results in the area of enterprise interoperability. IWEI provides an excellent platform for discussing the ideas that have emerged from IFIP WG5.8 meetings, and, reversely, to transfer issues identified at the conference to the IFIP community for further contemplation and investigation.

The proceedings of IWEI 2013 are contained in this volume. Out of 35 submissions, a total of 15 full papers were selected for oral presentation and publication. The selection was based on a thorough review process, in which each paper was reviewed by at least three experts in the field. The papers are representative of the current research activities in the area of enterprise interoperability. The papers cover a wide spectrum of enterprise interoperability issues, ranging from foundational theories, frameworks, architectures, methods and guidelines to applications and case studies.

The proceedings also include an invited paper and the abstracts of two keynotes. The invited paper by Lea Kutvonen, professor at the University of Helsinki, addresses the need of further maturing open service systems and inter-enterprise collaboration. The keynotes were given by Richard Mark Soley, chairman and chief executive officer of OMG, and Manfred Reichert, professor at the University of Ulm and author of the book *Enabling Flexibility in Process-Aware Information Systems*. Dr. Soley talked about the phenomenon of information explosion and the challenge it brings to enterprise interoperability. Prof. Reichert's keynote explored collaboration and interoperability support for agile and networked enterprises.

We would like to take this opportunity to express our gratitude to all those who contributed to the IWEI 2013 working conference. We thank the authors for submitting content, which resulted in valuable information exchange and stimulating discussions; we thank the reviewers for providing useful feedback to the submitted content, which undoubtedly helped the authors to improve their work; and we thank the attendants for expressing interest in the content and initiating relevant discussions. We are indebted to IFIP TC5 as well as INTEROP-VLab for recognizing the importance of enterprise interoperability as a research area with high economic impact, and acting accordingly with the establishment of WG5.8. Finally, we are grateful to the University of Twente and Novay for hosting the working conference.

January 2013

Marten van Sinderen
Paul OudeLuttighuis
Erwin Folmer
Steven Bosems

Organization

IWEI 2013was organized by IFIP Working Group 5.8 on Enterprise Interoperability, in cooperation with INTEROP VLab.

General Chairs

Paul Oude Luttighuis	Novay, The Netherlands
Erwin Folmer	University of Twente, The Netherlands

Program Chair

Marten van Sinderen	University of Twente, The Netherlands

IFIP Liaison

Guy Doumeingts	INTEROP-VLab/Université de Bordeaux, France

Local Arrangements Chair

Steven Bosems	University of Twente, The Netherlands

International Program Committee

Stephan Aier	University of St. Gallen, Switzerland
Markus Aleksy	ABB, Germany
João Paulo A. Almeida	Federal University of Espirito Santo, Brazil
Khalid Benali	LORIA – Nancy Université, France
Peter Bernus	GriffithUniversity, Australia
Arne J. Berre	SINTEF, Norway
Fred van Blommestein	University of Groningen, The Netherlands
Ricardo Chalmeta	University of Jaume I, Spain
Yannis Charalabidis	University of the Aegean, Greece
Vincent Chapurlat	EMA, France
David Chen	Université de Bordeaux 1, France
Antonio De Nicola	ENEA, Italy
Yves Ducq	Université de Bordeaux 1, France
Ip-Shing Fan	Cranfield University, UK
Luís Ferreira Pires	University of Twente, The Netherlands
Parisa Ghodous	University of Lyon, France
Ricardo Goncalves	New University of Lisbon, UNINOVA, Portugal
Claudia Guglielmina	TXT e-solutions, Italy

Axel Hahn	University of Oldenburg, Germany
Jenny Harding	Loughborough University, UK
Maria Iacob	University of Twente, The Netherlands
Kai Jacobs	RWTH Aachen University, Germany
Roland Jochem	University of Kassel, Germany
Paul Johannesson	KTH, Sweden
Pontus Johnson	KTH, Sweden
Leonid Kalinichenko	Russian Academy of Sciences, Russian Federation
Stephan Kassel	Westsächsische Hochschule Zwickau, Germany
Bernhard Katzy	University of Munich, Germany
Lea Kutvonen	University of Helsinki, Finland
Marc Lankhorst	Novay, The Netherlands
Peter Linington	University of Kent, UK
Jean-Pierre Lorr	Petals Link, France
Michiko Matsuda	Kanagawa Institute of Technology, Japan
Robert Meersman	Free University of Brussels, Belgium
Kai Mertins	Fraunhofer IPK, Germany
Andreas Opdahl	University of Bergen, Norway
Angel Ortiz	Polytechnic University of Valencia, Spain
Boris Otto	University of Sankt Gallen, Switzerland
Hervé Panetto	UHP Nancy I, France
Raquel Sanchis	Polytechnic University of Valencia, Spain
Ulrike Stefens	OFFIS, Germany
Raymond Slot	Hogeschool Utrecht, The Netherlands
Bruno Vallespir	Université de Bordeaux 1, France
Jack Verhoosel	TNO, The Netherlands
Harris Wu	Old Dominion University, USA
Xiaofei Xu	Harbin Institute of Technology, China
Milan Zdravkovic	University of Niš, Serbia
Hongwei Zhu	Old Dominion University, USA

Additional Reviewers

Stefan Bischoff	Petals Link, France
Markus Buschle	KTH, Sweden
Amira Ben Hamida	Petals Link, France
Thomas Knothe	Fraunhofer IPK, Germany
Julien Lesbegueries	Petals Link, France
Mario Lezoche	Research Centre for Automatic Control (CRAN), France
Eduardo de F.R. Loures	Pontifical Catholic University of Parana, Brazil
Thomas Morsellino	Université de Bordeaux, France
Sonja Pajkovska Goceva	Fraunhofer IPK, Germany
Johan Ullberg	KTH, Sweden

Sponsoring Organizations

IFIP TC5, www.ifip.org
INTEROP-VLab, www.interop-vlab.eu
OMG, www.omg.org
University of Twente, www.utwente.nl
Novay, www.novay.nl
TNO, www.tno.nl

Table of Contents

Keynotes

Modeling Enterprise Interoperability: Taming the Information Explosion 1
  Richard Mark Soley

Collaboration and Interoperability Support for Agile Enterprises in a Networked World: Emerging Scenarios, Research Challenges, Enabling Technologies 4
  Manfred Reichert

Invited Paper

Enhancing the Maturity of Open Service Ecosystems and Inter-enterprise Collaborations 6
  Lea Kutvonen

Enterprise Service Interoperability

An Interoperability Points Based Interoperability Approach for SaaS Applications 22
  Yanyan Han, Lei Wu, Shijun Liu, and Xiangxu Meng

Similarity Evaluation Based on Intuitionistic Fuzzy Set for Service Cluster Selection as Cloud Service Candidate 36
  Jorick Lartigau, Xiaofei Xu, Lanshun Nie, and Dechen Zhan

Enterprise Interoperability in Sectors

Achieving Flexible Process Interoperability in the Homecare Domain through Aspect-Oriented Service Composition 50
  Duc Viet Bui, Maria Eugenia Iacob, Marten van Sinderen, and Alireza Zarghami

On the Extended Clinical Workflows for Personalized Healthcare 65
  Milan Zdravković and Miroslav Trajanović

Cross-Organizational Business Processes Modeling Using Design-by-Contract Approach 77
  Malik Khalfallah, Nicolas Figay, Parisa Ghodous, and Catarina Ferreira Da Silva

Interoperability Methodology

Fit for Purpose: Toward an Engineering Basis for Data Exchange
Standards 91
   Arnon Rosenthal, Len Seligman, M. David Allen, and
   Adriane Chapman

P^{2}AMF: Predictive, Probabilistic Architecture Modeling Framework.... 104
   Pontus Johnson, Johan Ullberg, Markus Buschle, Ulrik Franke and
   Khurram Shahzad

Business Model Risk Analysis: Predicting the Probability of Business
Network Profitability 118
   Pontus Johnson, Maria Eugenia Iacob, Margus Välja,
   Marten van Sinderen, Christer Magnusson, and Tobias Ladhe

Interoperability for Specific Application Types

Linked Services for Enabling Interoperability in the Sensing
Enterprise 131
   Matthias Thoma, Alexandru-Florian Antonescu,
   Theano Mintsi, and Torsten Braun

Business Rules Management Solutions: Added Value by Effective
Means of Business Interoperability 145
   Martijn Zoet and Johan Versendaal

Behavioural Evaluation of Reputation-Based Trust Systems 158
   Sini Ruohomaa and Lea Kutvonen

Strategic and Tactic Aspects of Enterprise Interoperability

Mass Customization Oriented and Cost-Effective Service Network 172
   Zhongjie Wang, Xiaofei Xu, and Xianzhi Wang

Toward a Methodology to Control Interoperability Improvement
Projects Execution 186
   Abderrahim Taoudi, Bouchaib Bounabat, and Badr Elmir

Ontology-Based Interoperability

A Panorama of the Semantic EAI Initiatives and the Adoption of
Ontologies by these Initiatives 198
   Julio Cesar Nardi, Ricardo de Almeida Falbo, and
   João Paulo A. Almeida

Using Metamodels and Ontologies for Enterprise Model
Reconciliation 212
   Sabina El Haoum and Axel Hahn

Author Index 225

Modeling Enterprise Interoperability: Taming the Information Explosion

Richard Mark Soley

Object Management Group, Inc.
109 Highland Avenue, Needham, MA 02494, U.S.A.
soley@omg.org

Abstract. The problems of enterprise interoperability, portability, maintenance and integration are not exactly new. From the first time code was stored in memory, the problems of legacy integration with new users and new uses of computing systems began. The explosion of computing vendors and tools hasn't exactly made the problem any easier. In fact, it's the explosion of information in general that is causing the problem. We expect information at our fingertips, but somehow we expect that to come about magically, despite different developers, different development styles, different coding languages, operating systems, instruction set architectures -- and a general lack of planning (or indeed, reading of the literature). The most important problem is the enormous explosion of information available in the world, and the increasing demands for globalized, mobile, agile, connected business processes across newly digital value chains. The resulting complexity makes integration even harder than it was before -- and it was near impossible before. There is some hope, however. That hope is formal modeling, with associated metrics and continuous improvement of processes based on customer and supplier feedback. That is much easier to achieve, however, when those business models are "live" -- that is, rather than simply documenting the business process, they in fact are the business process. This requires not only formal models, but formal models with well-defined semantics. The combination of Business Process Modeling (BPM) with Model Driven Architecture (MDA) promises just that. This keynote will discuss the driving factors for BPM and MDA, and the standards that support the approach.

Keywords: Enterprise Interoperability, information explosion, Business Process Modeling, Model Driven Architecture.

1 Brief Biography

Richard Mark Soley, Ph.D is Chairman and CEO of the Object Management Group, Inc. (OMG). Dr. Soley was instrumental in the founding of OMG in 1989 (as the founding Chief Technology Officer), and since 1997 has led the organization as Chief Executive Officer.

As CEO, Dr. Soley is responsible for the vision and direction of the world's largest consortium of its type. After joining the nascent organization in 1989, Dr. Soley led the development of OMG's world-leading standardization process and the original

CORBA® specification. In 1996, he led the effort to move into vertical market standards (starting with healthcare, finance, telecommunications and manufacturing) and modeling, leading first to the Unified Modeling Language™ (UML®) and later the Model Driven Architecture® (MDA®). He also led the effort to establish the SOA Consortium in January 2007, leading to the launch of the Business Ecology Initiative (BEI) in 2009. The Initiative focused on the management imperative to make business more responsive, effective, sustainable and secure in a complex, networked world, through practice areas including Business Design, Business Process Excellence, Intelligent Business, Sustainable Business and Secure Business. In addition, Dr. Soley is the Executive Director of the Cloud Standards Customer Council, helping end-users transition to cloud computing and direct requirements and priorities for cloud standards throughout the industry. He was also directly involved in the creation of both the Eclipse Foundation and Open Health Tools.

Since 1989, OMG has become one of the world leaders in the creation of international software industry standardization, building worldwide communities to deliver software standards that have changed the face of the software development field. Hundreds of member companies (approximately half software vendors and half software users, with government agencies & research institutions as well), volunteering thousands of product management and software development professionals, are currently developing some hundred software standards in fields as diverse as business processing modeling languages & methodologies, systems modeling languages, cloud computing, software modernization & real-time & embedded systems, but also vertically-oriented standards in financial services, insurance, healthcare, manufacturing, life sciences, military command & control, military & civil communications, civil government management and new areas like smart energy grids and systems safety assurance for consumer devices from automobiles to consumer electronics.

In more than two decades at OMG, Dr. Soley has led the development of a leadership community on the OMG Board of Directors that has included high-level executives from IT vendors including IBM, Hewlett Packard, Oracle and Microsoft but also key vertical-market leaders like THALES, Citigroup, HSBC, Lockheed Martin, Northrop Grumman, John Deere & Company and many others, including many small and medium-sized firms as well. Through relationships around the world, Dr. Soley has become quite well known in the speaking circuit, giving hundreds of speeches in support of OMG's best-practices & technology programs in North & South America, all over Asia, Europe, Africa and the Middle East, on issues relevant to standards, the adoption of new technology and creating successful companies. Dr. Soley also serves on numerous industrial, technical and academic conference program committees all over the world. Before helping to found OMG, Dr. Soley was a successful entrepreneur, participating in and leading startups in the computer software and hardware arena. Start-up companies included A.I. Architects (the first leader in acceleration hardware for personal computers, and originator of the DOS extender), Symbolics (the most successful start-up in artificial intelligence hardware & software), PictureTel (the early leader in video telephony, now part of Polycom) and many others. Dr. Soley continues this early entrepreneurial focus with an active participation in venture investment & advising, with companies including United

Villages (the leader in rural delivery of fast-moving consumer goods in India, with a recent partnership with Oxigen), rollApp (a Ukrainian/US leader in rapid application virtualization for cloud delivery), Polymita (a Spanish company which was focused on being the world leader in business process automation, recently sold to Red Hat), Strategic Security Air (delivering lightweight, long-endurance, low-cost surveillance aircraft for civil and light military usage), ProcessUnity (a world leader in business process modeling for regulatory compliance and other innovative risk solutions), SpaceCurve (the leader in real-time geospatial-temporal databases for location services), ClinicalBox (the leader in automated surgical coordination), and so forth.

A native of Baltimore, Maryland, U.S.A., Dr. Soley's academic background includes the SB, SM and PhD degrees in Computer Science & Engineering from MIT, with undergraduate minor in Spanish and graduate concentration in business (with coursework from MIT's Sloan School and Harvard Law School). Dr. Soley has continued his academic & research relationships worldwide with associations as an advisor, Visiting Professor or Adjunct Professor at the Curtin University in Perth, Australia, Colorado State University, Wuhan University in the People's Republic of China, Bentley College near Boston, the Software Engineering Methods and Tools (SEMAT) international project, Fraunhofer Institut für Software- und Systemtechnik in Berlin, Goethe Universität Frankfurt am Main and others. Dr. Soley is a Life Member of the national engineering honor fraternity Tau Beta Pi; a Member of the national electical engineering honor fraternity Eta Kappa Nu, and a Life Member of the scientific research honor fraternity Sigma Xi, as well as a member of AAAI, ACM and IEEE; he is also a Founding Member of the Boston CTO Club, and a Member of the New York City CTO Club.

Collaboration and Interoperability Support for Agile Enterprises in a Networked World: Emerging Scenarios, Research Challenges, Enabling Technologies

Manfred Reichert

University of Ulm, 89069 Ulm, Germany
manfred.reichert@uni-ulm.de

Abstract. The economic success of enterprises increasingly depends on their ability to react to changes in their environment in a quick and flexible way. Examples of such environmental changes include regulatory adaptations (e.g. introduction of Sarbanes-Oxley or Basel II), market evolution, altered customer behavior, process improvement, and strategy shifts. Companies have therefore identified business agility as a competitive advantage required for coping with business trends like increasing product and service variability, faster time-to-market, and increasing division of labor along the supply chain. In particular, the agile enterprise should be able to quickly set up new business processes as well as to adapt existing ones. However, networked enterprises must not accomplish such business process changes independent from the interactions they have with their partners and customers; e.g., business contracts and business compliance rules must be ensured after business process changes as well. This keynote will discuss major research challenges to be tackled in this context. Further, it will present advanced methods, concepts and technologies enabling collaboration and interoperability support for the agile enterprise in a networked world.

Keywords: networked enterprises, collaboration, interoperability, agility, business process change, business process compliance.

1 Brief Biography

Manfred Reichert is professor at the University of Ulm, Germany and co-director of the Institute of Databases and Information Systems.

His major research interests are next generation process management technology (e.g., adaptive processes, process variability, data-driven and object-centric processes, mobile processes), service-oriented computing (e.g., service interoperability, service evolution), and advanced applications for flexible information systems (e.g., e-health and automotive engineering).

Together with Peter Dadam he pioneered the work on the ADEPT process management technology and he is co-founder of the AristaFlow GmbH. Manfred has been participating in numerous research projects in the BPM area and contributed more than 200 scientific papers on BPM-related topics. His book entitled "Enabling

Flexibility in Process-Aware Information Systems" was published by Springer in September 2012. Manfred has been PC Co-Chair of the BPM'08, CoopIS'11, and EDOC'13 conferences and General Chair of the BPM'09 conference.

References

1. Reichert, M., Weber, B.: Enabling Flexibility in Process-Aware Information Systems: Challenges, Methods, Technologies. Springer (2012)
2. Reichert, M., Rinderle-Ma, S., Dadam, P.: Flexibility in Process-Aware Information Systems. In: Jensen, K., van der Aalst, W.M.P. (eds.) ToPNoC II. LNCS, vol. 5460, pp. 115–135. Springer, Heidelberg (2009)
3. Dadam, P., Reichert, M.: The ADEPT Project: A Decade of Research and Development for Robust and Flexible Process Support - Challenges and Achievements. Computer Science – R & D 23(2), 81–97
4. Knuplesch, D., Reichert, M., Mangler, J., Rinderle-Ma, S., Fdhila, W.: Towards Compliance of Cross-Organizational Processes and Their Changes. In: La Rosa, M., Soffer, P. (eds.) BPM Workshops 2012. LNBIP, vol. 132, pp. 649–661. Springer, Heidelberg (2013)
5. Fdhila, W., Rinderle-Ma, S., Reichert, M.: Change Propagation in Collaborative Processes Scenarios. In: Proc. 8th IEEE Int'l Conf. on Collaborative Computing (CollaborateCom 2012), Pittsburgh, USA (2012)
6. Knuplesch, D., Pryss, R., Reichert, M.: Data-Aware Interaction in Distributed and Collaborative Workflows: Modeling, Semantics, Correctness. In: Proc. 8th IEEE Int'l Conf. on Collaborative Comp (CollaborateCom 2012), Pittsburgh, USA (2012)
7. Rinderle, S., Wombacher, A., Reichert, M.: Evolution of Process Choreographies in DYCHOR. In: Meersman, R., Tari, Z. (eds.) OTM 2006. LNCS, vol. 4275, pp. 273–290. Springer, Heidelberg (2006)
8. Rinderle, S., Wombacher, A., Reichert, M.: On the Controlled Evolution of Process Choreographies. In: Proc. 22nd Int'l Conf. on Data Engineering (ICDE 2006), Atlanta, USA, p. 124. IEEE Comp Society Press (2006)
9. Ly, L.T., Knuplesch, D., Rinderle-Ma, S., Göser, K., Pfeifer, H., Reichert, M., Dadam, P.: SeaFlows Toolset – Compliance Verification Made Easy for Process-Aware Information Systems. In: Soffer, P., Proper, E. (eds.) CAiSE Forum 2010. LNBIP, vol. 72, pp. 76–91. Springer, Heidelberg (2011)
10. Mutschler, B., Reichert, M., Bumiller, J.: Unleashing the Effectiveness of Process-oriented Information Systems: Problem Analysis, Critical Success Factors and Implications. IEEE Trans. on Systems, Man, and Cybernetics (Part C) 38(3), 280–291 (2008)

Enhancing the Maturity of Open Service Ecosystems and Inter-enterprise Collaborations

Lea Kutvonen

University of Helsinki, Department of Computer Science
lea.kutvonen@cs.helsinki.fi

Abstract. The present business era is labeled by collaborations across enterprise boundaries and by utilisation of service-based computing. Pervasive computing utilities are created to match the basic business activities, such as contracting and breach management, adaptation of innovative business models, and collaboration management. Categories of computer assisted breeding environments and automated service collaboration management ecosystems have been developed to address these needs. However, a maturity framework is required for comparing solutions and indicating gaps in systems development and standardisation, and for adoption of a sufficient set of multidisciplinary research and evaluation methodologies. This paper first introduces steps towards a maturity model, focusing on features that contribute to the correctness of collaborations and scalability of the ecosystem. Second, it introduces the choices made in Pilarcos ecosystem. Finally, it discusses the need for standards and maturity models on this domain, and raises issues on the research methodologies required.

1 Introduction

The present business era is labeled by collaborations across enterprise boundaries and by utilisation of service-based computing. Computing utilities are created to match the basic business activities, such as contracting and breach management, adaptation of innovative business models, and collaboration management.

These needs are addressed by trends of i) systems where breeding of collaborations across enterprise boundaries is facilitated by glocal applications (glocal= global + local aspects meet to make a pervasive environment) and ii) systems where business services are automatically composed using collateral business processes (choreographies) across organisational boundaries.

Roughly, we can consider the first one to be focused on enterprise interoperability. Enterprise interoperability solutions are likely to be run by human decision-makers, because the aim is to address unexpected, new business opportunities that require very close planning and implementation phases to become profitable. The latter focuses on service interoperability, expecting enterprise and business concerns to be used as governance policies, rules and decision-making input. Service interoperability solutions are likely to be allowed to run automatically, addressing new, but expected business cases for which a sufficient amount of software modules are available for runtime composition in a self-administrative manner. Essentially, the technical computing and engineering solutions are very similar, but the expected users of these technical facilities differ; this caricature indicates how the themes of enterprise interoperability, service interoperability and service ecosystems complement each other.

A third pattern to observe is the emergence of ecosystems, such as i) software ecosystem by Amazon, Nokia or Apple, ii) eBusiness networks as in supply chains, and iii) social networking platforms, like Facebook or LinkedIn. Each of these bring in elements of discovering new partners for collaboration with explicit or implicit behaviour patterns, business models of explicitly agreed nature and roles of involved partners, and capability of easy evolution. However, each of them addresses only one side of the expected mature ecosystem concerns.

For a mature business service ecosystem we expect i) overcoming innovation boundaries [1]; ii) explicit contracting on business and technology level while preserving partner autonomy in the ecosystem and in collaborations [2]; iii) trust management system to support private decision-making while allowing introduction of new partners into the ecosystem [3]; iv) breach detection and management in an automated, business situation sensitive way (for which the present business transaction techniques are not suitable [4]).

In the CINCO group, we have developed an open business-service ecosystem [2,5,6,1,3] architecture and supporting ecosystem infrastructure services [7], and furthermore, focused on the essential viewpoints and lifecycles [1] that generate correctness criteria for collaborations [6]. This is to address the key problems in inter-enterprise computing today: i) ad-hoc engineering and integration, either directly or through engineering tools that do not have sufficient scientific basis; ii) insecure and misplaced decision-making, e.g., engineers implementing fixed strategies affecting business model or user experience, and iii) missing control and governance of the composed collaboration.

This paper first introduces a comparison framework as a step towards a maturity model, focusing on features that contribute to the correctness of collaborations and to the scalability of the ecosystem. Second, we outline the choices made in the Pilarcos ecosystem infrastructure as an example. Thirdly, we discuss the need for standards and maturity models on this domain, and finally raise issues on the research methodologies required.

2 Ecosystem Comparison Framework

For the purposes of comparison we assume the concepts of (business) service, business process, collaboration, and interoperability to be present and that there is vocabulary for declaring their more detailed properties. In addition to these, as ecosystems have different focal areas, we split the comparison framework into three sections: i) innovation and engineering, ii) collaboration lifecycle and iii) ecosystem infrastructure concepts and service. Further, we must note how the ecosystem key concepts are connected across these viewpoints in each case.

Interoperability. We define interoperability, i.e. the capability to collaborate, as the effective capability to mutually communicate information in order to exchange proposals, requests, results, and commitments. Technical interoperability is concerned with connectivity between the computational services, allowing messages to be transported from one application to another. Semantic interoperability means that the message content becomes understood in the same way by senders and receivers, both in terms of information representation and messaging sequences. Pragmatic interoperability captures the willingness of partners to perform the collaborative actions. This willingness to participate refers both to the capability of performing a requested action, and to policies dictating whether it is preferable for the enterprise to allow that action to take place.

This differs from the standard definitions deliberately by bringing in terms that are important in business terms (like contracts and negotiations), and enforcing concepts from speech act theories to be utilised, due to their suitability for expressing business needs and their technical support.

Due to parallel work, the definition also deviates from the term conceptual interoperability that is split into integrability (technical and syntactic), interoperability (semantic, pragmatic) and composability (dynamic, conceptual). Our definition captures the same levels but places composability as a goal of pragmatic interoperability.

The comparison framework will include the questions about the support for conceptual, dynamic, pragmatic and semantic interoperability.

Innovation and Engineering. The traditional software engineering process produces monolithic artefacts that are built with the concepts supported by the engineering tools and the computing platform on which the artefacts are to be run. The process is based on knowledge on computer science and software engineering science, but omits key concepts from other scientific areas; there is little support for solving business issues, for addressing user experience alternatives, and crafting software module composability and management of compositions. Often, the hardest problems are on areas where the engineering phase is not the right time for solving the problem, but should allow operational time decision-making, because the decisions can depend on the presence of suitable partners, control of nonfunctional properties such as trust and privacy or transactionality, or regulations forced on the ecosystem to govern all its collaborations. Furthermore, the ecosystem evolution should not be considered only as a software versioning problem, just because the traditional engineering processes are not capable of handling other aspects.

Service-oriented software engineering (SOSE) [8] enhances the perspective by enriching the engineering process with lessons learned in service sciences in terms of requirements, and SOC platforms [9] and development tools in terms of development environment needs. The environment needs to be aware of the memberships, regulation systems and pervasive infrastructure services for runtime compositions. These facilities allow services supported by software artefacts to be composed together to a manageable entity that is aware of its business context and its users' situational preferences.

Special business-level challenges to address during the shared innovation and design phases include i) development of collaborative business models for independent partners; ii) partitioning of cost, risk and gained assets in the collaboration contract pattern; iii) trust between partners on being impartial at the design phase; and iv) management of collaborations being made possible by different collaboration and ecosystem members as their roles in the ecosystem requires.

The innovation phase creates declarations of business processes and collaboration models for the collaboration lifecycle support processes to utilise. Thus this is one of the collaboration correctness criteria sources, which furthermore is preferably to be considered impartial of ecosystem member incentives.

Collaboration Lifecycle. The collaboration lifecycle includes traditional phases of i) establishment, ii) operation (or enactment) and control, and iii) dissolution, but also furthermore, iv) collection of experience information for the improvement of further ecosystem activities. Activities in these phases can be mapped to business terms like tenders, proposals, commitments, breaches, and opinions. The collaboration contract is an essential concept for making all the correctness criteria cumulated into the contract from the ecosystem, and collaboration partners. The classifying questions are captured in Table 1.

The essential differences in system architectures according to our surveys include splitting to i) enterprise interoperability or service interoperability systems;

Table 1. Classification questions for collaboration lifecycle

All phases
Is the process a human process with computing support, or automated with human interventions supported?
Is the contract involved a multiparty contract or client-server-based?
Do the processes always allow partners to make subjective decisions, or is there a centralised decision-making point? Is the decision-making logic binary or deontic?
Is the contract dynamic? Does it involve business or technology details or both?
Collaboration establishment
Nature of information involved: i) partners and their roles in the collaboration pattern;
Nature of processes involved: i) Decision-making on trust for the suggested partners or services; ii) interoperability checking; iii) agreement process: level of automation, distribution of the control, quality of the resulting agreement.
Enactment and control of a collaboration
Levels of interoperability considered;
Equality of partners in enactment or centralisation of orchestration control; support for subjective monitoring of processes and NFPs
Whether expectations on the communication platform are implicit, explicitly stated, or requirements by which an open binding can be constructed at operational time.
Collaboration dissolution
Can be triggered by any partner at completion of the task or notification of a breach?
Experience collection
Metrics for successes and failures; Generation of experience information for reputation systems; Feedback generation for BPR and service improvement

Table 2. Classification questions for infrastructure facilities

Collection of partner information
Process of collecting: i) How is the required information produced and published? Granularity of services? Notation suitable (conceptual coverage), extendable, efficient? ii) Does it cover processes, collaboration models, service behaviour /interfaces, NFPs? **Information collected**: i) How partners are identified? Trustworthy tracking of service offers for contractual needs? ii) Does service knowledge carry explicit requirements information about the runtime service bindings? **Information made available**: i) Suitability to predefined collaboration structures information available? Collaborations evolvable or fixed? ii) Kind of semantic interoperability support? Does the available information in the ecosystem level databases suffice for interoperability testing? iii) Matching of services to collaboration structure is supported by an ontology or type system? iv) Is there any reputation information associated? Are the services trustworthy, traceable, attributed on their quality? Is the partner/service repository impartial?
Partner discovery process
Directed for browsing or automated matching, discovery by demand? Client-server or multiparty search with aim to contracting? Quick temporal partner selection or forming strategic networks? Private agent or third party or distributed? Considers interoperability and NFPs?
Partner/service selection:
Level of automation? If automated, areas of metapolicies for decisions (in what kind of situations automated decisions are permitted)? Style of trust decisions taken? Business needs addressed? Provides for automated eContract negotiation? For contract enforcement? Considers performance and utility aspects?
Service selection
Do service offers carry interface syntax; behaviour description; service provider; location; type description availability; awareness of resources; awareness of trust; dynamic properties in offers? correctness of information, traceability of announcements? Security and trustworthiness of offers covered?
Enactment and monitoring:
Scope: external processes only or integrated internal processes? Enactment: active agents or WFMC engine (workflow management engine) or model interpreter or translated process description to implementation? Semantic data transformations explicit or implicit? Breach detection: immediate or delayed? NFP with business issues vs technical SLA? Who are the controllers?
Dissolution:
BPI metrics? Who provides reports and when? How is information utilised? Reputation information model and processes?

ii) dynamism of the collaboration contract and the availability of control interfaces at the enactment phase, iii) multiparty vs client-server constellations, and iv) methods for keeping the membership of the ecosystem in control.

Ecosystem Infrastructure Facilities. We take the ecosystem infrastructure as an unbiased, trusted party, and all ecosystem members have systemic trust into its services for each of the collaboration lifecycle phases. The questions investigating the variance within available services are shown in Table 2. In addition, the comparison of solutions should take into account how different threat scenarios have been addressed.

Conceptual Connectivity between Viewpoints. While creating ecosystem models, a small set of essential concepts appear in closely related forms in different viewpoints. For example, a collaboration model under design in the engineering viewpoint will reappear as a contract structure during the collaboration, and eventually will enforce structure for distributing gains and losses for the collaboration members at the dissolution.

For a mature ecosystem model, we require these related concepts in different viewpoints be bound together in the lifecycle models. Connectivity should be defined for main concepts, such as contract, business service, breach recovery processes, and NFP (nonfunctional property) frameworks, just to name a few. In a mature ecosystem, the connectivity is managed by metainformation governance, and can be evolved as needed at the ecosystem level.

These connections are mostly missed when projects focus on one viewpoint only, but the consequences are serious: Interoperability and correctness failures are often caused by ad hoc transitions from one phase to another.

3 Pilarcos Open Service Ecosystem Architecture

The Pilarcos open service ecosystem architecture intertwine engineering, governance and operational needs of collaborations and thus involves:

- enterprises providing and needing each others' business services, with their published business service portfolios [2,1];
- business-domain governing consortia, with their published business scenarios and business models [1];
- infrastructure service providers of individual functions such as service discovery and selection, contract negotiation and commitment to new collaborations, monitoring of contracted behaviour of partners, breach detection and recovery [7,2,10] and reputation flows from past collaborations [3];
- consortia and agencies that define legislative rules for acceptable contracts [6] and joint ontology about vocabulary to be used for contract negotiation, commitment and control [11,6]; and
- infrastructure knowledge-base providers that maintain the information underlying the ecosystem infrastructure functions; this role is essential in enforcing all conformance rules of all ecosystem activities [7,11,1].

3.1 Key Concepts and Functionality

Three key concepts in the Pilarcos open service ecosystems are those of inter-enterprise collaborations, eContract agents and ecosystem infrastructure. The Pilarcos architecture views *inter-enterprise collaboration* as a loosely-coupled, dynamic constellation of business services; it involves multiple partners through their software-based business services and their mutual interactions.

A *business service* is a software-supported service with a functionality suitable for a business need on the market and thus relevant for the networked business. In itself, each business service is an agent, in terms of being able to take initiative on some activity, being reactive to requests by other business services, and being governed by policies set by its owner. The relationship between business service and software supporting it resembles the relationship between an agent and web service [12]. Each business services provides business protocol interfaces for each other, but also utilise locally provided agents for connecting to peer services through channels with appropriately configured properties (e.g., security, transactionality, nonrepudiation).

The type of the service constellations is declared as *business network model* (BNM), expressed in terms of the roles and interactions within the collaboration, the involved member services, and policies governing the joint behaviour [2]. Intuitively, a BNM describes a business scenario.

The *eContract agent* governs the inter-enterprise collaboration and captures both business- and technical-level aspects of control, as well the large-granule state information to govern the dynamism of the collaboration. The eContract is structured according to a selected BNM.

An essential part of the ecosystem is its *ecosystem infrastructure*, a set of CaaS agents (Collaboration-as-a-Service) that provide shared utilities for enterprises to discover and select services available in the ecosystem, negotiate and establish collaborations, govern those collaborations through eContract agents, and utilise reputation information and collaboration type information.

From the business point of view, the Pilarcos ecosystem provides for the maturity of ecosystems by addressing at the same time four intertwining tiers [13], as illustrated in Figure 1. The main ecosystem activities involve service engineering (left and bottom), ecosystem and collaboration governance (left and right), operational-time collaboration support (right and bottom), and ecosystem governance (rules within infrastructure in the bottom), as discussed below.

The left side of Figure 1 depicts processes related to engineering steps at each involved enterprise or consortia. Here, metainformation is brought to the system by designers and analyzers: i) available services are published by service providers (enterprises including public and private sector providers), ii) the publicly known BNMs are created by teams of designers and published after acceptability analysis, and iii) regulations for conducting collaboration at administrative domains are fed in by enterprise and ecosystem administrators knowledgeable about local and international laws and business domain practices.

This body of knowledge accumulates into metainformation repositories within the globally accessible infrastructure layer. The repositories only accept models that fulfil the set consistency criteria, thus providing a point of control. All created collaborations inherit suitable correctness criteria to be monitored at the operation time. This *modeling tier* is where service and collaboration innovation take place, utilising the skills of designers and the feedback gathered

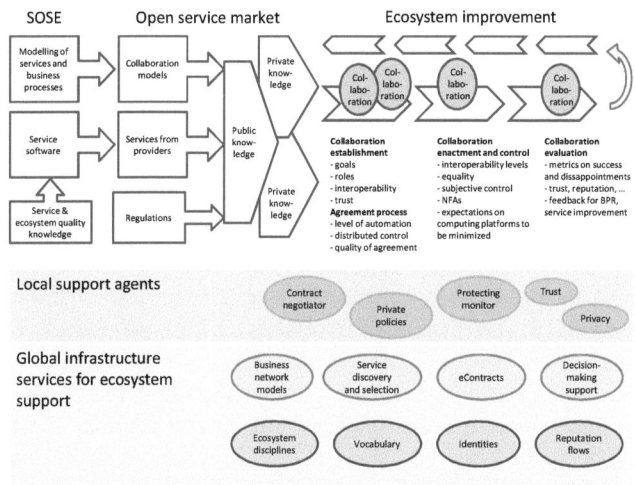

Fig. 1. An overview of the Pilarcos open service ecosystem

from collaborations already operational. The methodologies to be used here apply service-oriented software engineering (SOSE) and model driven engineering (MDE) methods and tools.

The modeling tier and ecosystem repositories together give a basis for evolution of the ecosystem with service and collaboration models [11,1].

The right side of Figure 1 depicts the *collaboration tier* supporting the lifecycles of collaborations from the establishment to the termination phase. The collaboration lifecycle management is automated in all routine cases, and triggers human intervention in new or undefined situations. The automated management decisions can be commitments to collaborations or refusals to participate. In practice, the collaboration establishment is initiated by one of the partners suggesting the use of commonly known BNM that can be picked from the infrastructure repositories. Further, the infrastructure services help in discovery and selection of suitable partner services for the collaboration and running a negotiation protocol between the selected partners. Within the negotiation step, the local, private support agents of each partner consider especially the suitability of the collaboration for the enterprises' strategies and sufficiency of trust in partners. In the enactment and control phase, the local support agents provide protective monitoring and the required contract-related communication.

In this way, the CaaS tier services become usable by enterprises or other organisations for making tenders, proposals, commitments, and to react to breaches, as well as initiating, negotiating, committing, and dissolving collaborations, and even, helping the subjective control of new kind of business transactions. The individual eContract is the key element for each collaboration as it governs that multiparty, dynamic agreement with details from business level to communication technology. The eContract also provides interfaces for each partner to notify their observations of the collaboration behaviour, deviations of the expected behaviour, their refusals to accept the recent progression of the collaboration, or their approvals on completing business transactions. The Pilarcos architecture emphasises on subjective and private decision-making support for partners on all collaboration phases.

The arrows leading to the left at the right side of Figure 1 depicts the experience information gathered from all the collaborations in the ecosystem and providing feedback information for re-engineering and future decision-making processes in the ecosystem.

The bottom part of Figure 1 represents the global, federated infrastructure services that participates the governance, engineering and collaboration management processes, i.e. the *CaaS tier (Collaboration-as-a-service)*. The CaaS tier includes ecosystem-widely available infrastructure services, such as service discovery and selection [2], eContracting [2], breach management [2], and reputation-based trust management system [3] that allows the scaling of the ecosystem membership. The scaling can be achieved only by creating incentives for parters to behave according to their contracts, and especially according to expectations at the ecosystem maintenance processes like reputation exchange and helps enterprises in adjusting to rapidly changing business situations and participation in natural competition between collaborations and ecosystem members.

The reputation-based trust management concept facilitates the scalability of the ecosystem. Here we can rely on social ecosystem studies [14]: The number of potential partners in the ecosystem is very limited if there are no established behaviour norms, and only slightly higher if misbehaviour is sanctioned. However, if also leaving misbehaviour unreported is considered as misbehaviour, an increasingly large ecosystem can be kept alive. The reputation production mechanism together with the negotiation step, where partners can reflect the collaboration suitability for their strategies and the potential risk predicted with reputation information, creates a cycle that has this necessary control function. It effectively emulates the social or legal system pressure of business domain. This functionality is much missing from other approaches.

Further, the *ecosystem tier* is the source of ecosystem level regulations, thus forming an explicit ecosystem engineering discipline. For each ecosystem this discipline has to be specialised individually.

3.2 Comparative Details

Within the above frame, we take a more detailed look at Pilarcos using the maturity framework aspects. Comparisons to other systems in e.g. [13].

Innovation and engineering are addressed by the SOSE processes [1] producing BNM and service types into the infrastructure repositories (service offer repository, service type repository, BNM repository). Service type definitions form a basic vocabulary for declaring BNMs and publishing service offers, and can be reused. The BNMs can be designed collaboratively between multiple impartial organisations, and be then verified and validated for their suitability for the market domain. The vocabularies created by service types and BNMs eventually support the checking of pragmatic interoperability at the operational phase, as the business services in a collaboration do not have a joint inheritance hierarchy that would enforce interoperability.

The decisions on the partner selection and trust are postponed to collaboration establishment time. We have separated the model design phases from the collaboration establishment phase, to enable automation at the commitment phase and to separate the innovation phase as the actor sets involved in these phases differ. The traditional virtual organisation breeding environment way (e.g., in ECOLEAD and CrossWork [15]) of first choosing the partners and base the business processes on their capabilities actually forces the design phase for each individual collaboration, and the actors be shared in these two phases.

For acquiring correctness of collaborations [6], the infrastructure repositories must control the publication of offers or models following the rules provided by the ecosystem management. The control must consider traceability of the declaration makers, acceptability of the models in terms of best practices on a business domain, regulatory rules, and securing the coherence of the repository contents, especially the asserted relationships between stored concepts.

For the **collaboration lifecycle management** the key agents are the the private agents representing the involved enterprises and the eContract agent that governs the collaboration itself. The local support agents subjectively represent the enterprise, and provide a local interface to the ecosystem infrastructure services for the local business services. The enterprise agents are needed for tasks of i) contract negotiation, ii) monitoring during collaboration operation, and iii) experience reporting when the collaboration terminates either having reached its purpose or terminating prematurely due to breaches.

A contract negotiator provides interfaces for application software or administrative interfaces to initiate collaboration establishment, or for responding to suggestions from other enterprises. The contract negotiator first utilises the populator for helping in the the initial service selection that is based on public information. As the populator provides suggestions for sets of interoperable partner services for the collaboration, the contract negotiator initiates the negotiation phase that involves private decision-making by all suggested partners. In the negotiation phase each suggested collaborating party can agree to join the collaboration, or refrain. The decisions are split to automatic rejections and approvals, and grey area cases that are forwarded for human decision-making with a kind of expert tool support [10,3]. The decision-making is governed by enterprise policies [10,3] related to i) strategic policies indicating what type of collaborations or which partners are of interest and worth investing the resources to collaborate with; ii) reputation-based trust that weights the anticipated risk and tolerated risk level [3]; and iii) privacy-preservation that may overrule otherwise acceptable collaborations due too high privacy costs involved.

Although trust and privacy are closely related, the decision-making processes on the issues are separate and parallel. Trust decisions weight expected benefits against anticipated losses in a specific business case; privacy decisions guard access to private information, metainformation and behaviour patterns. We define trust as the extent to which one party is willing to participate in a given action with a given partner in a given situation, considering the risks and incentives involved. Trust decisions are subjective evaluations made by the trustor, targeting a given trustee and a given action in terms of standard assets shared between organizations: monetary, reputation, control and satisfaction [3]. We define privacy as the right of subjects to determine themselves for whom, for what purpose, to what extent, and how information about them, or information held by them, is communicated to others [16]. Here, the subject can be a person, social group organisation or organisational group.

As the result of negotiation phase, eContract agent is created. It comprises of the collaboration metamodel thus providing a shared-language view on the collaboration structure, behaviour, policies and abstracted state. The eContract provides interfaces for the collaboration partners for renegotiation, epoch changes (where membership or responsibilities can be changed), progressing to defined milestones in the business processes, and declaring detected breaches. The logical eContract is physically replicated to the computing systems of each collaboration member. The private contract agents are responsible of keeping the local services in their governance in synchrony with the committed eContract.

The eContracts include policies as rules of expected behaviour patterns. For policy expressions we use deontic logic [17]. Deontic logic is not binary (denied/compulsory), but uses rules of prohibition, obligation and permission instead. This is necessary in an environment where there is no single policy maker or enforcer of the policies but the actors are independent of each other. Thus it is not possible for force a partner to refrain from an action, or to force that partner to take another action. However, it is possible to agree that it is a violation of a prohibition to take certain actions, and in addition, to agree on the consequences of violations. The detailed behaviour on functional or nonfunctional aspects of the partners cannot either be (practically) agreed on, but some optional behaviour patterns can be allowed without causing violation management. This area is where permissions clarify the behaviour: something is optional to take place, and there is a specification in existence about the followup behaviour.

In the enactment and control phase monitoring agents check the acceptability of the behaviour (messaging) [7]. The monitors receive rules from eContract and from their local enterprise policy repositories. The deontic-logic policy approach allows us to make clear distinction between violations of the contracts and acceptable behaviour according to that contract [18]. However, each partner in the collaboration uses subjective rules for decision-making on whether to join the collaboration, or on whether to report to the eContract some violation detected in the sequence of actions they get exposed to.

The private enterprise rules and eContract based rules can be contradictory. At the negotiation phase only those policies are checked that are explicated both in the eContract and in the enterprise policies. The enterprises may change their local policies during the collaboration and the arising contradictions can cause breaching business obligations, or failing quality of service agreements, such as availability, timeliness, and privacy-preservation, or as non-repudiation and immutability. At detected breach situations, the partner needs to decide (automatically or through human intervention) whether the breach is serious enough for terminating or leaving the collaboration. In case of an essential breach, the eContract is notified for triggering recovery steps. The breach recovery process is defined as part of the eContract, as there are different categories of theoretical recoverability capabilities.

At collaboration termination, successful or unsuccessful, experience reporting is required [3]. The local agent feeds reports to reputation flow agents that aggregate reputation information, arranged into several asset aspects including monetary, reputation, and control assets. The reputation information becomes available for future trust-decisions throughout the ecosystem. Therefore, a dynamic incentive mechanism is effectively created for ecosystem members to keep to their service offers and eContract commitments (including privacy rules), and especially to the reporting protocols [3,16].

The **ecosystem infrastructure** provided by Pilarcos differs from related approaches. Instead of a simple service offer repository, in Pilarcos the service discovery and selection is supported by a *populator agent*. The collaboration initiator selects a model from the public BNM repository and invokes the populator to find matching service offers for remaining roles [2]. The populator returns a contract proposal that ensures that the set of services it proposes do match to the roles for their service types, are not denied to work together by regulations, and are interoperable on technical, semantic and pragmatic levels. Furthermore, the populator checks that the additional requirements indicated in all the involved service offers do not inhibit collaboration. New contract proposals can be picked within selected resource limits.

In comparison with other service offer repositories (UDDI [19], ODP/OMG trader [20]) the fundamental difference is the populator service providing a multi-partner matching instead of a client-server setup, and also checks not only technical and semantic interoperability but also takes into account pragmatic interoperability aspects. The pragmatic aspects include views to BNMs, acceptable role combinations and environment contract information (i.e., requirements of the communication channel properties). The information base utilized by the populator agent is based on ODP trading service.

Further, the negotiation phase is only refining the populator suggestion in terms of policy agreements and choices at the communication channel structures needed for dynamically configuring open bindings between business services. An open binding provides a constellation where distribution transparencies, transactionality support elements and security levels are selectable, and where a management interfaces stays available for the users of the binding [21].

For the enactment phase, Pilarcos does not include a business process execution engine, but business services are active agents able to independently trigger business process actions on each other. As the capabilities of the technical software supporting the service may be wider, policies and monitoring is needed to restrict that behaviour to the contracted or enterprise-widely accepted limits. Naturally, contracted behaviour limits are monitored only in the scope of external processes. Monitoring is enhanced towards the business-level NFPs [5].

Breach detection is designed to allow immediate resolution to take place, although each collaboration contract may have differently designed breach recovery processes captured in the eContract.

Conceptual connectivity is one of the cornerstones of Pilarcos development. For consistency enforcement, the ecosystem repositories are governed by several ontologies or heaps of metamodel hierarchies [11,1]. The purpose is to connect innovation time and enactment time concepts together, and thus ensure that there is no conceptual misunderstandings caused by the change of modeling team tools to enactment time monitors. The conceptual connectivity facilities are based on a conceptual analysis that captures the key concepts and processes required by all ecosystems, and a methodology for creating tailored, evolvable ecosystems for a certain business domain [1].

4 Discussion

Our experiments on developing the Pilarcos ecosystems have created some opinions on the direction of future work, standards, and expectations on the requirements on the scientific base on the field.

The CINCO group mission is to develop a mature, dynamic ecosystem architecture for protecting organisations from interoperability mistakes, future needs of major collaboration platform change, and for supporting easy innovation in multiple, governed inter-enterprise environments. The Pilarcos contributions address the key problems in inter-enterprise computing: i) ad-hoc engineering and integration (can be within tools); ii) insecure and misplaced decision-making; and iii) missing control and governance of the systems composed.

We expect **mature open service ecosystems** to provide

- ecosystem infrastructure with management functionality involving embedded model verification and validation;
- private and public decision-making points that address the needs of business stakeholders and can be policy-driven but allow intervening;
- scalability through automation for breach detection and limiting of misbehaviour of the ecosystem members (incl. trust, privacy);
- systematic support and automation on collaboration lifecycle management involving autonomous parties;
- enhanced safety/correctness of collaboration lifecycles based on eContracts and underlying metamodel hierarchy; and
- a subjective, relaxed view to business transactions.

Open service ecosystems provide an environment in which enterprises (or organisations, even individuals) can easily pick a collaboration model, find potential partners beyond their normal strategic networks, and manage the lifecycle of the dynamic collaboration.

In order to adopt and trust ecosystem services, these enterprises need to preserve their autonomy and to gain understanding on how, and to which extent, the ecosystem services can ensure the correctness of collaborations. Correctness of collaborations can intuitively be connected to freedom of deadlocks and livelocks, fairness, consistency of the partners view on the state of affairs at each milestone of the collaboration, and conformance of the collaboration behaviour to the subjectively set policy requirements for the collaboration. Only some of these properties the enterprises themselves can enforce while the others must be produced by collaborative engineering and control functionalities at the ecosystem or at the collaboration level.

Furthermore, for the sustainability of the ecosystems it is essential that the evolution of the ecosystem is supported and the facilities provided by the ecosystem are scalable in terms of the ecosystem membership and service numbers and capacity of learning from experience. A future challenge is to appropriately interface organisational processes with the ecosystem agents.

Existing **standards** on the field are limited to singular business domains where tailored dictionaries and processes, or technological solutions are defined. In addition, trials of description languages for services and business processes have been made, leading much to the same expressive power. Inclusion of semantics notes is still not resolving the needs of composability, but a more systemic, and unfortunately, rather complex solution is required. This requires the courage to view all elements of the ecosystems at the same time. Some of the major cornerstones lie within the conceptual metamodeling hierarchy that is not prone to standardisation as such, but more likely to appear in forms of ecosystem engineering methodologies [1].

In order to choose appropriate candidate areas for standardisation, we must understand the evolution path of large systems. At present, this field has seen individual environments built, focused on one or two of the essential viewpoints. In addition, interoperability solutions based on tools and modeling have been tried; much of the present EU-level research is working with problems of the model and tool interoperability. This provides for collaboration management from a design perspective. The next major step is to push the capabilities generated by these tools into a common infrastructure in a generic form. This provides for ecosystem engineering and intertwining above-discussed perspectives. The new standards should not hinder this step, but the standards should be chosen from the areas supporting both the ecosystem engineering and the collaboration management tiers. It is likely that those standards may indicate different maturity levels for systems in different phases.

Good standard candidates include contract structuring, domain-specific collaboration modeling methods, innovation support, and an open binding infrastructure to mature ESBs.

The field is multidisciplinary in nature, which causes debates on the **science base or research and evaluation methodologies**. This interdisciplinary nature forces us to solutions constructed from elements from more than one scientific field. Considering our work with Pilarcos, we have applied several underlying computer science disciplines (such as extended state machines and protocol verification, even coloured Petri nets lately; patterns of reflective systems to control software artefacts with models; multi-agent technologies and type disciplines), complex adaptive systems theories, speech act theories with multi-agent systems, and basics of business, economy and psychology.

An essential goal in our work is that the ecosystem innovation and collaboration management environment should protect the engineers and especially the business-oriented users of the ecosystem facilities from most of these scientific considerations. Complexity should be hidden within the tools and methodologies, and the metainformation hierarchies built so that the complex rules are taken into consideration automatically, in the guidance of expert systems.

Considering the evaluation methods, the situation is equally complex. With Pilarcos, we started from constructive research, building prototypes and measuring their performance and balancing the cost with the achieved automation. We also had ATAM-like discussions with collaborating companies for validating question setting, focus of interest, and thresholds for adoption. On the side, we made threat analyses to understand security weaknesses of the introduced services. For the architecture as a whole we have done ODP-based modeling for major parts, giving concepts and processes a formalism beyond the functional verification. Recently some group members have taken the direction of design science. In addition, we have been pondering if there should be a basic benchmark defined for trust management and ecosystem governance [22].

Researchers can only make sure to catch for each project people with solid research skills in different, supporting disciplines and evaluation processes, and furthermore, ensure efficient cooperation despite the seemingly different goals. More importantly, researcher educators and funders should recall that overly multidisciplinary groups do not provide sufficient support for most researchers. Unfortunately, many of the current research financing instruments fail by requiring too much simultaneous multidisciplinary work that leads to progress by additional detail where structural innovation is needed.

Acknowledgements. This paper draws from work in the CINCO group (Collaborative and Interoperable Computing, http://cinco.cs.helsinki.fi/) at the University of Helsinki. Over the years, the group has been funded by various company-related projects through TEKES, and the Academy of Finland.

References

1. Ruokolainen, T.: A Model-Driven Approach to Service Ecosystem Engineering. PhD thesis, Department of Computer Science (accepted for defence, 2013)
2. Kutvonen, L., Metso, J., Ruohomaa, S.: From trading to eCommunity management: Responding to social and contractual challenges. Information Systems Frontiers 9(2-3), 181–194 (2007)
3. Ruohomaa, S.: The effect of reputation on trust decisions in inter-enterprise collaborations. PhD thesis, Univ. of Helsinki, Dept. of Computer Science (2012)
4. Kutvonen, L., Norta, A., Ruohomaa, S.: Inter-enterprise business transaction management in open service ecosystems. In: EDOC 2012 (September 2012)
5. Ruokolainen, T., Kutvonen, L.: 21: Framework for managing features of open service ecosystems. In: Handbook of Research on Non-Functional Properties for Service-Oriented Systems: Future Directions. IGI Global (December 2011)

6. Kutvonen, L.: ODP RM reflections on open service ecosystems. Computer Standards & Interfaces (February 2012) (in press)
7. Kutvonen, L., Ruokolainen, T., Metso, J.: Interoperability middleware for federated business services in web-Pilarcos. International Journal of Enterprise Information Systems, Special issue on Interoperability of Enterprise Systems and Applications 3(1), 1–21 (2007)
8. Stojanovic, Z., Dahanayake, A. (eds.): Service-Oriented Software System Engineering: Challenges and Practices. Idea Group Publishing (2005)
9. Papazoglou, M.: Web Services and SOA: Principles and Technology, 2nd edn. Prentice Hall (2012)
10. Kutvonen, L., Ruohomaa, S., Metso, J.: Automating Decisions for Inter-Enterprise Collaboration Management. In: Camarinha-Matos, L.M., Picard, W. (eds.) Pervasive Collaborative Networks. IFIP, vol. 283, pp. 127–134. Springer, Boston (2008)
11. Ruokolainen, T.: Modelling framework for interoperability management in collaborative computing environments. Licentiate thesis, University of Helsinki, Department of Computer Science (2009)
12. Payne, T.: Web services from an agent perspective. IEEE Intelligent Systems 23(2), 12–14 (2008)
13. Kutvonen, L.: Multi-tier agent architecture for open service ecosystems. In: Proceedings of First International Conference on Agreement Technologies, Dubrovnik, Croatia (October 2012)
14. Fehr, E., Fischbacher, U.: The nature of human altruism. Nature (October 2003)
15. Mehandjiev, N., Afsarmanesh, H., Camarinha-Matos, L., Kutvonen, L., Norta, A.: Dynamic Business Process Formation for Instant Virtual Enterprises. In: Comparable Approaches to IVE. Advanced Information and Knowledge Processing. Springer (2010)
16. Shen, Y., Miettinen, M., Moen, P., Kutvonen, L.: Privacy preservation approach in service ecosystems. In: EDOC 2011 Workshops, pp. 283–292 (2011)
17. von Wright, G.H.: Deontic logic. Mind 60(237), 1–15 (1951)
18. Ruohomaa, S., Kaur, P., Kutvonen, L.: From Subjective Reputation to Verifiable Experiences — Augmenting Peer-Control Mechanisms for Open Service Ecosystems. In: Dimitrakos, T., Moona, R., Patel, D., McKnight, D.H. (eds.) IFIPTM 2012. IFIP AICT, vol. 374, pp. 142–157. Springer, Heidelberg (2012)
19. Bellwood, T., Clément, L., Ehnebuske, D., Hately, A., Hondo, M., Husband, Y.L., Januszewski, K., Lee, S., McKee, B., Munter, J., von Riegen, C.: UDDI Version 3.0. UDDI Spec Technical Committee Specification (July 19, 2002)
20. ISO/IEC: IS13235-1: Information technology - Open distributed processing – Trading function: Specification (1998)
21. Fitzpatrick, T., Blair, G.S., Coulson, G., Davies, N., Robin, P.: Supporting adaptive multimedia applications through open bindings. In: Configurable Distributed Systems, pp. 128–135 (1998)
22. Ruohomaa, S., Kutvonen, L.: Behavioural Evaluation of Reputation-Based Trust Systems. In: van Sinderen, M., Luttighuis, P.O., Folmer, E., Bosems, S. (eds.) IWEI 2013. LNBIP, vol. 144, pp. 158–171. Springer, Heidelberg (2013)

An Interoperability Points Based Interoperability Approach for SaaS Applications

Yanyan Han, Lei Wu, Shijun Liu, and Xiangxu Meng

School of Computer Science and Technology, Shandong University
250101, Jinan, P.R. China
sduhyy@foxmail.com, {i_lily,lsj,mxx}@sdu.edu.cn

Abstract. SaaS applications have been widely adopted especially by small and medium enterprises. At the same time, the features "multi-tenancy" and "loosely coupled" bring new challenges to enterprises interoperability. On the basis of the layered interoperability model, the paper presents an approach based on interoperability points to implement interoperation between SaaS applications in the service layer. After carrying out the interoperability point matching algorithm, the intermediary Enterprise Service Bus (ESB) performs dynamic selection of interoperability points dictated by Quality of Service (QoS) attributes. In the premise of a comprehensive consideration of the functional and non-functional preferences and constraints, dynamic interoperation between SaaS applications is realized. Finally, this paper shows a case study of applying the interoperability approach.

Keywords: enterprise interoperability, SaaS, interoperability point.

1 Introduction

In the current industrial and economic context, enterprises should be capable of seamlessly interoperating with other enterprises across organizational boundaries to gain more benefits. Enterprise Interoperability (EI) has therefore become an important area of research to ensure the competitiveness and growth of enterprises [1].

At the same time, SaaS (Software as a Service) [2] has been widely accepted as a popular way to carry out the software service delivery. SaaS applications have been adopted by more and more business partners, especially by small and medium enterprises (SMEs). Software delivered in a SaaS model is no longer running exclusively for one customer at a customer's premise but supports multi-tenants over the Internet, which is called "multi-tenancy". Enterprises once accomplish their business through the interaction between traditional on-premise software must face with the interoperability issues between SaaS applications hosting anywhere. The feature of "loosely coupled" means that interoperability bridge between two SaaS applications must be services with standard interfaces. The above two features are exactly two main challenges of interoperability between SaaS applications [3].

In this paper, we focus especially on the new framework and approach to implement interoperation between SaaS applications in the service layer. In our proposed framework, a SaaS application which wants to interoperate with other SaaS applications should expose a standardized web service interface as an interoperability point which acts as a source interoperability point. After searching among other interoperability points according to the basic attribute constraints analyzed from the interoperation request, we can gain several related interoperability points. On a basis of an interoperability point matching strategy, we put forward an interoperability point matching algorithm. The algorithm takes the operation interfaces of the related interoperability points as input, and produces some target interoperability points sorted by matching degree. The intermediary ESB performs dynamic selection of these target interoperability points dictated by QoS attributes and gains the optimum interoperability point to interoperate with. The dynamic interoperation between SaaS applications is realized finally.

The following parts of the paper are organized as follows: Section 2 introduces the previous work on the layered interoperability model as well as the research actualities of enterprise interoperability. In section 3, we present an overview of the interoperability framework in the service layer and the main components, which is followed by section 4 that describes the process of interoperability point discovery. Section 5 discusses the implement of dynamic interoperation based on ESB. Section 6 presents a case study. Finally, conclusions and future work directions are shown in the last section.

2 Related Work

Researchers have presented many initiatives which are concerned with the elaboration of an enterprise interoperability framework. Kassel [4] presents some foundations for introducing a decision support model into a model-driven interoperability architecture for services. Arafa et al. [5] set out a framework for a high-level approach to software component integration. For another work, Yang et al. [6] provide a novel service and data management platform called DSP (Data Service Portal) that facilitates the integration of applications by sharing their information in a loosely coupled manner. Other significant pieces of work such as the LISI approach [7], the IDEAS interoperability framework [8] and the European Interoperability Framework (EIF) [9] aim at different concerns.

In previous work, we have designed an approach to develop SaaS applications and implemented a service based collaboration supporting platform (New Utility platform & Tools for Service, Nuts) [10] to deliver them to enterprises. With the ultimate aim to provide means to resolve all kinds of interoperability challenges that may hamper the effective usage of SaaS applications in supporting enterprise collaborations, we have given the definition of the "layered interoperability model" [11].

For the interoperability of independent SaaS applications must be implemented from the UI layer to the data layer underneath. The enterprise interoperability framework is designed as a layered model with 5 layers including data layer, service layer, process layer, business layer and presentation layer.

A modified Widget model is used to implement interoperation in the presentation layer. Service layer interoperability refers to discover, composite different kinds of application functions or services for well collaborative work, which is the core interoperability of the five layers. The goal of interoperability in the process layer is to make various processes work together. Interoperability for the business layer is on the standpoint of organization and company, and it deals with the interoperation barriers causing by diverse business rules, policies, strategies, legislation and culture. Business layer interoperability is established by negotiation mechanism and monitoring facilities, which makes the use of a federated analogous interoperability form. Data synchronization toolkit and message engine are implemented to address the integration issues in data layer.

The interoperability in the same layers is interconnected by two or several interoperability points. The interoperability point is defined as an interface between two interoperability entities and has different forms in different interoperability layers. To implement interoperation between two SaaS applications, we should detect and define the interoperability point for different SaaS applications in different layers. Focusing on the interoperability approach for SaaS applications in the service layer, this paper outlines an interoperability framework and gives the formal definition of the interoperability point in the service layer.

3   The Interoperability Framework in the Service Layer

In the subsections below, we give a brief overview of the key components in the framework as shown in figure 1.

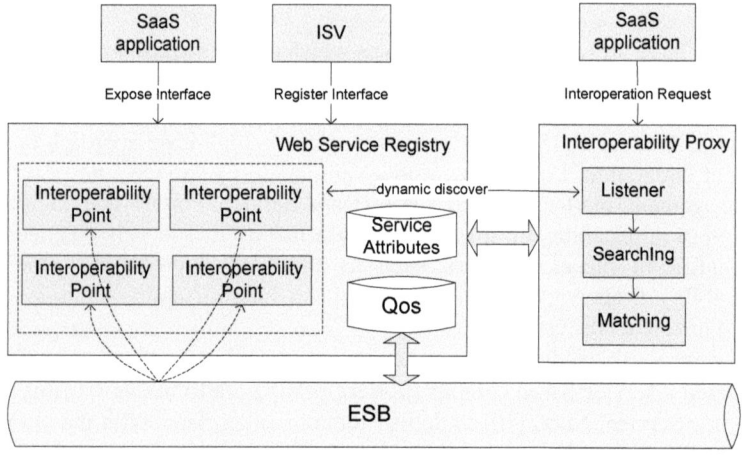

Fig. 1. The interoperability framework in the service layer

3.1   Web Service Registry

This module mainly includes two components:

1. Register Interface
Web Service (WS) technologies rapidly become the de facto standard to expose the functions of business application. The ISVs (independent software vendors) package

and publish the business functional modules as web services ahead of registering to the web service registry on the platform. The platform automatically extracts the service metadata information from the given WSDL, such as service name, operations, input/output parameters, etc. On this basis, the ISVs need to add some other service attributes to complete the registration, such as service description and service type.

Our Web Service formalization definition is given below:

Definition 1 (Web Service): A Web Service is a tuple WS = (SA, OPs), where: SA delegates the public attributes of service, including service name, service description and service type; OPs is a finite set of operations, then for every OP ∈ OPs, OP = (Oname,Ins,Os), Oname is the operation name; Ins represents the input parameters of OP; Os represents OP's output parameters, for each I ∈ Ins, O ∈ Os, I = (Ipname,Iptype), O = (Opname,Optype). Ipname and Opname are respectively the input parameter name and the output parameter name. Iptype and Optype are the input parameter type and output parameter type.

The web service registry realizes the service classification, the standards and specifications of the service description and enhanced service discoverability. Through the unified classified standard, services that registered in web service registry can be searched by name or other constraints.

2. Expose Interface

The interoperability point is the interface between two interoperability entities, namely two SaaS applications. In order to fully realize interoperation among SaaS applications, we should define interoperability points formally and analyze the procedure of searching, matching and selection of interoperability points.

The SaaS application can selectively expose the registered web service as an interoperability point. Only by the exposure operation will the SaaS application be possible to interoperate with other SaaS applications. The interoperability point not only inherits all the attributes of the web service, but also appends several new attributes, such as enterprise attributes, QoS attributes and URI. The enterprise attributes can be used as one of the conditions of interoperability point searching. By identifying the enterprise attributes, SaaS applications can interoperate with related enterprise's SaaS applications. Interoperation between SaaS applications should be based on mutual trust. In some cases, SaaS applications only hope to interoperate with their partner enterprises' SaaS applications. The QoS attributes can be updated by the monitor on the Nuts platform in real-time and can be used as the basis for the ESB-based dynamic selection among target interoperability points. The URI uniquely identifies the interoperability point which serves as the entry point for the interoperation call.

The formalization definition of Interoperability Point:

Definition 2 (Interoperability Point): A Interoperability Point is a tuple IP = (SA, OPs, QoS, EA, URI). It inherits the whole attributes of Web Service. QoS, EA and URI are three new attributes, where: QoS attributes including response time, reliability and usability; EA means the enterprise attributes; URI uniquely identifies an interoperability point and serves as the entry point for the interoperation call.

3.2 Interoperability Proxy

The interoperability proxy is responsible for interoperability point discovery. Similar with web service discovery, the interoperability point discovery in this paper refers to obtaining target interoperability points which both satisfy the users' basic attribute constraints and match with the source interoperability point according to the operation interface constraints.

The proxy briefly includes several following components:

1. Listener Component
1) Listening interoperation request
This component carries on the analysis of the interoperation request and obtains the basic attribute constraints of interoperability points, such as service name, service type, enterprise attributes and so on.

The formalization definition of Interoperation Request:

Definition 3 (Interoperation Request): IR = (SN, SD, ST, EA, w), where: SN: service name; SD: service description; ST: service type; EA: enterprise attributes; w: the threshold value of matching degree between interoperability points.

2) Listening fresh exposure of interoperability points
The framework is also able to support run-time interoperability point discovery. The listener component can dynamically discover new interoperability points exposed by SaaS applications. According to the current interoperation request, it determines whether the new interoperability points can be used as new target interoperability points.

2. Searching Component
In a large scale of interoperability points, how to discover the target interoperability points rapidly, accurately and efficiently is a tough problem. In order to reduce the time consuming of the interoperability point matching algorithm, we divide the process of interoperability point discovery into two phases, namely the searching phase and the matching phase. In the searching phase, the proxy obtains several related interoperability points after querying according to the basic attribute constraints in the interoperation request. An operation interface matching algorithm is applied to related interoperability points in the next step. This strategy can effectively filter out the irrelevant interoperability points, reduce the input range of the matching algorithm and improve the efficiency of the algorithm.

3. Matching Component
To enable interoperability points seamlessly interact with each other, the way how to design the interface matching algorithm is a key. We put forward a matching algorithm for the operation interfaces of interoperability points. On the basis of related interoperability points get from the last searching phase, we can get a set of target interoperability points ranked according to the matching degree. A number of different business processes will be formed after invoking the matching algorithm.

The same web service exposed by different SaaS applications may become different interoperability points which have the same web service attributes. For example, the interoperability points IP5, IP6 and IP7 in the figure 2 are exposed from the same web service WS2, but they belong to different SaaS applications.

At the same time, the same SaaS application may deploy multiple instances, so there may also exist interoperability points possessing the same web service attributes. For example, the interoperability points IP1, IP2 and IP3 in the figure 2 which belong to the different instances of the same SaaS application also possess the same web service attributes.

The target interoperability points which have the same web service attributes possess the same matching degree after matching with the source interoperability point, so the searching and matching process can be omitted. Meanwhile, they generate the same business process, the user can choose according to their actual needs as well as the matching degree obtained. As shown in figure 2, after interoperability point searching and matching, two processes have been generated: IP0—>{IP1, IP2, IP3, IP4}; IP0—>{IP5, IP6, IP7}.

After performing the selected process, ESB perform dynamic selection of these target interoperability points dictated by QoS attributes.

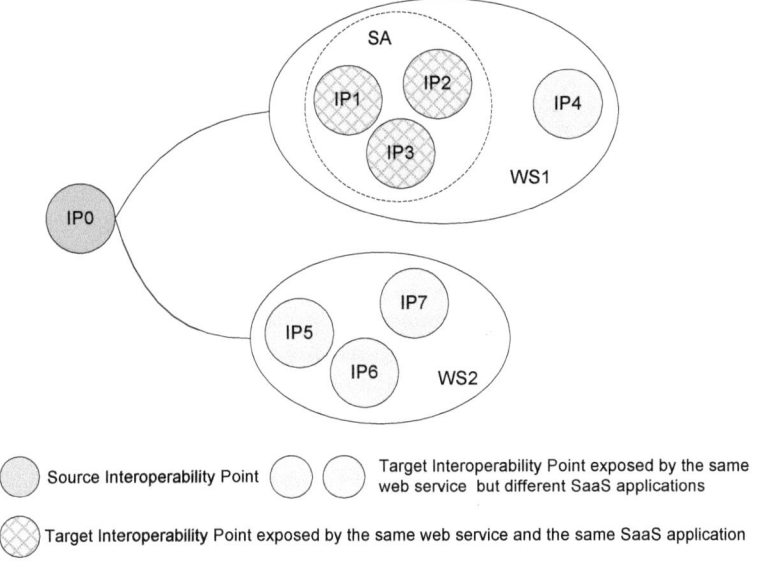

Fig. 2. The target interoperability point in a different case

3.3 ESB Routing Engine

Through the searching and matching performed by the interoperability proxy, we have get some target interoperability points which meet the goal of a business process. From the above, we know that there may be multiple target interoperability points, and new interoperability points that meet the request and matching rules may be exposed, and some target interoperability points may be no longer available or can no longer respond to the request. In these cases, to obtain a fast response and high quality service, we need an intermediary to conduct the dynamic selection and the discovery of target interoperability points.

ESB is the core and basis of SOA, and one of its core functions is message routing [12]. Message routing mainly refers to the delivery of messages between request endpoint and provider endpoint according to certain rules and logic. In addition, ESB supports transport protocol conversion and message format conversion and applications are able to flexibly connect with each other, regardless of the platform and technical differences.

Consequently, we use ESB in our framework to determine an optimum interoperability point from candidates based on the QoS attributes in that we think the quality of the target interoperability point is one of the main concerns.

3.4 The Process

Using the interoperability framework, the process could be illustrated as follows:

1. The ISVs package the business functional modules in the SaaS applications, publish as web services according to defined rules and norms and register to the web service registry on the platform after determining some service attributes.

2. SaaS applications can selectively expose the registered web service as an interoperability point. Only by the exposure operation will the SaaS application be possible to interoperate with other SaaS applications.

3. The interoperability proxy obtains several related interoperability points after querying according to the basic attribute constraints in the interoperation request. On this basis, according to the operation interface matching rules, some target interoperability points and several business processes will be gained after invoking the matching algorithm.

4. After the searching and matching phase, ESB performs dynamic selection of these target interoperability points dictated by QoS attributes and obtain the optimum interoperability point ultimately.

4 Interoperability Point Discovery

Web service discovery is based on web service matching. The functionality provided by web services is accomplished by calling the operations. The operation is the basic functional entity of web services. Every web service comprises a number of operations. Service matching is ultimately reflected in the operation matching.

We have acquired a set of related interoperability points after the searching phase. In order to further find the target interoperability points that can actually interact with the source interoperability point, we make full use of the service operation structure information provided by the current standard service description language WSDL, establish matching rules and design the interoperability point matching algorithm based on operation interface descriptions.

4.1 Interoperability Point Matching Rules

Each web service has an associated WSDL document, describing the service functionality and interface. Every service contains a series of operations and each operation is a set of names corresponding to the operation's input and output parameters. WSDL document describes the name and data type of each parameter in more detail.

The main content of the WSDL description document of a web service can form a tree structure logically. As shown in Figure 3, there are four layers in the figure. The root node represents an interoperability point. The nodes in layer 2 represent the operations. The nodes in layer 3 represent the input or output messages. And the nodes in layer 4 represent the parameters of the messages.

The input and output parameter types of operations are defined with XML Schema. The parameter type can be divided into simple data type and complex data type. Simple data type needs only parameter name and internally defined parameter type such as int and string. Each parameter is presented in the form of <name, type>. But for complex data type, the model group tags which nest other simple data types or complex data types are used.

We begin with the input and output parameters of operations and match them in three aspects: the number of parameters, parameter name and parameter type.

When the matching degree calculated by matching the output parameters of a source interoperability point and the input parameters of a related interoperability point in the aforementioned three aspects reaches the threshold user preset, the two interoperability points match successfully. And the related interoperability point can be treated as a target interoperability point.

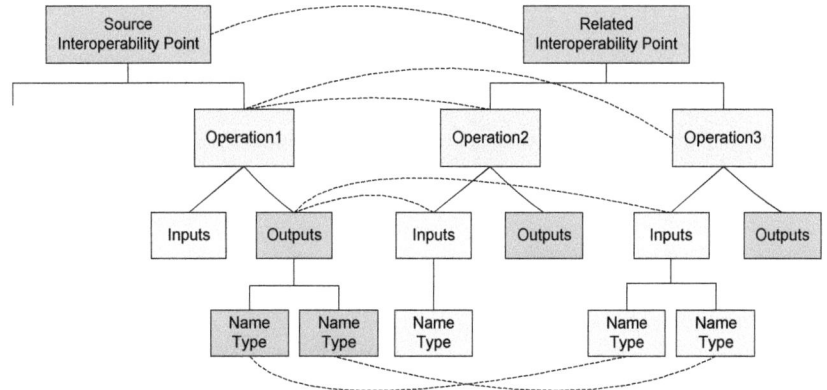

Fig. 3. Matching between two interoperability points based on the operation interface descriptions in the WSDL document

The concrete matching rules are shown as follows:

1) The number of the output parameters of the source interoperability point has to be the same with that of the input parameters of the related interoperability points. That is the precondition of the following matching processes.

2) The simple data type parameters are shown in the form of <name, type>, so matching degree is the combination of parameter names matching degree and parameter types matching degree. For parameter names, we can match them according to semantic similarity. For example, we can use the existing WordNet [14] semantic dictionary. For parameter types, we can reference the classification method in article [15].

3) The complex data type parameters nest other simple or complex data type parameters. So we implement algorithm with recursive.

4.2 Interoperability Point Matching Algorithm

The following are the main matching algorithms.

```
Algorithm 1 getTargetIPs
Input: SIP, the source interoperability point
       RIPs, the set of related interoperability
       points
       W, the threshold value of matching degree
Output: TIPs, the set of target interoperability points
Set sp as the operation of the source
interoperability point;
Set OPs as the set of target operations in target
interoperability points;
Set MD=0;
For each interoperability points RIP in RIPs{
   For each operation p∈ RIP{
   MD= getMatchDegree(sp,p);
     If(MD>w){
        RIP.OPs.add(p);
           If(RIP is not in TIPS)
              TIPs.add(RIP);
   }
}
```

Algorithm 1 matches the operations of source interoperability point with all the operations of the related interoperability points. The interoperability point whose calculated matching degree is greater than the threshold value user preset will be added to the set of target interoperability points.

Algorithm 1 calls Algorithm 2 to calculate the matching degree between operations.

```
Algorithm 2  getMatchDegree
Input:   sp, the source operation
         P, the target operation
Output:  MD, the matching degree between two
         operations
If(|sp.Os|==|p.Is|){
```

```
      For each parameter pairs{
      If(isSimpleType(sp.o)&&SimpleType(p.i)){
         nameMD=getNameMD(sp.o.name,p.i.name) ;
         typeMD=getTypeMD(sp.o.type,sp.i.type) ;
         MD=getMD(nameMD,typeMD)
      }
      Else if(isComplexType(sp.o)&&ComplexType(p.i)){
         If(|sp.o.groupLength|==|p.i.groupLength|){
            For each parameter pairs in model group
            getMatchDegree(sp.o.groupi,p.i.groupi);
          }
         ELSE MD=0;
      }
      Else MD=0;
      }
  }
  Else   MD=0;
```

Algorithm 2 is used to calculate the matching degree between the operations of interoperability points. Firstly it judges whether the number of parameters are the same. Secondly, the operation matching degrees of simple data type and complex data type are calculated respectively. The returned value is used in Algorithm 1.

The calculation of the matching degree of parameter names and parameter types is not the emphasis in the paper and no more words about it here.

5   ESB-Based Dynamic Interoperability

On the basis of functional matching, target interoperability points must guarantee some kind of quality. So we use QoS attributes information, such as response time, reliability and usability, as the basis of dynamic target interoperability points selection. NUTs platform provides a monitor which can update the QoS attributes information of interoperability points in real-time and the monitor can select the interoperability point with optimum performance according to some certain rules.

We need an intermediary to receive the request messages and route the messages to the target interoperability points. ESB implements message routing that receives and dispatches messages from source to the target. In addition, ESB establishes transport protocol conversion and message format transformation. Among several ESB implementations, we choose Mule and integrate it to our interoperability framework to realize the interoperation between SaaS applications.

Web Service Proxy is one of the commonest scenarios in ESB and also one of the four pattens of Mule.

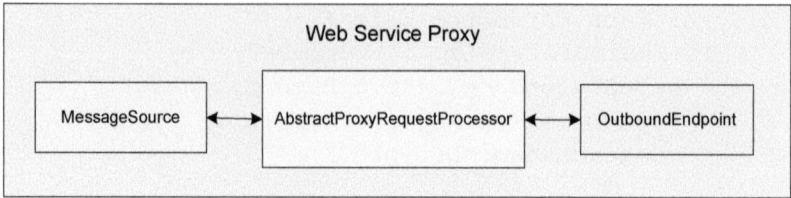

Fig. 4. The Web Service Proxy Pattern of Mule

There are three components in the Web Service Proxy, as shown in Figure 4.

1. MessageSource
MuleMessage is received or created by MessageListener. For example, If the DefaultInboundEndpoint is adopted as the MessageSource, SOAP messages will be received from the socket.

2. OutboundEndpoint
It is in charge of receiving and distributing messages.

3. AbstractProxyRequestProcessor
It is responsible for handing MuleEvent and rewriting WSDL addresses. There are two implementation classes, which are StaticWsdlProxyRequestProcessor and DynamicWsdlProxyRequestProcessor respectively.

By the following codes, we get the optimum interoperability point's address based on QoS analyzation and add an output endpoint with the new address dynamically. Then Mule can transfer the request messages to the optimum interoperability point.

```
//Clone a Global service
EndpointBuilder endpointBuilder =
muleContext.getRegistry().lookupEndpointBuilder("
originBuilder");
EndpointBuilder cloneEndpoint = (EndpointBuilder)
endpointBuilder.clone();
//Get the uri of optimum interoperability point
  from the QoS analyser
String uri=getUri(TIPs);
cloneEndpoint.setURIBuilder(new URIBuilder(uri));
//Rewrite the info for clone endpoint
muleContext.getRegistry().registerEndpointBuilde
r("optimumUri", cloneEndpoint);
//Get the OutboundRouter, clear the message and
add the new endpoint
OutboundRouter outboundRouter = ((OutboundRouter)
service.getOutboundRouter().getRouters().get(0));
outboundRouter.getEndpoints().clear();
outboundRouter.addEndpoint(cloneEndpoint.buildOu
tboundEndpoint());
```

6   A Case Study

This section demonstrates the features of our interoperability framework by referring to an example. On the NUTs platform, there exists a good deal of SaaS applications. Many SaaS applications expose the standardized web service interfaces uniformly registered by ISVs as interoperability points.

For Example, there are two SaaS applications on the delivery platform, one is supply business management system (SBM) and the other is Advanced Plan Optimization (APO). Several organizations tenant these SaaS applications and maintain their own instances. We can observe from figure 4 that SBM_A, APO_B and APO_C are three typical SaaS applications which expose some web service interfaces as interoperability points. If Tenant A which rents SBM_A wants to optimize the result plans list queried by PurchasePlanQuery, it can put forward an interoperation request. PurchasePlanQueryA should be treated as a source interoperability point and three target interoperability points will be figured out after the searching and matching process. Two different business process "Purchase Plan Query—>Supply Forecast" and "Purchase Plan Query—>Plan Optomize" will be presented to Tenant A.

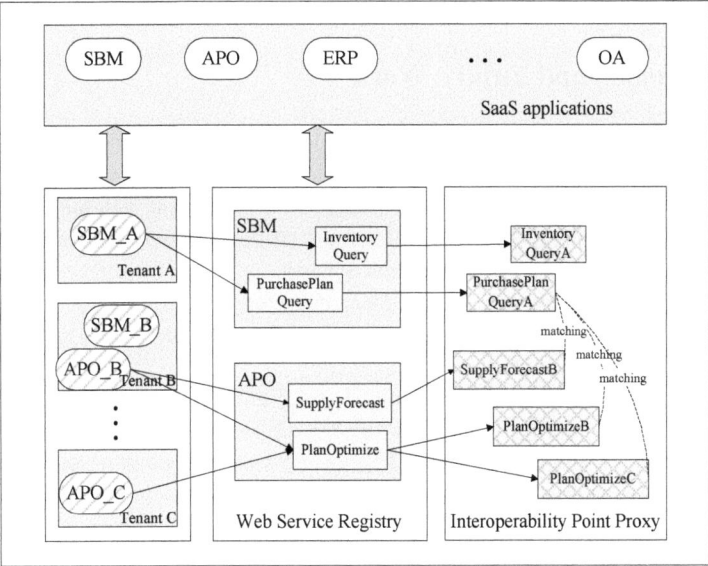

Fig. 5. An example process of interoperability point discovery

Tenant A should choose one of the business processes based on own preferences. Then ESB will dynamically select interoperability points and perform transport protocol conversion and message format transformation simultaneously.

The Inbound which serves as the request client of Mule receives the request messages. Web Service Proxy receives not only request message but also the optimum interoperability point address selected by the monitor on Nuts platform.

Web Service Proxy creates a dynamic endpoint and rewrite the OutboundAddress as the new endpoint address. When the call is triggered, Mule will deliver the request message to the optimum interoperability point and the dynamic interoperation between two SaaS applications is realized finally.

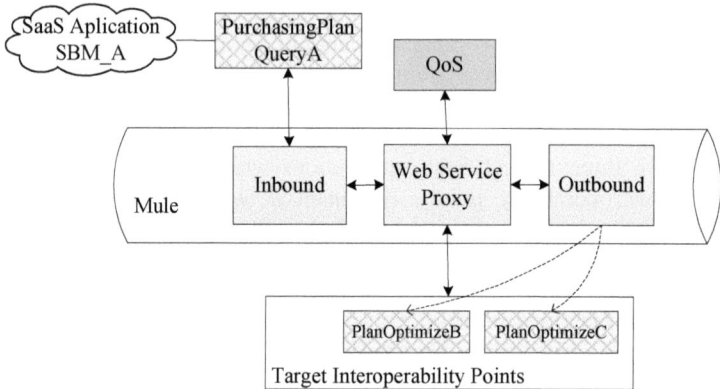

Fig. 6. An example process of dynamic interoperation between two SaaS Applications

7 Conclusion and Future Work

The paper presents an approach to implement interoperation between SaaS applications in the service layer. We provide the formalization description of the interoperability point and put forward an interoperability point matching algorithm on a basis of an interoperability point matching strategy. After interoperability point matching, the intermediary ESB performs dynamic selection of interoperability points dictated by QoS attributes. In the premise of a comprehensive consideration of the functional and non-functional preferences and constraints, we finally realize dynamic interoperation between SaaS applications.

In our algorithm, interoperability points are sorted in a particular order. We need match each interoperability point with the source interoperability point one by one exhaustively. The matching algorithm will meet efficiency problem when the number of interoperability points reaches some order of magnitudes. In our future job, index mechanism will be introduced to build the function index of interoperability points and a matching algorithm based on index will be provided.

Acknowledgment. The authors would like to acknowledge the support provided by the National High Technology Research and Development Program of China (2011AA040603, 2012AA040904), the National Key Technologies R&D Program of China (2012BAF12B07), the Natural Science Foundation of Shandong Province (ZR2009GM028, ZR2011FQ031) and Independent Innovation Foundation of Shandong University (IIFSDU).

References

1. Charalabidis, Y., Gionis, G., Hermann, K.M., Martinez, C.: Enterprise Interoperability Research Roadmap (2008)
2. Dubey, A., Wagle, D.: Delivering Software as a Service. In: The McKinsey Quarterly, Web Exclusive (2007)
3. Liu, S., Wang, L., Meng, X., Wu, L.: Dynamic Interoperability Between Multi-Tenant SaaS Applications. In: Enterprise Interoperability V. Proceedings of the IESA Conferences, vol. 5, Part 4, pp. 217–226 (2012)
4. Kassel, S.: An Architectural Approach for Service Interoperability. In: International Conference on Interoperability for Enterprise Software and Applications China, IESA 2009, pp. 212–218 (2009)
5. Arafa, Y., Boldyreff, C., Tawil, A., Liu, H.: A High Level Service-Based Approach to Software Component Integration. In: Sixth International Conference on Complex, Intelligent, and Software Intensive Systems (2012)
6. Yang, J., Anand, R., et al.: Data Service Portal for Application Integration in Cloud Computing. In: Emerging Technologies for a Smarter World, CEWIT (2011)
7. The C4ISR Architecture Working Group (AWG) (CAWG): Levels of Information Systems Interoperability, LISI (1998)
8. IDEAS: Interoperability Development for Enterprise Application and Software Roadmaps, Annex 1—Description of Work (2002)
9. EIF: European Interoperability Framework, White Paper. Brussels (2004)
10. Nuts, http://www.nutsplatform.cn
11. Liu, C., Yang, C., Liu, S., Wu, L., Meng, X.: A Process Interoperability Method for SMEs. In: van Sinderen, M., Johnson, P. (eds.) IWEI 2011. LNBIP, vol. 76, pp. 50–60. Springer, Heidelberg (2011)
12. Keen, M., Acharya, A., Bishop, S., et al.: Patterns: Implementing an SOA Using an Enterprise Service Bus, Redbooks. IBM Press (2004)
13. Mule, http://www.mulesoft.org
14. Miller, G.: WordNet: A lexical database for english. Communications of the ACM 38(11) (1995)
15. Yu, S., He, F., Le, J.: Automatic Web Service Composition Based on Interface Matching. Computer Science (2007)
16. Paolucci, M., Kawamura, T., Payne, T.R., Sycara, K.: Semantic Matching of Web Services Capabilities. In: Horrocks, I., Hendler, J. (eds.) ISWC 2002. LNCS, vol. 2342, pp. 333–347. Springer, Heidelberg (2002)
17. Zhou, C., Zhang, X.: A Policy-Confgurable Dynamic Routing Mechanism in Enterprise Service Bus. In: International Conference on Educational and Information Technology, ICEIT, pp. 480–485 (2010)
18. Ziyaeva, G., Choi, E., Min, D.: Content-based intelligent routing and message processing in Enterprise Service Bus. In: Proceedings of the International Conference on Convergence and Hybrid Information Technology, pp. 245–249 (2008)

Similarity Evaluation Based on Intuitionistic Fuzzy Set for Service Cluster Selection as Cloud Service Candidate

Jorick Lartigau, Xiaofei Xu, Lanshun Nie, and Dechen Zhan

School of Computer Science and Technology, Harbin Institute of Technology
92 Xi Dazhi Str. Nangang District, Harbin 150001 China
jorick@hotmail.fr, {xiaofei,nls,dechen}@hit.edu.cn

Abstract. Cloud manufacturing (CMfg) provides new opportunities toward the servitization, and embeds a set of functional features to enhance the collaboration among various service providers and their resources. The main target is to compose dedicated manufacturing cloud, by encompassing a set of cloud services, to manufacture a requested service. CMfg is a recent concept, but already widely spread in the academic and industrial researches in China. The paper firstly focuses on the manufacturing environment background to understand its purpose. Thus as an introduction, the concept of CMfg is discussed. Finally, we present a method based on intuitionistic fuzzy set for the similarity evaluation between cloud services and service clusters. The objective is to match the best service cluster to provide composite resource services as cloud service candidates. Our method is ABC (Artificial Bee Colony) optimized, and its performance are discussed through experiments.

Keywords: Cloud manufacturing (CMfg), Service cluster, Cloud service, Intuitionistic fuzzy set (IFS), Artificial bee colony (ABC).

1 Background

Modern manufacturing industries are facing a major change in their organization, conducted by an unpredictable competition on a worldwide scale [1], the emergence of new information technologies, and cloud technology. Indeed, IoT (Internet of Things) / IoS (Internet of Services), Future Internet, Cloud computing and Virtualization techniques offers many new possibilities to remodel the manufacturing environment significantly. Meanwhile, during the past two decades, many advanced manufacturing models and technologies have been proposed in order to realize the aim of TQCSEFK (i.e. faster time-to-market, higher quality, lower cost, better service, better environment, greater flexibility, and higher knowledge) for manufacturing enterprises. Typical examples include computer integrated manufacturing (CIM), lean manufacturing (LM), digital manufacturing, agile manufacturing (AM), networked manufacturing (NM), virtual manufacturing (VM), application service provider (ASP), collaborative manufacturing network, industrial product-service system (IPS), manufacturing grid (MGrid), crowd sourcing and supply chain [2]. But the modern manufacturing faces new challenges, especially toward the survival of the SMEs (Small-Medium Enterprise).

1.1 The Servitization and the Needs of Innovation

Servitization is a change process where manufacturing companies embrace service orientation and/or develop more and better services, with the aim to satisfy customer's needs, achieve competitive advantages and enhance firm performance [3]. The servitization tends to a high number of implied resource service providers collaborating and inter-connected for the value creation. According to [4], 58% of US manufacturers had servitized in 2007 and less than 20% of Chinese manufacturers had servitized in 2011. For actual major industries, servitization is a valuable source of expenditures. For instance, services represented the main part of IBM capital expenditures since 2010 [5].

The goal of servitization is to create a product-service shift. It implied a circular relationship where products create service opportunities. This relationship improves business opportunities and also has a fundamental impact on the product leading to transformation and innovation. It becomes a major change agent and driver of product innovation. In a world of competition and global market, the innovation is the constraint driver for expending its business, and maintaining its impact. The innovation is extended by the interplay of various service providers and demanders in a high collaborative level environment within many time zones, distances, or enterprise organizations. The need of intermediary core platform among the service providers, their related service centers and demander, to manage and orchestrate the operations is a key for innovation. In our days, from a business perspective, manufacturing companies sense that the core competitiveness of their product gravitates around all the service package offered as additional services (e.g. machinery maintenance, human resources training) (Fig. 1.).

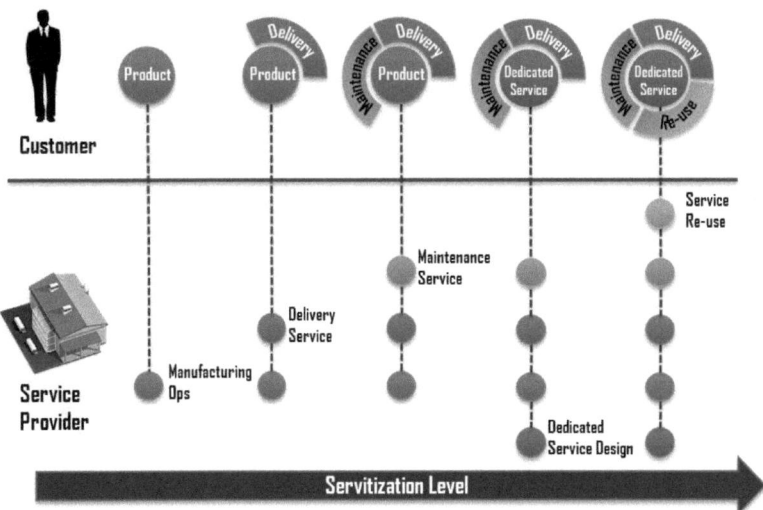

Fig. 1. Service provider / Customer relationship on a servitization scale

1.2 High-Performance and Precision Equipment

In a world of competition with a wide range of offers, a service demander may give priority to the "*best of breed*". This phenomenon necessarily stimulates the enterprises to invest in better equipment and manufacturing resources, to enhance the service or product quality. Such investment can be unreachable for SMEs, especially with a large number of machineries and resources implied. As a result, collaboration between SMEs becomes an undeniable fact for their survival and expansion. On another hand, enterprises willing to invest might face under utilization of high-performance and precision equipment. From a business view, an interesting fact will be to offer the use of these equipments on demand, enabling a full sharing and open new business opportunities.

1.3 Enhance the QoS (Quality of Service), with Interoperability, Collaboration and Standardization

As mentioned above, collaboration appears to be one of the main factors to succeed in modern manufacturing. Along the collaboration setups, come the interoperability and standardization challenges. The required manufacturing resource is transmitted among the enterprises, which employs different standardization strategies [6]. Considering a third-party platform, the core service has to insure the interoperability and standardization coverage of the shared resources among the service providers. The objective is to enhance the quality of the requested service, by evolving the best resources and equipments, while maximizing the collaboration between the service providers and their occupancy.

1.4 The Emergence of Cloud Computing

Cloud computing is a concept consisting to dispatch computer programs to distant servers rather than local server or customer computer. The users are not anymore the host or the manager of the computer services, but can access from anywhere to online services without the need of managing the infrastructure model, often very complex. Cloud computing is changing the way industries and enterprises do their businesses in the meaning that dynamically scalable and virtualized resources are provided as a service over the Internet. Enterprises currently employ Cloud services in order to improve the scalability of their services and to deal with resource demands [7]. The concept of Cloud computing can be extended to the manufacturing field, providing on-demand service from remote resource service providers. Cloud computing mainly emerged to satisfy the needs of long time follow-up and service quality [8].

2 Cloud Manufacturing

Cloud Manufacturing (CMfg) service-oriented manufacturing model is been developed in order to satisfy the new paradigms and orientation of the manufacturing industries and market globalization. CMfg combines around a service-oriented architecture, new technologies and theory concepts [9]. CMfg realize the full sharing and circulation, high utilization, and on-demand use of various manufacturing resources and capabilities by providing safe and reliable, high quality, cheap and on-demand used manufacturing services for the whole lifecycle of manufacturing [2].

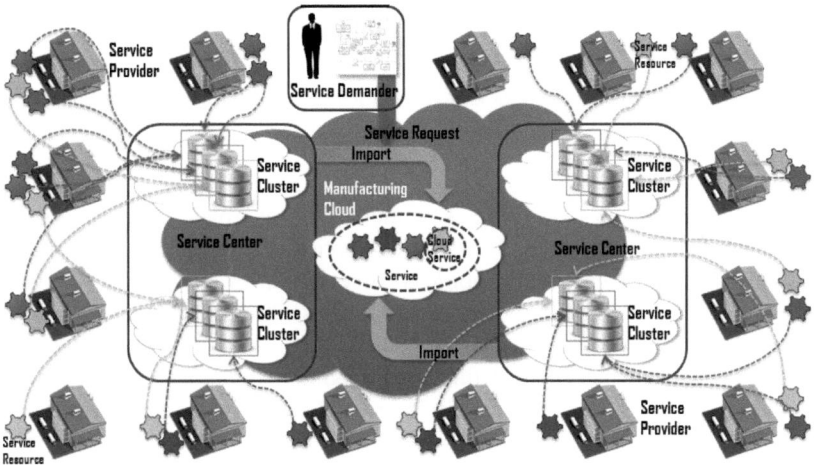

Fig. 2. CMfg concept model

The figure 2 presents the concept model of CMfg, based on resource service transaction. From the virtualization perspective, the physical service resources from various service providers are classified and characterized, to enable their encapsulation into service clusters. The service clusters are monitored and governed within one or several service centers. Thus, through a composition and evaluation process by an agent broker; here denoted as Cloud Platform, the system is able to build a set of cloud services to fulfill the functional and non-functional demander's service requirements. The four main parameters are defined as follow:

(a) *Resource Services* encompass a large set of resources, e.g. material resources, human resources, computational resources, equipment resources; which can interplay in collaboration to build existing and new services.

(b) *Service Clusters* gather the logical resource according to their functional parameters but also their non-functional QoS parameters, within preset ranges. Logical resources are the result of resource virtualization, transforming physical resources into logical. Service clusters embed a set of data associated to the functional definition of the resources and non-functional parameters denoted as QoSs, e.g. cost, reliability, and flexibility. QoS parameters are provided by the related service provider to the resource services, recorded and monitored from previous service operations.

(c) *Service centers* are responsible for the governance of the service clusters, and the agent services gravitating through the architecture layers to provide and share the needed information along the service processing.

(d) *Cloud services* are the representation on the cloud layer of the service tasks to perform. A service to provide is a chain of several Cloud services which can be the combination of several models (e.g. sequential, parallel, selective and cycle). A cloud service can be fulfilled by a single resource service within the same functional properties and non-functional QoSs minimum requirements.

3 Similarity Evaluation between Eligible Service Clusters and Cloud Services Based on Intuitionistic Fuzzy Set (IFS)

3.1 Problem Statement

One of the main features of CMfg is to enable the interplay of several composite resource services through a cloud service association, to model a new manufacturing service. Thus, the driven consideration is to set up an evaluation and composition strategy concerning the cloud service candidates. Cloud service candidates are ful-filled by composite resources encompassed in service clusters with the same function-al characteristics and non-functional QoSs satisfying the service demander's mini-mum requirements. The composition process can be very exhaustive in term of com-putational time for cloud service chains involving a high number of resource services. Therefore, the problematic is to compose the best selection of resource services, with-out browsing all the possible solutions.

The advantage of a CMfg organization is to enable the resource virtualization and encapsulation into service clusters. Taking in account this specificity, an efficient approach is to pre-select eligible service clusters to provide the best resource services must be envisaged.

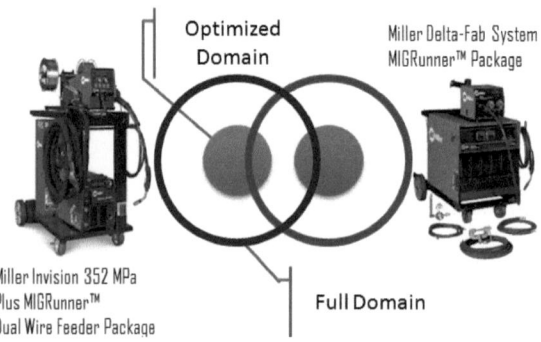

Fig. 3. Welding resources application domain model

To launch the composition and evaluation process, the CMfg system has to match the service clusters which can provide the right composite resource service. Along with the composition process, we have to keep in mind the diversity of Mfg resource services and their possible scalability toward several inputs and outputs, which might complicate the notion of candidate selection for a given cloud service. Indeed, a manufacturing machine is designed and optimized for a set of given inputs to generate a set of outputs, but can often manufacture services out of these bounds (Fig. 3.). However this process is not recommended since the machine is not optimized out of the bounds, and needs probably new calibrations and maintenance operations. Therefore, the membership definition of a manufacturing resource to a given set of inputs generating related outputs remains very fuzzy and cannot be expressed in full logical consideration.

In this paper, we propose a method based on IFS (intuitionistic fuzzy sets) to analyze the similarity degree between a requested set of cloud services and the available service clusters, within the same application domain (e.g. power supply, journal bearing) with optimized computational time, without going through all the possible solutions. The objective of our method is to select for each cloud service the best match among the service clusters. To illustrate the problematic, we model the whole composition process (Fig. 4.).

In the frame of manufacturing, the similarity evaluation between cloud services and service clusters enable to overview the input and outputs, to insure the correlation among them, for an optimal service clusters selection.

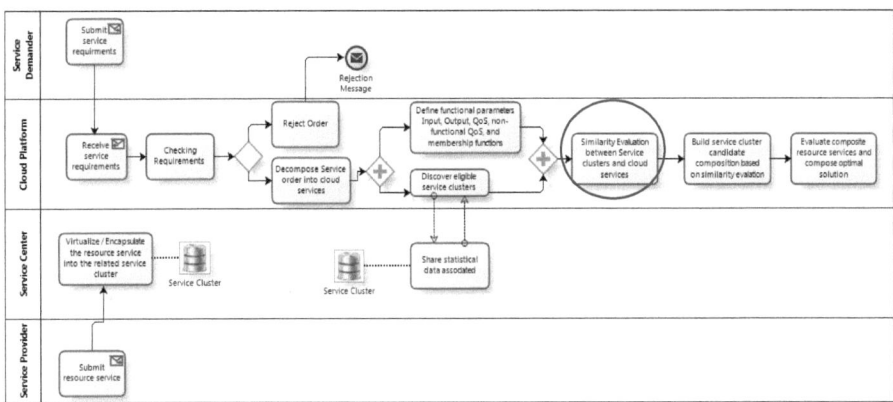

Fig. 4. The whole cloud service composition BPMN representation

The similarity evaluation can also be extended, for the consideration of interoperability (e.g. standards), and the non-functional QoSs requirements (e.g. reliability).

3.2 Introduction to IFS

Fuzzy set theory was introduced by L.A. Zadeh [10], by extension to set theories, where a given element is not anymore characterized by a binary (0 or 1) assessment to define its membership or not to a given set, but by a gradual assessment. The gradual assessment is the result of a membership function in the interval [0, 1] to characterize the strength of its membership to this set. The fuzzy set theory can be used in a wide range of domains in which information is incomplete or imprecise [11].

Let $X = \{x_1, x_2, ..., x_i, ... x_n\}$ be a fixed set of cardinality n. A fuzzy set A is expressed as:

$$A = \{\langle x, \mu_A(x)\rangle | x \in X\} \tag{1}$$

where $\mu_A: X \to [0,1]$ is the membership function of A and $\mu_A(x) \in [0,1]$ is the membership of $x \in X$ in A.

The notion of Intuitionistic Fuzzy Set (IFS) was introduced as generalization of the notion of fuzzy set [12].

Let $X = \{x_1, x_2, ..., x_i, ... x_n\}$ be a fixed set of cardinality n. An IFS A is expressed as:

$$A = \{\langle x, \mu_A(x), v_A(x)\rangle | x \in X\} \tag{2}$$

where respectively $\mu_A: X \to [0,1]$ and $v_A: X \to [0,1]$ are the membership degree and the non-membership degree of A, as $\mu_A(x) \in [0,1]$ is the membership degree of $x \in X$ in A and $v_A(x) \in [0,1]$ is the non-membership degree of $x \in X$ in A.

Naturally is introduced $\pi_A(x)$ the degree of indeterminacy [13] of x to A, determined as:

$$\pi_A(x) = 1 - \mu_A(x) - v_A(x) \tag{3}$$

If $\pi_A(x) = 0$, for all $x \in X$, then the IFS A is reduced to a fuzzy set, else $\pi_A(x) > 0$, thus an indeterminacy occurs for the element x.

The similarity between two IFSs A and B is defines as [14]:

$$S(A, B) = 1 - \frac{|\mu_A(x) - \mu_B(x)| + |v_A(x) - v_B(x)|}{2} \tag{4}$$

with $S(A, B) \to [0,1]$ expressing the similarity degree.

3.3 Environment Definition

A service to manufacture S is a set of cloud services as $S = \{CS_1, CS_2, ..., CS_i, ... CS_N\}$. Then, let's consider $In_i = \{in_1^i, in_2^i, ..., in_j^i, ... in_{J_i}^i\}$, the set of input relative to the cloud service CS_i, where $i = 1,2, ..., N$ and $j = 1,2, ..., J_i$, with $N, J_i \in \mathbb{N}$. As well, $Out_i = \{out_1^i, out_2^i, ..., out_k^i, ... out_{K_i}^i\}$ is the set of output relative to CS_i, with $k = 1,2, ..., K_i$ and $K_i \in \mathbb{N}$. Both input and output can globalize functional and non-functional parameters. The proposed approach is then, fully customizable and scalable to any type of cloud services.

Thus, an IFS $CSFin_i$ is introduced to characterize the degree of membership of the elements from the set In_i within CS_i based on eq.(2).

$$CSFin_i = \{\langle x, \mu_{CSFin_i}(x), v_{CSFin_i}(x)\rangle | x \in In_i\} \tag{5.a}$$

And a second IFS to characterize the membership of the elements from the set Out_i to CS_i.

$$CSFout_i = \{\langle x, \mu_{CSFout_i}(x), \upsilon_{CSFout_i}(x)\rangle | x \in Out_i\} \quad (5.b)$$

The objective is to evaluate the similarity for each element between a given CS_i and a set of service cluster eligible, within the same domain (e.g. power supply, journal bearing).

Therefore, we consider $SC_i = \{sc_1^i, sc_2^i, \dots, sc_m^i, \dots sc_{M_i}^i\}$ the set of service clusters associated to the same domain than CS_i. The two IFSs to characterize the elements x membership from the two sets In_i and Out_i within a given sc_m^i are defined as:

$$scFin_m^i = \{\langle y, \mu_{scFin_m^i}(x), \upsilon_{scFin_m^i}(x)\rangle | x \in In_i\} \quad (6.a)$$

and

$$scFout_m^i = \{\langle y, \mu_{scFout_m^i}(x), \upsilon_{scFout_m^i}(x)\rangle | x \in Out_i\} \quad (6.b)$$

3.4 Membership, Non-membership and Indeterminacy Functions Generation

The membership functions $\mu_{scFin_m^i}(x)$, $\mu_{scFout_m^i}(x)$ and the non-membership $\upsilon_{scFin_m^i}(x)$, $\upsilon_{scFout_m^i}(x)$ can be obtained through different methods; e.g. consult specialists, use predefined membership functions, sort of the membership functions automatically [15]. In our case they will express the degree of optimization and ownership of a given set of inputs or outputs to a given manufacturing resources. The advantage is to define the domain of capabilities and optimization for the whole set of service cluster candidate according to the cloud service definition.

However, for the sake of simplicity, we consider the intervention of several specialists to evaluate the membership of an element $x \in In_i$. That's why we setup the following matrix for membership and non-membership function generation process for a given sc_m^i and the set of input In_i and the set of output Out_i as:

$$InGen_m^i = \begin{bmatrix} ePos_{m,1}^i & eNeg_{m,1}^i & eInd_{m,1}^i \\ ePos_{m,2}^i & eNeg_{m,2}^i & eInd_{m,2}^i \\ \cdot & \cdot & \cdot \\ ePos_{m,j}^i & eNeg_{m,j}^i & eInd_{m,j}^i \\ \cdot & \cdot & \cdot \\ ePos_{m,J_i}^i & eNeg_{m,J_i}^i & eInd_{m,J_i}^i \end{bmatrix}_{3 \times J_i} \quad (7.a)$$

$$OutGen_m^i = \begin{bmatrix} ePos_{m,1}^i & eNeg_{m,1}^i & eInd_{m,1}^i \\ ePos_{m,2}^i & eNeg_{m,2}^i & eInd_{m,2}^i \\ \cdot & \cdot & \cdot \\ ePos_{m,k}^i & eNeg_{m,k}^i & eInd_{m,k}^i \\ \cdot & \cdot & \cdot \\ ePos_{m,K_i}^i & eNeg_{m,K_i}^i & eInd_{m,K_i}^i \end{bmatrix}_{3 \times K_i} \quad (7.b)$$

where $ePos_{m,j}^i$ is the number of positive evaluation for the membership of the element in_j^i in the IFS $scFin_m^i$ associated to the service cluster sc_m^i, $eNeg_{m,j}^i$ the number of negative evaluation (non-membership), and $eInt_{m,j}^i$ the number of indeterminacy; e.g. specialist who did not evaluate the parameter membership of in_j^i.

Therefore we can setup the functions $\mu_{scFin_m^i}(x)$, $\nu_{scFin_m^i}(x)$ and $\pi_{scFin_m^i}(x)$, $\forall x \in In_i$. Let's consider the case $= in_j^i$, with $j = 1, 2, \dots, J_i$:

$$\mu_{scFin_m^i}(in_j^i) = \frac{ePos_{m,j}^i}{(ePos_{m,j}^i + eNeg_{m,j}^i + eInd_{m,j}^i)} \tag{8.a}$$

$$\nu_{scFin_m^i}(in_j^i) = \frac{eNeg_{m,j}^i}{(ePos_{m,j}^i + eNeg_{m,j}^i + eInd_{m,j}^i)} \tag{8.b}$$

and

$$\pi_{scFin_m^i}(in_j^i) = \frac{eInd_{m,j}^i}{(ePos_{m,j}^i + eNeg_{m,j}^i + eInd_{m,j}^i)}$$
$$= 1 - \mu_{scFin_m^i}(in_j^i) - \nu_{scFin_m^i}(in_j^i) \tag{8.c}$$

By analogy, we setup the functions $\mu_{scFout_m^i}(x)$, $\nu_{scFout_m^i}(x)$ and $\pi_{scFout_m^i}(x)$ using $OutGen_m^i$.

3.5 Similarity Evaluation between CS_i and sc_m^i

We propose the following framework (Fig. 5.) to illustrate the similarity evaluation process between a given CS_i and sc_m^i. For the sake of readability, we only consider the set In_i. Our approach is to evaluate the similarity separately (heuristic approach) between all the elements from $\mu CSin_i$, $\nu CSin_i$ and $\mu scin_m^i$, $\nu scin_m^i$ respectively the set of membership and non-membership functions from the elements In_i in CS_i, and the set of membership and non-membership functions from the elements In_i in sc_m^i. Thus, the similarity evaluation for the element x_j is defined using eq.(4) as:

$$S\left(CSFin_i(x_j), scFin_m^i(x_j)\right)$$
$$= 1 - \frac{\left|\mu_{CSFin_i}(x_j) - \mu_{scFin_m^i}(x_j)\right| + \left|\nu_{CSFout_i}(x_j) - \nu_{scFout_m^i}(x_j)\right|}{2} \tag{9}$$

Finally, the overall similarity between the IFS $CSFin_i$ and $scFin_m^i$ is linearized and computed as:

$$S_m^i = \sum_{j=0}^{J_i} \left[S\left(CSFin_i(x_j), scFin_m^i(x_j)\right) \times \omega_j\right] \tag{10}$$

with ω_j the weight associated to the importance of the element x_j as $\omega_j \in \mathbb{R}_0^+$ and $\sum_{j=1}^{J_i} \omega_j = 1$.

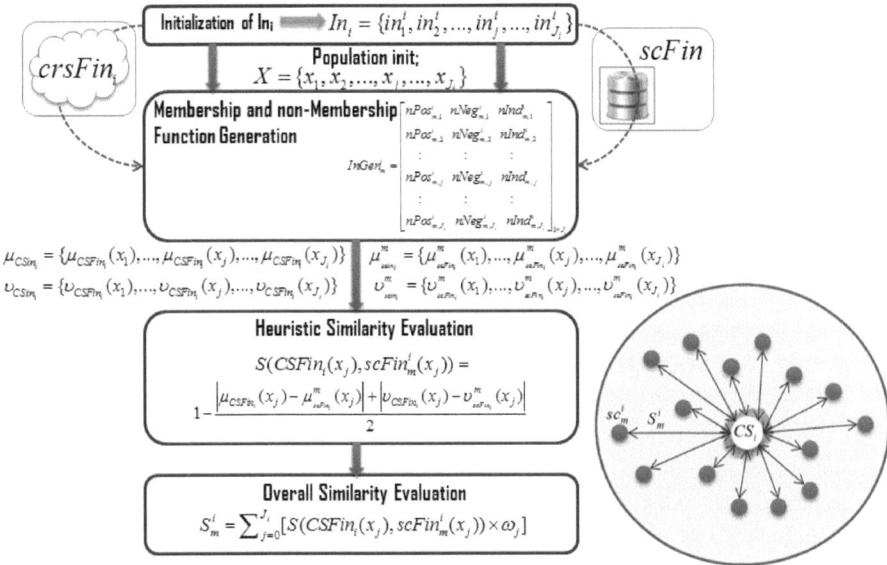

Fig. 5. Similarity evaluation Framework between Cloud service and Service cluster candidate based on IFS

4 Computational Experiments

4.1 Introduction to Artificial Bee Colony (ABC) Optimization for Similarity Evaluation

Our first objective is to reduce the computational time for the similarity evaluation, and find the service cluster with the highest service cluster for each cloud service of the N cloud service chain. However, we deliberately avoid a full heuristic similarity evaluation. Instead our approach evaluates the whole chain of service clusters, allowing the integration of additional features (e.g. correlation analysis among service clusters). To realize this objective, we compute our method through Artificial Bee Colony (ABC) optimization.

For the best understanding, we only introduce the features of ABC, where a modification is needed to fit to our similarity evaluation between service clusters and cloud services.

ABC is one of the most recently introduced swarm-based algorithms, which present higher performances than ES (Evolution Strategies), GA (Genetic Algorithm), DE (Differential Evolution Algorithm) and PSO (Particle Swarm Optimization) [16].

ABC route execution is inspired by the behavior of honeybee swarm. The population of bees is divided into three categories:

(a) *Employed Bees*, who search for food sources and evaluate their nectar, in order to share their information in the hive with onlooker bees.

(b) *Onlooker Bees*, who position themselves on food sources presenting higher nectar amount.
(c) *Scout Bees*, who search to discover new food sources area.

The route of the algorithm is defined as [17]:

```
1    Initialization; set cycle
2    Repeat
3        Place the employed bees on their food sources
4        Place the onlooker bees on the food sources depending on
         their nectar amount
5        Send the scouts to search new areas for new food sources
6        Memorize the best food source found so far
7    Until cycle=0
```

Here the food source represents the possible solution, which in our case is an eligible service cluster, and the nectar amount the fitness, which is related to the similarity of the service cluster to a given cloud service.

An onlooker bee selects its food source according to the probability value p_m^i associated with that food source as:

$$p_i = \frac{fit_i}{\sum_{n=1}^{SN} fit_n} \quad (11)$$

with SN the population number equal to the number of possibilities, and fit_i the fitness value of the solution i. In our case:

$$SN = \prod_{i=1}^{N} M_i \quad (12)$$

$$\forall m \in [1, M_i]; fit_i = \sum_{i=1}^{N} S_m^i \quad (13)$$

Thus, the objective is to minimize fit_i, $\forall i \in [1, N]$ and $\forall m \in [1, M_i]$.

In ABC, as the search approaches the optimal solution in the given population of service clusters, the research area is adaptively reduced.

There are three controlled parameters to setup the search and evaluation environment:

(a) The *limit* is the number of cycle, during which one, each bee will search for better food sources in its neighborhood. If the fitness is not improved by then; the food source is abandoned.
(b) The *NP*, the number of colony size (employed bees + onlooker bees).
(c) *MCN* (Maximum Cycle Number) set up the number of time the sequence of foraging will last.

These parameters are settled arbitrarily, and can influence the performances of the algorithm significantly. But as an advantage, ABC has only three [18].

4.2 Performance Evaluation

We evaluate the performances of our method optimized through ABC, and the same similarity evaluation method using LP (linear programming) through all the possible solutions, enabling us to identify the optimal solution. During these experimentations we study the performances by modifying the numbers M_i of service clusters per cloud services, while the number of parameters N, J_i of In_i and K_i of Out_i are set to 10. For all the run, the setup parameters of ABC are $NP = 2N$, $Limit=50$, and $MCN = NP \times \overline{M_i}$.

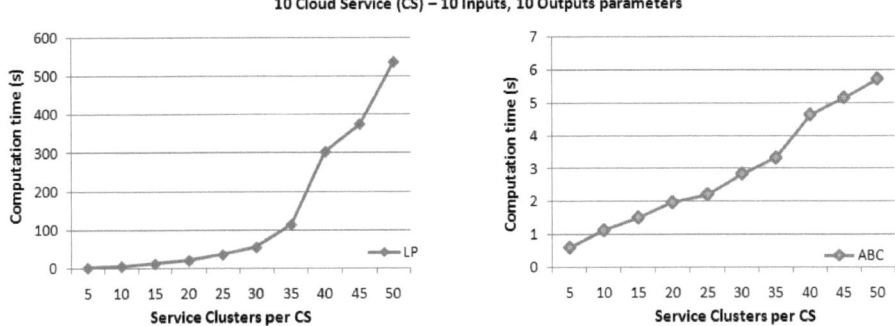

Fig. 6. Computational time comparison for Similarity evaluation using LP and ABC

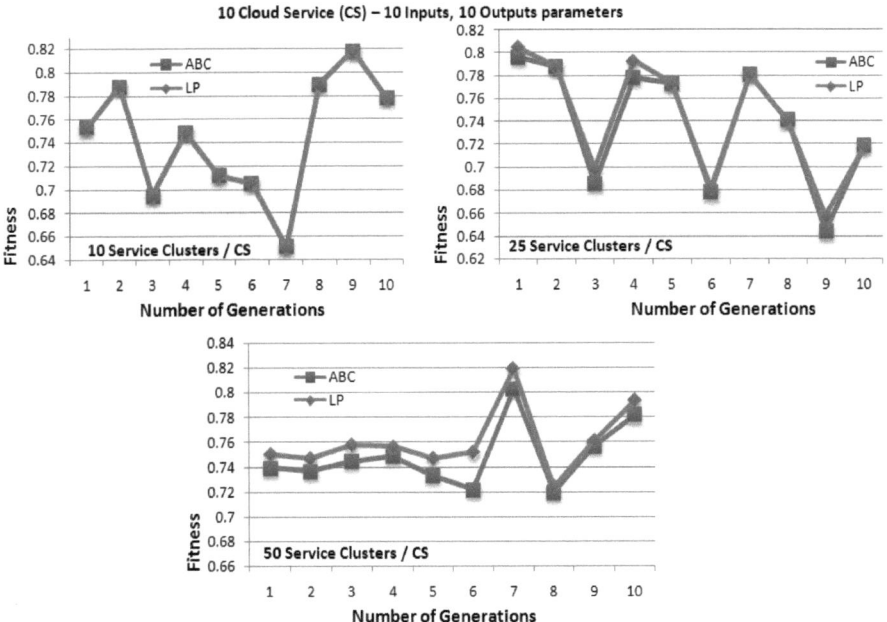

Fig. 7. Fitness comparison for Similarity evaluation using LP and ABC

We conducted these experiments on a computer equipped with an Intel Core i3-2100 3.10GHz processor and 4GB RAM. The machine is running under Windows 7 pro and Java 1.7.

We can easily remark that the LP method becomes unrealistic while the problem size is increasing (Fig. 6.). The computational time is growing exponentially toward the number of possible solutions, whereas the ABC optimization offers a faster computation, especially for large scale problem.

However, the LP method consisting to browse all the solutions to match the optimal one presents the best fitness possible. While the problem size is increasing our similarity evaluation ABC optimized shows a distance between its best fitness and the optimal fitness (Fig. 7.). The discrepancy is linked to the number of MCN. Since ABC is based on a probability selection process, it is impossible to define a sure value of MCN according the problem inputs. Nevertheless, the CMfg system can train a neural network aiming to define the best MCN. But of course, MCN has a strong influence on the computational time.

Therefore, the advantage of our similarity evaluation ABC optimized is to scale the computational time and the quality of the fitness evaluation, according to the equipment restriction and / or quality fitness requirements.

5 Conclusion and Future Work

The research work presented in this paper proposes a method to evaluate the similarity between service clusters and cloud services, to match the service cluster with the highest similarity value, according to a set of definition (In_i and / or Out_i). The ABC optimization offers satisfying computational time for the proposed method.

However, this method has to be considered in the whole problematic of cloud service composition. As mentioned, this process represents the core value of the CMfg system, enabling the creation of services and innovations. Therefore, the CMfg system has to select the best matches toward the functional parameters of the cloud services to manufacture, and also the non-functional parameter as QoSs, to satisfy the demander's requirements. In this purpose, our method represents an entry point to the whole composition process, enabling to select the best service cluster. Thus, a strategy concerning the evaluation of composite resource service within the same service cluster must be established. Since our method is mainly designed to insure the coordination among the requested inputs and outputs for a given cloud service, a strategy more QoS-aware oriented will be a relevant point to ponder.

Acknowledgement. This work has been partly funded by the MOST of China through the Project Key Technology of Service Platform for Cloud Manufacturing. The authors wish to acknowledge MOST for their support. We also wish to acknowledge our gratitude and appreciation to all the Project partners for their contribution during the development of various ideas and concepts presented in this paper.

References

1. Tao, F., Hu, Y.F., Zhou, Z.D.: Study on manufacturing grid and its resource service optimal-selection system. Int. J. Adv. Mfg Technology 37, 1022–1041 (2008)
2. Tao, F., Zhang, L., Venkatesh, V.C., Luo, Y., Cheng, Y.: Cloud manufacturing: a computing and service-oriented manufacturing model. Proceedings of the Institution of Mechanical Engineers, Part B: Journal of Engineering Manufacture, 1–8 (August 2011)

3. Ren, G., Gregory, M.: Servitization in manufacturing Companies – Literature Review, Research Progress and Cambridge service Research. Cranfield Product-Service Systems Seminar (November 2007)
4. Neely, A., Benedetinni, O., Visnjic, I.: The servitization of manufacturing: Further evidence. In: 18th Euro. Ops. Management Association Conf., Cambridge (July 2011)
5. Loughridge, M.: IBM Financial Model. IBM Investor Briefing (2010)
6. Ning, F., Zhou, W., Zhang, F., Yin, Q., Ni, X.: The Architecture of Cloud manufacturing and its key technologies research. In: Proceedings of IEEE Cloud Computing and Intelligence Systems (CCIS), pp. 259–263 (September 2011)
7. Buyya, R., Yeo, C.S., Venugopal, S.: Market-Oriented Cloud Computing: Vision, Hype, and reality for delivering it services as Computing Utilities, vol. 07, pp. 7–9. University of Melbourne, Australia (2008)
8. Xu, X.: From Cloud computing to Cloud manufacturing. Rob. and Comp. Mfg (July 2011)
9. Mou, T., Nie, L., Zhan, D., Xu, X.: Task Scheduling and Assignment Methods for Cloud Enterprises. In: Enterprise Interoperability V, pp. 427–437 (2012)
10. Zadeh, L.A.: Fuzzy sets. Information and Control 8, 338–553 (1965)
11. Liang, L.R., Lu, S., Wang, X., Lu, Y., Mandal, V., Patacsil, D., Kumar, D.: FM-test: A Fuzzy-Set-Theory-Based Approach to Differential Gene Expression Data Analysis. BMC Bioinformatics 7(4) (2006)
12. Atanassov, K.T.: Intuitionistic Fuzzy Sets. Fuzzy Sets and Systems, 87–96 (1986)
13. Tao, F., Zhao, D., Zhang, L.: Resource service optimal-selection based on intuitionistic fuzzy set and non-functionality QoS in manufacturing grid system. Knowledge and Information Systems 25(01), 185–208 (2010)
14. Xu, Z.: Some similarity evaluations of intuitionistic fuzzy sets and their applications to multiple attribute decision making. Fuzzy Optim. Decision Making 6(2), 109–121 (2007)
15. Genari, A.C., Guliato, D.: Similarity evaluations based on fuzzy sets. Federal University of Uberlandia, Brazil
16. Karaboga, D., Akay, B.: A comparative study of Artificial Bee Colony algorithm. Applied Mathematics and Computation 214(1), 108–132 (2009)
17. Karaboga, D., Gorkemli, B., Ozturk, C., Karaboga, N.: A comprehensive survey: artificial bee colony (ABC) algorithm and applications. Artificial Intelligence Review (March 2012)
18. Anandhakumar, R., Subramanian, S., Ganesan, S.: Modified ABC Algorithm for Generator Maintenance Scheduling. Int. J. of Comp. and Elec. Engineering 3(6), 812–819 (2011)

Achieving Flexible Process Interoperability in the Homecare Domain through Aspect-Oriented Service Composition

Duc Viet Bui[1], Maria Eugenia Iacob[2], Marten van Sinderen[2], and Alireza Zarghami[2]

[1] Cape Groep
[2] Centre for Telematics and Information Technology,
University of Twente
Enschede, The Netherlands
d.bui@capegroep.nl,
{m.e.iacob,m.j.vansinderen,a.zarghami}@utwente.nl

Abstract. In elderly care the shortage of available financial and human resources for coping with an increasing number of elderly people becomes critical. Current solutions to this problem focus on efficiency gains through the usage of information systems and include homecare services provided by IT systems. However, the current IT systems that integrate homecare services have difficulties in handling the user-context dynamicity and the diversity of needs and preferences of care-receivers. This makes the available homecare services hardly interoperable at the process level, particularly due to the lack of support for process flexibility. In this paper, we present an approach capable of dealing with such interoperability issues based on aspect-oriented service composition. We demonstrate the feasibility of our approach and of the proposed architecture by implementing a prototype for a reminder service scenario.

Keywords: process interoperability, process flexibility, aspect-oriented service composition, homecare services, orchestration.

1 Introduction

European countries are experiencing a rapidly growing number of elderly people. According to European Union's Health portal, by 2050, "the number of people aged 65 and above is expected to grow by 70% and the number of people aged over 80 by 170%" [1]. Consequently, healthcare systems are under pressure to address the increasing demands for elderly care. Information systems offering and integrating IT homecare-services for elderly [2] are believed to have the potential of reducing healthcare costs by supporting independent living of elderly in their own home.

There are already several providers of commercial services for remote monitoring services, such as bio-signals monitoring (e.g., blood-pressure, heart-rate and oximetry), and contextual information services (e.g., location and temperature). However, these services fail to deliver the expected benefits since they are to a large extent offered and used as isolated services. In addition, such services cannot cope with the diversity of needs and preferences of the user (e.g., in the case of a reminder service, one user may prefer a light signal to announce a reminder, while another prefers the vibration from a cell-phone), nor with the dynamicity of the user's context (e.g., change of the user's location or of the activity in which the user is engaged [3]).

Thus, an important challenge is to integrate existing homecare services through a single platform that allows user-driven service composition according to personal needs and preferences and that can automatically adapt the execution of a service composition according to the user-context at hand. We approach this challenge from the enterprise interoperability perspective [21] applied to the homecare domain [4, 24]: homecare services from different organizations should be able to work together or side by side, flexibly coordinated through an independent platform as required by needs, preferences and context. Our focus is not on syntactic or semantic interoperability, but on process interoperability. More precisely, we target *flexible process interoperability*, here defined as *the ability to coordinate different services in order to fulfill a complex user need in a dynamic environment*. User needs are complex since they require multiple services and may be context-dependent. Context-dependency arises from the dynamic nature of the environment in which the user consumes the services.

We propose an aspect-oriented service composition architecture which is based on the principles of service orientation, and is able to deal with context dynamicity and user requirements diversity [4]. We argue that the use of aspect-orientation facilitates the maintenance and management of complex processes and business rules. Also, we adhere to the design science research methodology as proposed in [19, 20].

The remainder of the paper is organized as follows. In Section 2, the reminder service scenario is presented that will serve as illustration, running example and test case for the approach and prototype we further propose in the paper. Then, a review of the existing web-service composition approaches will be presented in Section 3. In Section 4, our aspect-oriented service composition architecture will be presented. The implemented prototype described in Section 5 demonstrates the feasibility of our approach. The proposed architecture has been instantiated in a prototype, which in turn has been tested in two situations arising from the chosen scenario. Finally, in Section 6, we address the advantages and weaknesses of our approach, draw some conclusions and give some pointers to future work.

2 Scenario

To capture the dynamicity and diversity of user-context in the homecare domain, we use the following "reminder service" scenario:

Jan is an elderly person who lives in an apartment which equipped with the necessary infrastructure to support homecare applications. For example in the apartment two medicine dispensers are available, which are connected to the internet and can exchange information with our homecare service platform. Jan has to take some medication at 11:50 PM, on a daily basis. Among other things, the homecare system must remind him to take the medication. A reminder is sent to Jan three times up to 15 minutes later than the scheduled intake time. If the medication is not removed from any of the available medicine dispensers, an alarm will be sent to the care center. Jan also has a hearing impairment and uses a wheelchair, so the doors inside the apartment open automatically. He prefers to take the medication from the closest medicine dispenser (MD) at night. Two MDs, filled with the required medication, have been installed, one in the kitchen and the other one in the bedroom. The MD inside the kitchen has embedded light. The TV installed in the bedroom, the lights in the apartment and a wristwatch can all be used as reminder devices for taking medication. However, Jan prefers not to be reminded by lights after midnight.

Linda, another care-receiver, prefers her PDA as reminders.

Nancy, as a care-giver, wants to create the desired application for both Jan and Linda. Because she understands better than IT specialists her patients' situation and requirements, she must tailor the application for both of them.

3 Background

In this section, we give first identify the requirements imposed by the homecare application domain to the future service composition architecture, and we give an brief overview of the existing web-service composition approaches.

3.1 Homecare Constraints

Besides the dynamicity of user-context and the diversity of users' preferences and needs, there are three major requirements imposed on applications used in the homecare domain, namely, safety, non-intrusiveness for care-receivers and limited technical skills of care-givers and users. Safety constrains require healthcare systems to be error-free [6] due to ethical and legal considerations regarding the impact such systems may have on human lives. Hence, safety means that any reaction/behavior of the system is controllable. In other words, care-givers have to know exactly how the system behaves. The non-intrusiveness requirement refers to the fact that the system should have no impact on the normal life of care-receivers [7,8]. The limited technical skills of care-givers and care-receivers require the system to be designed such that it can be used and tailored by persons with no technical knowledge [6].

3.2 Existing Web-Service Composition Approaches

A web-service composition is "an aggregate of services collectively composed to automate a particular task or business process" [9]. According to Rao, et al. [10], there are three approaches to service compositions: static workflow-based compositions, dynamic workflow-based compositions and Artificial Intelligence (AI) planning - based compositions. In the case of the static workflow-based composition approach, a predefined process model has to be specified before the actual composition of web services takes place. Thus, in this type of composition the selection and binding of web services is realized upfront [10]. The dynamic workflow composition approach is based on the generation (at run time) of process models and selection of web services [10]. Based on logical theorem provers or on AI planners, AI-planning approaches produce service compositions automatically without a predefined workflow [10].

3.3 Why Dynamic Workflow Composition and Aspect-Oriented Approach

The specific homecare constraints influence the way in which suitable web-service compositions are determined. AI planning approaches allow the creation of the web-service composition in an automatic manner with minimum interactions with care-givers, and, thus, diminishing the impact of limited IT skills of care-givers. However, practically, it is not feasible to generate service compositions automatically in all cases with high accuracy due to the highly complex web service environment and the difficulty in capturing behavior in sufficient detail [10, 11]. Therefore, from the perspective of safety criteria, AI planning approaches have serious disadvantages due to unreliability and lack of control/predictability of the system's behavior.

Static workflow composition approaches serve safety criteria much better because the care-givers know exactly the behavior of system. However, the static approaches seriously constrain the adaptability and flexibility of the service compositions. As the result, the care-givers have to aid the system in dealing with new changes of care-receivers' needs. Furthermore, mostly such compositions will become intrusive, by forcing care-receivers to adapt to the system.

Taking the considerations above into account we have chosen the dynamic workflow composition approach because of the following reasons:

- It is based on a generated workflow. Thus the care-givers can still control the system's main activities and behavior.
- It is capable to capture changes in the user-context or the user needs, and to generate accordingly different composition workflows, by adding extra services into a predefined reference workflow. Which services are inserted into the reference workflow is determined by a set of business rules. In this way, by external changes, the rules may evaluate differently, and consequently the resulting compositions are adjusted accordingly. In this way, diversity and dynamicity are also partly supported.

There are many techniques that focus on the idea of dynamic workflow composition as described above. Inspired by aspect-oriented programming (AOP), Charfi and Menzini [12] propose an approach to externalize business rules from processes by proposing an extension of BPEL (AO4BPEL). This approach requires the modification of process engines to make it possible to handle the so-called pointcuts, advices and aspects [13].

Rosenberg and Dustdar [14] propose a Rule Interceptor Service which intercepts all incoming and outgoing Web service calls, maps them to business rules, and then applies associated business rules. A mapping document is used to map a call to business rules. Eijndhoven et al. [15] exploit the power of a business process engine (Aqualogic BPM Studio) and ILOG business rule engine. At variability points in the process, the process engine sends a request to the rule engine. Based on the input data from the request and the current context, the rule engine evaluates its business rules and the returns the result to the process engine. In [23], a tuple space has been proposed to provide more flexibility with respect to data flows. In this approach, the data can be added and shared by a process or rule engine on the fly. This approach, is somewhat similar to [15], in the sense that it also assumes that the process engine only needs to call the rule engine at some specific variability points. In [24], the decision-making rules have been wrapped and provided as a so-called decision service which can be called by the process engine. Moreover, the decision service can notify the processes asynchronously to update their behavior.

In the homecare domain, the process specifying the behavior of the system in case of a user-context change can be very complex. For example, the process to aid care-receivers with Alzheimer disease to go out for physical exercise can be very complex and may involve many rules and activities. In addition, in order to be able to manage service compositions for care-receivers with different diseases, we need a method that can diminish the maintenance tasks. Taking this into account and the specific requirements imposed by the homecare domain, we argue that a service composition approach in should be capable 1) to execute the rules anywhere and anytime during the process instead of limiting that to some variability points and 2), to insert new services anywhere in the process (if necessary) as a reaction of system to a context change. Both requirements cannot be satisfied by approaches such as [15, 23], since both the invocation of rules and the adaptation of processes is limited to variability points. Using the Aspect-Oriented approach (AOA) by Charfi and Menzini [12] would enable us to support these capabilities. However, AOA should be applied in such a way it can be used in combination with existing implementation platforms.

4 An Aspect-Oriented Service Composition Architecture

4.1 Aspect-Oriented Approach

Before presenting our architecture, we start with description of the AOA [12] and the basic constructs used in aspect orientation.

As mentioned above, in all dynamic workflow composition approaches, there are two basic elements: general workflows and business rules. More exactly, the general workflow captures the non-variable part of the service composition, and models the basic control flows, services and the dataflow. Business rules are used to represent policy-sensitive aspects of the composition, which are likely to change over time. Charfi and Menzini [12] introduce the AOA in order to separate business rules from business processes by using three elements: aspects, joint points and advices. Aspect information encoded in XML files (so-called aspect files) includes a set of joint points. A joint point is a specific point, after or before one activity in the workflow. A joint point also links to advices, which are external services or processes that have to be executed when the process execution reaches that joint point. Conditional statements can be embedded in the joint point to check the inputs taken from the general workflow and decide which advices are deployed. In a similar way, aspect information may also describe the computation rules which are applied to calculate new values of certain business process variables according to user-context changes [13]. Figure 1 shows the relation between the elements mentioned above.

It is worth noticing that an aspect is different from a business rule because besides containing a business rule, an aspect also specifies where the business rule is applied by its joint points list. Thus, one can separate business rules from specific processes and can increase the reusability of business rules.

For example, the general process shown in Figure 8 involves some mandatory services, such as a service to activate the reminder and a service to check whether the

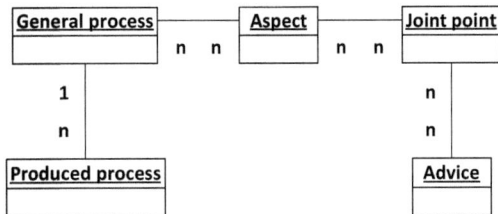

Fig. 1. Relationship between AOA elements

medicine is taken. One possible business rule (in the form of an aspect) may concern saving user-context after each activity of the general process. When reaching the joint points (following all activities of the general process), the process executor will invoke the respective advice and save the user-context.

4.2 The Proposed Architecture

In this section, we propose the aspect-oriented service composition architecture that enables the interoperability and integration of homecare services. These third-party services providing information on bio-signals (heartbeat rate and blood pressure) and location are assumed to be available and can be exposed through their interfaces. It should be noted that we do not intend to design such services.

To support aspects, joint points and advices, we introduce the following three components. First, an *advice repository* is introduced to store advices. An advice, as mentioned earlier, is an external service or process which is written in BPEL and can be executed by a process engine. Second, an *aspect repository* is used to store aspect files. Third, we develop an *aspect manager* with two main functions – calculating new values for variables in general processes and determining advices. When determined, the advices are then handled by the process executor.

To support dynamicity and diversity, besides the components above, the system also needs the following infrastructure components.

Adaptor: this component has the ability to "provide connectivity, semantic disambiguation and transition services" between our application and 3-rd party services [16]. Therefore, not only it can enable communications in two directions between third party services and the system but it can also convert the different interfaces, protocols, data formats of different parties into the standardized ones for the system and vice versa.

Context Server: the context server has four functions: listening to the user-context changes from adaptors, storing context information of users and devices in a database, allowing querying of context information by the aspect manager and informing the aspect manager about user-context changes.

Process Executor: the process executor takes care of the execution of general processes and of the external services/processes, as shown in Figure 2.

Service Discovery Manager: in case there are many third-party services offering the same functions, the service discovery manager aims to assist care-receivers by searching services, prioritizing them and select the most suitable ones.

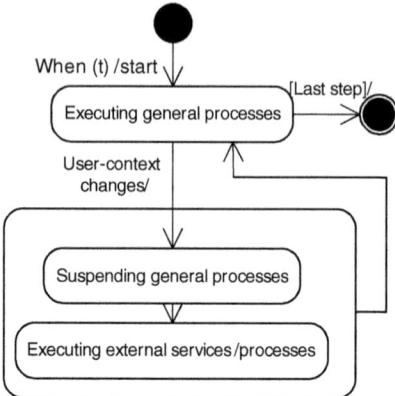

Fig. 2. The behavior of the process executor

In the scope of this paper, we assume that the service discovery manager, adaptors and the context server are available and ready to use. We focus solely on the process executor, the aspect repository, the advice repository and the aspect manager. The proposed architecture is shown in Figure 3.

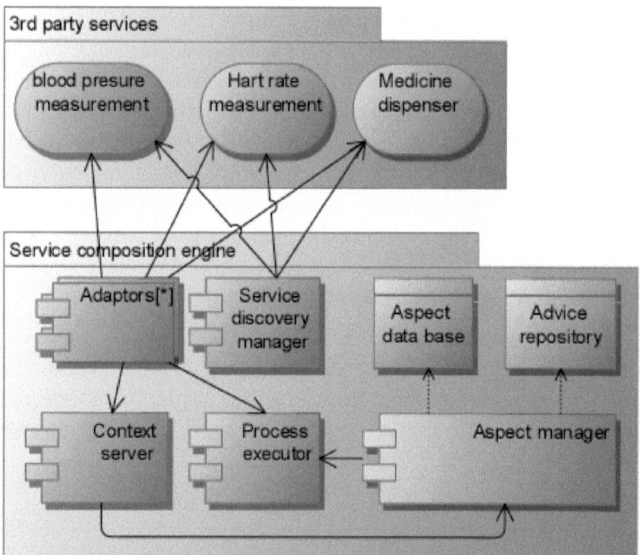

Fig. 3. The proposed SOA-based architecture

5 Implementation

To show the feasibility of our approach, we have implemented a prototype that follows the proposed architecture. In this section we discuss the development platforms we used and we explain the implementation of each element, with an emphasis on the aspect manager. Finally, we use in two scenarios to demonstrate how the prototype can handle user-context dynamicity and diversity of needs/preferences.

5.1 Development Platform

For building the prototype we have used the Lombardi process engine [17]: a business process manager that allows creating process models, implementing process steps, running and inspecting processes, optimizing and installing process applications [17]. Another feature of this engine we have used is its JavaScript API, which allowed us to invoke one process/service programmatically from another process.

5.2 Implementing the Architecture's Components

Below we discuss the implementation of the three elements supporting AOA.

Aspect Files' Structure: With respect to aspects, we follow the specification of AO4BPEL proposed by Charfi and Menzini [18] describing the structure of aspect files. In short, this structure starts with the name of the aspect, followed by pointcut element containing a set of joint points. An advice is a BPEL activity. Other elements like variables, partner links, fault handlers, structured and basic activities in AO4BPEL are inherited from BPEL.

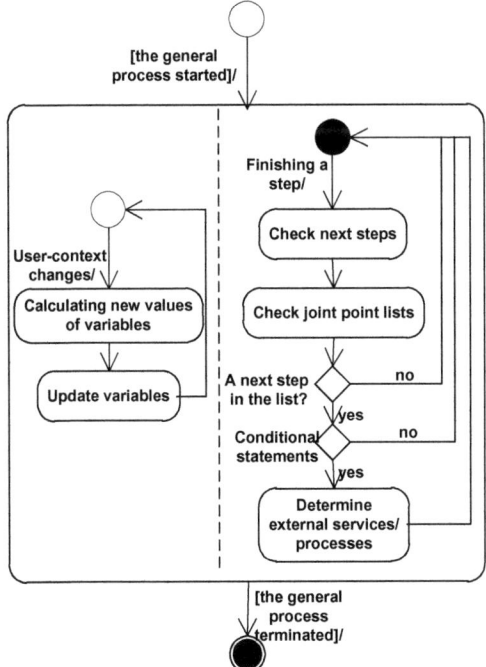

Fig. 4. The behavior of the aspect manager

58   D.V. Bui et al.

Advices: as mentioned above, advices can be defined in aspect files as BPEL activities. However, in our approach, we decided to define advices in separate files. In this way, it is possible to reuse advices in different aspects.

Aspect Manager: to avoid a modification of the process engine, we propose an independent aspect manager. This component is a Java script embedded before or after one step of a general process. Because of the predefined structure and the content of aspect files, the script can parse aspect files to archive information about joint points, conditional statements and advices. Then, it evaluates condition statements to determine suitable advices or calculates new values for variables in the general process according to user-context changes. The behavior of the aspect manager is depicted in the diagram shown in Figure 4.

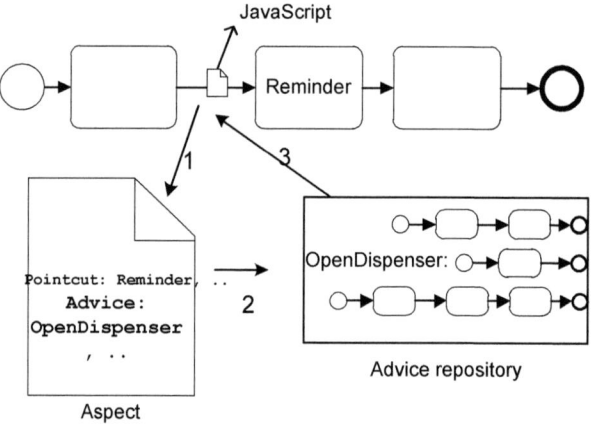

Fig. 5. Inserting a process in a general process

Figure 5 shows the location of an aspect in a general process and explains how external processes/services (in the form of advices) can be inserted, via aspects, between the steps of this process. The arrows in Figure 5 have the following significance:

1: The aspect manager (JavaScript code) parses aspect files
2: The advice is found in advice repository
3: The process engine executes the advice

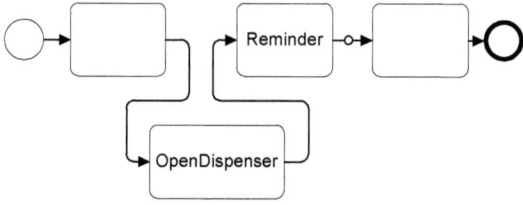

Fig. 6. The produced process

After the addition of the OpenDispenser external (advice) process to the general process, the actual generated and executed process is as depicted in Figure 6.

To update the variables of the general process, a java script is also placed in a parallel process such that the update task is performed independently without influencing or being influenced by the general process.

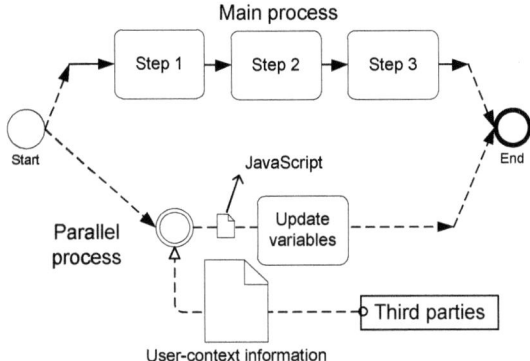

Fig. 7. Update variables

5.3 Test Cases

In this section, two situations related to the chosen scenario will be addressed. Each of them is associated with different types of requirements. The first one focuses on dynamicity aspects and refers to the case when the care-receiver (Jan) moves from the kitchen to the bedroom where the dispenser needs to be opened automatically (a service to open this dispenser should be available). The second case captures the diversity of preferences/needs of different care-receivers by introducing a second care-receiver. However, before discussing these situations in further detail, the general process for the reminder service scenario is presented.

The General Process for Reminder Service Scenario. In the reminder service scenario, the general process that is stable for all user-context changes and user preferences is depicted in Figure 8. The process is triggered by a care giver. The first activity is an inquiry of the user-context information to initialize the variables of the process. For example, based on the care-receiver's location information, the system can calculate t1, t2 and the endpoints of the web-service to invoke (i.e., the suitable reminder device). t1 is the waiting time from the moment the process is triggered until the first reminder is sent. After that, the system waits in t2 before checking whether the medicine is taken or not. If not, the process goes back to the reminder task. This loop is executed until the number of sent reminders is equal to a predefined number, resulting in one alarm sent to care-givers. The logic for the calculation is specified in an aspect file. The reason is that this variable calculation is a crosscutting concern occurring in many places: after the first inquiry and after any information update sent by the context server.

Situation 1: User-Context Dynamicity. In this paragraph, we describe the expected behavior of the system's in case of a context change and the results of the generated process execution.

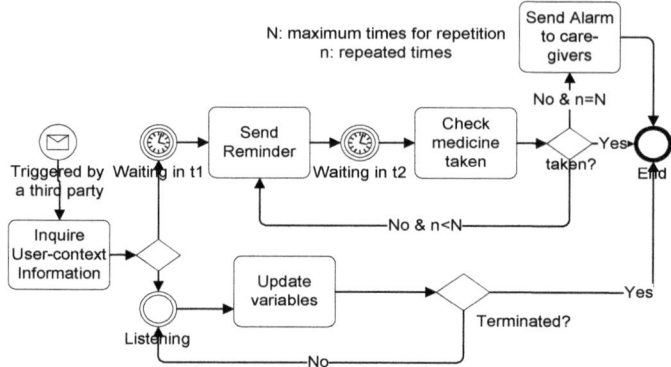

Fig. 8. The general process for the reminder service scenario

a) User-context change: Jan moves from the kitchen to the bedroom. In the kitchen, built-in lights are used as reminders while in the sleeping room the TV is used. The medicine dispenser in the bedroom needs to be opened automatically.

b) The process' variables are: t1, t2 as described above; an endpoint address pointing to a specific device (as reminder); user-context information including user' ID number, location and time.

c) Expected system behavior: in dealing with the change, the system needs to update the endpoint address to point to the TV in the bedroom. The external service to open the dispenser is required to be invoked before Jan can remove his medicine.

d) Aspect configurations: there are two aspect configurations: first, for calculating new values of variables; second, for inserting a service to open dispenser. For the sake of simplicity and to avoid the confusion that may be caused by XML tags, we simplify the two aspects' specification by using natural language as shown in Figure 9 and in Figure 10.

Aspect name: calculating variables		
Pointcut: inquire user-context information; listening		
Conditions: user's ID is "p104jan" (Jan's ID)		
Type: after		
Variable: location		
Location	Endpoint	Device
Kitchen →	http://130.89.227.130:9090/ws/Ucare_WS_notifyReminder/	Lights
Bedroom →	http://130.89.227.132:9090/ws/Ucare_WS_notifyReminder/	TV

Fig. 9. Calculate variables for Jan

Aspect name: open dispenser
Pointcut: send reminder
Conditions: user's ID is "p104jan"
Type: before
Variable: location
Conditions of advice: current location is "bedroom"
Advice: open dispenser

Fig. 10. Open dispenser

The first aspect, called calculating variables, states that the following action will be performed if the care-receiver is Jan and the current step is after inquire user-context information or listening in the general process. This aspect simply matches the user's location with the endpoint of services, which invokes the corresponding device at the user's location. Hence, when Jan is in the bedroom, the television becomes the reminder. This can be considered a computation rule without calling advice.

However, as the care-receiver changes his location to the bedroom, one advice (open dispenser) needs to be injected in the general process. This aspect (rule) is shown in Figure 10. This aspect, called *open dispenser,* means that for the user with ID "p104jan", if the current step is before *send reminder* step, an advice to invoke *open dispenser* will be performed.

e) Result: after applying these two aspects, the general process will change into the generated process shown in Figure 11.

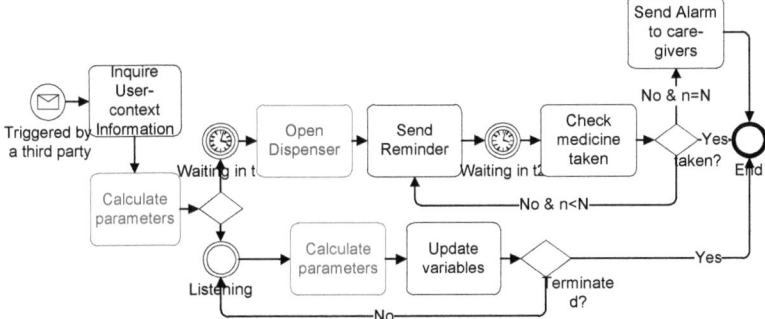

Fig. 11. Produced composition

Situation 2: Diversity of Preferences/Needs. To illustrate the behavior of the system in case of diversity of user preferences/needs, we use another example, in which a new care-receiver, Linda, is introduced, adding new references.

a) Different references: Linda, another care-receiver, prefers her PDA over lights or any other devices as reminders.

b) Aspect configuration: similar to the previous situation, by changing the conditional statements, a different preference is formed (see Figure 12).

Aspect name: calculating variables		
Pointcut: inquire user-context information; listening		
Conditions: user's ID is "p104Linda" (Linda's ID)		
Type: after		
Variable: location		
Location	**Endpoint**	**Device**
Kitchen →	http://**130.89.227.131**:9090/ws/Ucare_WS_notifyReminder/	PDA
Bedroom →	http://**130.89.227.131**:9090/ws/Ucare_WS_notifyReminder/	PDA
Corridor →	http://**130.89.227.131**:9090/ws/Ucare_WS_notifyReminder/	PDA

Fig. 12. calculate variables for Linda

c) Result: as the ID is a part of user-context information, composing aspects with different IDs reflect the diversity of users' preferences/needs.

6 Conclusions

In this paper, motivated by two current problems of the homecare domain, namely, dynamicity and diversity, we have applied an aspect-oriented approach to the design and implementation of an architecture for the dynamic workflow composition of services. By this approach, not only we have externalized business rules from business processes, but we have also ensured the flexible process interoperability of homecare services in complex processes. Moreover this approach facilitates enterprise interoperability through the composition of services and processes resulting in complex integrated applications. As demonstrated in the previous section, the combination of aspect orientation and SOA has many advantages. The diversity of user preferences is easily controlled by changing the aspect configuration as discussed in the second situation described in the previous section. With regard to the dynamicity of user-context, due to the separation of business rules (in aspect files) from processes, the care-givers can easily update or add new business rules to adapt the system's behavior according to different care-receiver needs or contexts. Furthermore, the idea of externalizing advices and storing them into an advice repository can increase the reusability of advices. This is particularly useful in complex processes where finding places to insert/remove services is time-consuming. Another advantage worth being noted is the fact that aspect manger provides a light-weight AOA implementation solution in the sense that it does not require a modification of the process engine to support aspects (as suggested by [12]), as long as a JavaScript API is supported. Finally, as a part of general processes, the aspect manager can access directly the its variables, minimizing the effort to pass data to external processes and services.

Our approach also has some limitations. Some are inherited from the aspect – oriented approach of Charfi and Menzini and concern the lack of support for complex and multiple business rules [12]. The usage Java script also raises concerns about its flexibility and about its ability to handle different types of business rules. We are currently improving our approach to also support inference rules. Regarding the non-intrusiveness criterion, it should be noted that only pre-defined changes can be handled by the system. In the case of unforeseen events, the care-givers have to assist system developers in defining new business rules and incorporate them in general processes.

References

1. Health-EU. Elderly (2011), http://ec.europa.eu/health-eu/my_health/elderly/index_en.html
2. Gaßner, K., Conrad, M.: ICT enabled independent living for elderly, A status-quo analysis on products and the research landscape in the field of Ambient Assisted Living (AAL) in EU-27 (October 2010)
3. Dey, A.K., Abowd, G.D., Salber, D.: A conceptual framework and a toolkit for supporting the rapid prototyping of context-aware applications. Hum.-Comput. Interact. 16(2), 97–166 (2001)

4. Zarghami, A., Zarifi Eslami, M., Sapkota, B., van Sinderen, M.: Service Realization and Compositions Issues in the Homecare Domain. In: 6th International Conference on Software and Data Technologies, ICSOFT 2011, Seville, Spain (July 2011)
5. O'Brien, L., Merson, P., Bass, L.: Quality Attributes for Service-Oriented Architectures. In: Proceedings of the International Workshop on Systems Development in SOA Environments, p. 3. IEEE Computer Society (2007)
6. Garde, S., Knaup, P.: Requirements engineering in health care: the example of chemotherapy planning in paediatric oncology. Requirements Engineering 11(4), 265–278 (2006)
7. Shin, J.H., et al.: Ubiquitous House and Unconstrained Monitoring Devices for Home Healthcare System. In: 6th International Special Topic Conference on Information Technology Applications in Biomedicine, ITAB 2007 (2007)
8. Eslami, M.Z., Sinderen, M.V.: Flexible Home Care Automation. In: Proceedings of PervasiveHealth 2009 Conference (2009)
9. Erl, T.: SOA Design Patterns. Prentice Hall (2009)
10. Rao, J., Su, X.: A Survey of Automated Web Service Composition Methods. In: Cardoso, J., Sheth, A.P. (eds.) SWSWPC 2004. LNCS, vol. 3387, pp. 43–54. Springer, Heidelberg (2005)
11. Hull, R., et al.: E-services: a look behind the curtain. In: Proceedings of the Twenty-Second ACM SIGMOD-SIGACT-SIGART Symposium on Principles of Database Systems, pp. 1–14. ACM, San Diego (2003)
12. Charfi, A., Mezini, M.: AO4PBEL: an aspect-oriented extention to BPEL. World Wide Web 10, 309–344 (2007)
13. Charfi, A., Mezini, M.: Hybrid web service composition: business processes meet business rules. In: Proceedings of the 2nd International Conference on Service Oriented Computing, pp. 30–38. ACM, New York (2004)
14. Rosenberg, F., Dustdar, S.: Business Rules Integration in BPEL – A Service-Oriented Approach. In: Proceedings of the Seventh IEEE International Conference on E-Commerce Technology, pp. 476–479. IEEE Computer Society (2005)
15. van Eijndhoven, T., Iacob, M.E., Ponisio, M.L.: Achieving Business Process Flexibility with Business Rules. In: 12th International IEEE Enterprise Distributed Object Computing Conference, EDOC 2008 (2008)
16. Papazoglou, M., van den Heuvel, W.-J.: Service oriented architectures: approaches, technologies and research issues. The VLDB Journal 16(3), 389–415 (2007)
17. IBM-InfoCentre. Lombardi tasks (2011), http://publib.boulder.ibm.com/infocenter/wle/v7r2/index.jsp (cited June 01, 2011)
18. Charfi, A.: Aspect-Oriented Workflow Languages: AO4BPEL and Applications. In: Fachbereich Informatik. TU Darmstadt, Darmstadt (2007); Smith, T.F., Waterman, M.S.: Identification of Common Molecular Subsequences. J. Mol. Biol. 147, 195–197 (1981)
19. Hevner, A.R., March, S.T., Park, J.: Design research in information systems research. MIS Quarterly 28(1), 75–105 (2004)
20. Peffers, K., Tuunanen, T., Rothenberger, M., Chatterjee, S.: A Design Science Research Methodology for Information Systems Research. Journal of Management Information Systems 24(3), 45–77 (2008)
21. Chen, D., Doumeingts, G., Vernadat, F.: Architectures for Enterprise Integration and Interoperability: Past, Present and Future. Computer in Industry 59, 647–659 (2008)
22. Zarifi Eslami, M., van Sinderen, M.J.: Flexible home care automation adapting to the personal and evolving needs and situations of the patient. In: 3rd Intl. Conf. on Pervasive Computing Technologies for Healthcare, PervasiveHealth 2009, pp. 1–2. IEEE (2009)

23. Sapkota, B., Asuncion, C., Iacob, M., van Sinderen, M.: A Simple Solution for Information Sharing in Hybrid Web Service Composition. In: 15th IEEE Int. Conf. on Enterprise Distributed Object Computing Conference, EDOC 2011, pp. 235–244 (2011)
24. Zarghami, A., Sapkota, B., Zarifi Eslami, M., van Sinderen, M.: Decision as a service: Separating decision-making from application process logic. In: 16th IEEE Intl. Conf. on Enterprise Distributed Object Computing, EDOC 2012, pp. 103–112 (2012)
25. Asuncion, C.H., Iacob, M.-E., van Sinderen, M.J.: Towards a flexible service integration through separation of business rules. In: 14th IEEE International EDOC Enterprise Computing Conference, EDOC 2010, pp. 184–193. IEEE Comp. Soc. (2010)

On the Extended Clinical Workflows for Personalized Healthcare

Milan Zdravković and Miroslav Trajanović

Faculty of Mechanical Engineering, University of Niš,
ul. Aleksandra Medvedeva 14, 18000 Niš, Serbia
{milan.zdravkovic,miroslav.trajanovic}@masfak.ni.ac.rs

Abstract. There are many cases in the clinical practice where using personalized medical products could decrease the cost of treatment and risk of possible complications. However, due to the large costs and long manufacturing lead time, the medical products are customized to the individual patient's needs only in a few critical treatments. One of the main cost factors of the collaboration between the clinical centres and custom medical product suppliers is uptake of human effort in exchange of knowledge between two domains and corresponding issues. In this paper, we use the concepts of the networked enterprises to define the extended clinical workflow which spans the medical and manufacturing practice. We identify the associated systems infrastructure of this workflow and related interoperability issues. The extended workflow is demonstrated on the case study for custom orthopedic implants manufacturing.

Keywords: Ontology, Enterprise Interoperability, Supply Chain Management, SCOR.

1 Introduction

Current fragmentation of health sciences and medical care along traditional boundaries is considered [1] as artificial and inefficient with respect to many scientific hypotheses that establish the correspondences between the concepts from the different scientific disciplines (biology, physiology, etc.) or clinical specialties (such as cardiology, neurology, etc.). This fragmentation can be considered at modeling level, where reductionist approach (modeling on a dimensional scale, such as organ, tissue, cellular and molecular) dominates over the systemic one [2].

It is foreseen that a more effective approach will integrate the different relevant areas according to the focus of the particular problem, unconstrained by scientific discipline, anatomical subsystem and temporal or dimensional scale [3]. The Virtual Physiological Human (VPH) paradigm [1] is intended to provide a unifying framework that enables and practically benefits from the integration of inter-disciplinary data and observations about human's biology. These observations may be collected, organized and shared across the laboratories and hospitals, so that clinical and non-clinical experts can collaboratively interpret, model, validate and understand the data. Thus, this unifying framework is expected to facilitate: 1) integration of physiological processes across different length and time scales; 2) integration of descriptive data with predictive models; and 3) integration across disciplines [4]. Then, this integration will eventually lead to the practical benefits of the future healthcare system, such as personalized care solutions; reduced need for experiments on animals; more holistic approach to medicine; and preventative approach to treatment of diseases [4].

The impact of the VPH on industry will first be felt in the medical device and pharmaceutical industries [1]. The prediction sets an interesting assumption that the knowledge relevant to VPH will be integrated faster across the boundaries of all organizations involved in a healthcare (including hospitals, clinical centers, as well as pharmaceutical and manufacturing industries), than within the clinical centers. The prediction is argued by the global distribution of innovation interest and knowledge and developing trend in providing personalized healthcare, which is often related to customization of the medical products.

As an effect of this integration, the traditional clinical workflows will be extended to involve all actors that contribute to delivery of a personalized healthcare, in systematic, efficient way. In addition, the rate of use of custom medical products, such as custom head and neck support systems [5], orthopedic implants [6], patient rooms [7], blood coagulants [8] and others will increase. As a consequence, more and more supply chains, and not only pharmaceutical ones [9] will span the clinical workflows. This effect will facilitate higher degree of customization of the medical products. It reduces the risk, efficiency and cost of treatment, due to increased similarity to the individual patient's anatomy and physiology. For example, standard bone implants are sometimes not sufficient because of abnormal joint anatomy or possible risks of postoperative complications [10], such as aseptic loosening which occurs due to uneven stress distribution on the bone surface. This problem can be addressed by custom design process in which the design of the implant is accommodated to the specific features of the patient's anatomy. However, the traditional approach to supply chain planning cannot be applied in the scenarios of custom medical products manufacturing, due to long delivery times.

Manufacturing of the custom medical products is considered as one-of-a-kind manufacturing, where the customization requirements often affect not only a principal manufacturer but also its suppliers. The manufacturing of a custom medical product could also include high-tech services by different suppliers, which are based on the models which need to be exchanged (for example, the reverse engineering of the missing part of a bone). Typically, some of these services precede supply chain planning phase because their results often determine the basic product's topology.

Because of such a complex scenario, clinicians often choose standard products, even at the cost of sacrificing the above listed benefits of custom ones. Exactly this, not always desirable compromise was the main motivation for the research presented in this paper. The key research problem was identified as "high complexity of the supply chain planning and execution in custom medical products manufacturing".

In our research, this problem is addressed by combining practices of collaborative networked organizations with clinical practices. As one of the results, an extended clinical workflow is proposed. Besides the traditional activities of the clinical practice, this extended workflow also encompasses planning, decision making, design, sourcing and manufacturing of custom medical products. It also considers systems' and knowledge infrastructures which facilitate the efficient execution of this extended workflow. In a way, the models and knowledge required to resolve interoperability issues of such a workflow can be considered as extension to VPH paradigm, because the topology and design of a custom medical product correspond to physiological and anatomical features of a patient, represented by VPH models.

The remainder of this paper is structured as follows. In part 2, the traditional clinical workflow is described in context of Electronic Health Record, a paradigm which is often used to integrate patient specific information throughout the history of medical care delivery. Part 3 presents the extended clinical workflow, associated resources, namely systems infrastructure; and analysis of interoperability issues of such infrastructure. In part 4, a study is presented, on the case of manufacturing the custom orthopedic implant for diagnosis of bone cancer of tibia. Finally, in part 5, the main conclusions are drawn.

2 Electronic Health Records and Clinical Workflows

In practice, the clinical workflows are often defined in context of Electronic Health Record (EHR). Health Information Management Systems Society's (HIMSS) defines EHR as[1] "the longitudinal electronic record of patient health information generated by one or more encounters in any care delivery setting..."

Many benefits from maintaining EHR are expected, such as automation and streamlining of the clinical workflow, evidence-based decision support for diagnosis or treatment prescription (based on accurate and complete record of a clinical patient encounter), support to other care-related activities such as billing, reporting and quality management. An EHR enables the hospital administrator to extract the billing data, the physician to assess the effectiveness of treatments, a nurse to monitor treatment and reactions and a researcher to analyze the efficiency of medications.

One of the main issues of EHR is the fact that it is not a record of all care provided to the patient in all facilities over time. It is generated and maintained within the single medical centre. Even so, one of the greatest challenges of maintaining EHR arises from the collaborative effort in collection and analysis of its data. Namely, medical centers can be considered as complex enterprises. They typically consist of multiple healthcare facilities, such as affiliated hospitals and clinics, diagnostic and treatment centers and laboratories. Managing all of these departments implies the complex business processes, for which EHR is fully associated.

2.1 Clinical Workflow

In a way, EHR is the patient specific representation of a clinical workflow, combined with information (from the observations) collected in the course of this workflow. It

---

[1] http://www.himss.org/ASP/topics_ehr.asp

typically connects administrative data with information from the relevant health information systems. Figure 1 illustrates a simplified representation of a clinical workflow for inpatient care.

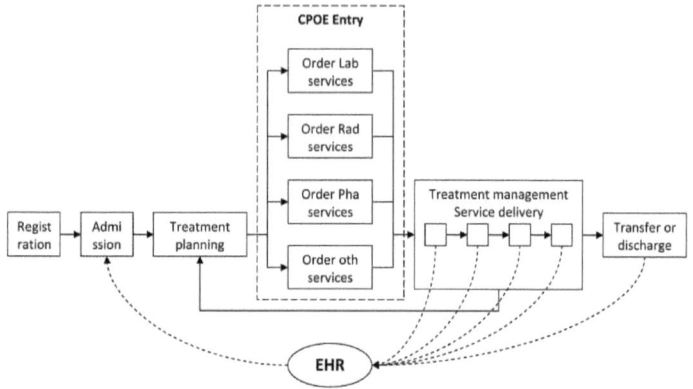

Fig. 1. Simplified representation of the clinical workflow for inpatient care

Registration, admissions, discharge, and transfer (RADT) data are the key components of EHRs. These data include vital information for accurate patient identification and assessment, such as name, demographics, employer information, etc. The registration portion of an EHR contains a patient identifier (master patient index - MPI), which is identifiable only inside the organization in which the EHR is maintained. EHR record for a specific patient is recovered during his/her admission. Admission notes are added in case that inpatient care need to be provided and include patient's status, reasons why the patient is being admitted and initial instructions for patient care.

An EHR can be considered as patient specific RADT data, integrated with respective information from Laboratory Information Systems, Radiology Information Systems, Electronic clinical documentation systems and pharmacy systems. This integration is carried out by Computerized Physician Order Entries (CPOE) which permits clinical providers to electronically order laboratory, pharmacy, radiology and other services.

CPOE entries are initially entered according to first patient observations and treatment plan. Once the treatments are launched, namely during and after entered orders execution, it may become necessary to require additional actions, such as pre-operation planning, other tests, etc. When all treatments (in one or multiple iterations) are carried out, the patient is discharged or transferred. All treatments' results and notes, including the administrative data on the discharge and transfer are added to a patient's EHR.

3   Extended Clinical Workflows and Associated Systems Infrastructure

In general, two of the most critical non-technical barriers to customization are: 1) lack of efficiency of manufacturing enterprise to handle one-of-a-kind production tasks;

and 2) lack of efficiency in transfer of multi-disciplinary knowledge, required for the design of custom product. Manufacturing enterprises refine their designs for simplicity and cost; they design their workflows for volume manufacturing. Hence, by default, they are not capable to handle one-of-a-kind manufacturing tasks efficiently.

One-of-a-kind manufacturing is considered as a case for the Virtual Enterprises. Virtual Enterprise (VE) is a temporary network of independent organizations, who join together quickly to exploit fast-changing opportunities and then dissolve [11]. It is characterized by a short-living appearance of a supply chain, capable to produce low volume of high variety of products, by drawing from the loosely-coupled, heterogeneous environment of available competences, capabilities and resources. This environment is sometimes called Virtual Breeding Environment (VBE), defined as a pool of organizations and related supporting institutions that have both the potential and the will to cooperate with each other, through the establishment of a long-term cooperation agreement and interoperable infrastructure [12]. In our research, VBE and VE paradigms are used to propose the interoperable infrastructure which will support the extended clinical workflows for custom medical products.

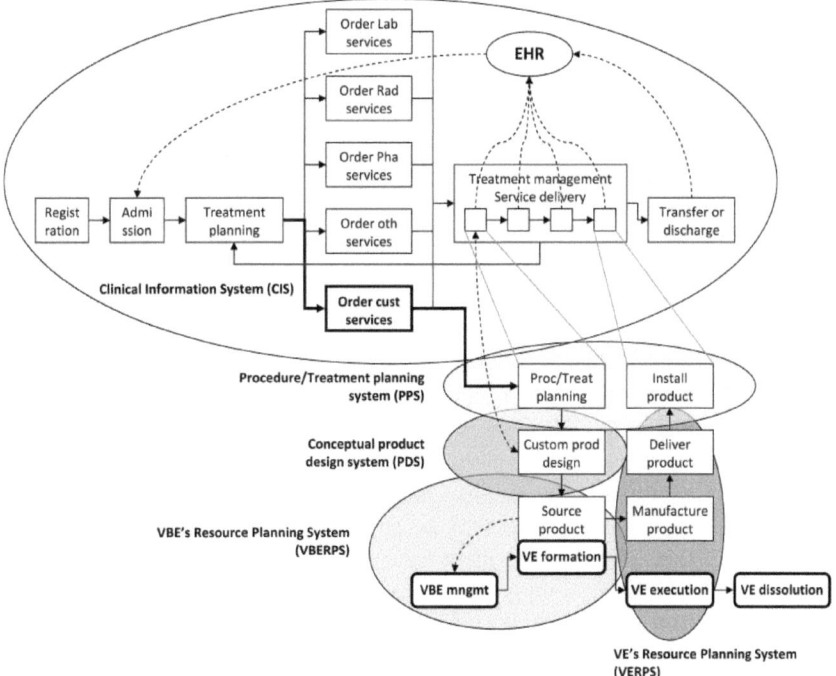

Fig. 2. Simplified representation of the extended clinical workflow

In traditional settings, the workflow for manufacturing of custom medical products includes many human analysis and decisions, such as interpretation and analysis of CT scans and lab results, mechanical analysis, collecting inputs and approvals, etc. The lack of efficiency to adapt their traditional workflows to these activities becomes even more critical when enterprises are required to subcontract the different parts or services suppliers. All this human involvement includes a number of interactions between different experts in which functional (medical), organizational and other perspectives to the custom manufacturing need to be considered. Hence, efficient design elaboration and mutual understanding on the complex variety of issues require involvement of experts with multi-disciplinary skills and knowledge.

In order to overcome the barriers above, the extended clinical workflow and associated systems infrastructure is proposed. Figure 2 illustrates simplified representation of the extended clinical workflow with associated systems, foreseen as facilitators of this workflow.

Traditional clinical workflows (see Fig. 1) are based on the order-delivery service sequences and/or cycles, where these services are related to specialized observations and/or treatments. In the extended clinical workflow, the manufacturing of a custom medical product (with all associated services) is considered as a single service which can be ordered by using CPOE entry in the Clinical Information System. For fulfillment of this entry, six key activities are required: 1) procedure/treatment planning; 2) custom product design; 3) source product; 4) manufacture product; 5) product delivery; and 6) product installment. While procedure/treatment planning and installment are fully integrated in the traditional clinical workflow, other activities are carried out in the shared or environment of VBE, which is the main supplier of the clinical center for custom medical products of a certain type. Each of the activities of the clinical workflow should be facilitated by specific (hypothetical) system, as it is illustrated appropriately on Figure 2.

3.1 On the Systems Infrastructure for Extended Clinical Workflows

The design of the custom medical product is never considered in isolation from the procedure of its installment or a treatment method; as it must take into account the constraints and requirements of the specific intervention (e.g. surgery). Typically, the procedure/treatment planning is not facilitated by the information system or a tool. The decisions made in this phase are used to select from a range of standard medical products. In most of the cases, the problem of selecting a standard product is trivial.

However, in case of custom medical products, the Procedure/Treatment Planning System (PPS) is considered as essential, because its output is later used by the system for a product design, to define the main features (mechanical, geometrical, chemical, etc.) and topology of the custom product. Namely, in great most of the cases, there are strong correspondences between these features and steps, micro-steps and assets used in the installment of the custom medical product or treatment process. Hence, PPS is intended to be used for developing and generating a kind of a process model, which significant features will be then mapped to the features of the custom medical product conceptual model. The product model is considered as conceptual because it includes only features which are necessary and sufficient for establishment of the above-mentioned correspondences (both with PPS and VBERPS) and is designed by using the Conceptual Product Design System (PDS).

VBE Resource Planning System (VBERPS) is foreseen to be used in the sourcing step of the extended clinical workflow, where the Virtual Enterprise (VE) is formed from the VBE, according to the features of the conceptual product model. VBERPS is expected to have access to the relevant information for determining the capacity and availability of each enterprise of VBE to carry out a specific role, according to the conceptual product model (including its Bill of Material) and associated requirements, defined by the features of the respective parts.

Finally, the lifecycle of this VE is managed by using VE Resource Planning System (VERPS), which is typical an ERP system of the VE's focal partner.

3.2 Systems Interoperability in Extended Clinical Workflows

Interoperability is one of the main enablers of the extended clinical workflow, because it facilitates the flexible collaboration; it reduces the time needed for the setup and discontinuation of the VE. Given the high requirements for the workflow's efficiency, it is of outmost importance to remove as many as possible preconditions for the collaboration and requirements for any kind of previous agreements in exchange of relevant information between its actors. Exactly these preconditions and requirements are considered as some of the most difficult challenges in implementing the extended clinical workflow.

Systems interoperability issues of the extended clinical workflow can be easily identified in the intersections of the systems' scopes from the proposed infrastructure (see Fig.2). They are related to the interoperations and data exchanges illustrated on Figure 3.

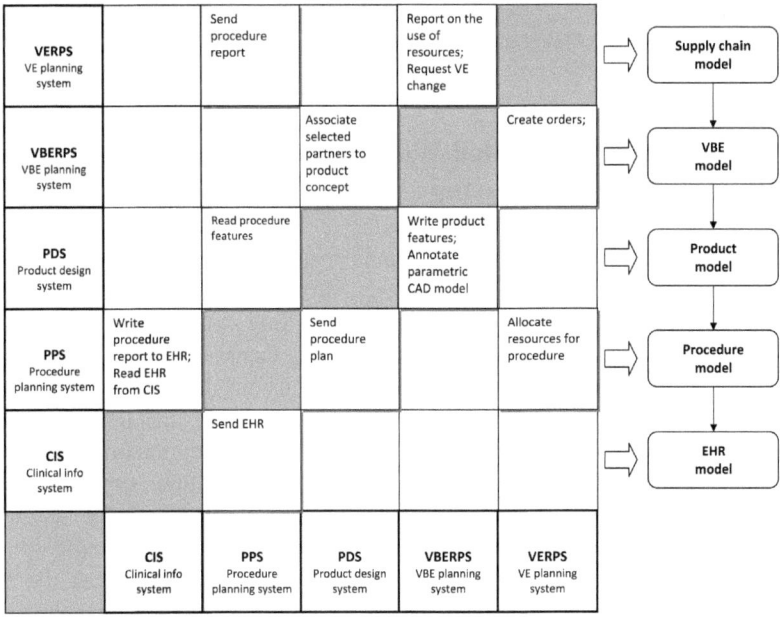

Fig. 3. Systems interoperations and models infrastructure in the extended clinical workflow

Since the capacity to interoperate is unidirectional capability of systems, the two-fold consideration of each interoperation is assumed. Namely, in every interoperation between two systems, each of these two systems must exhibit the non-interrelated, independent capabilities to send and receive (and interpret) the exchanged messages or invocation requests. However, the minimum requirement is considered as use of pre-determined or pre-selected dictionaries, vocabularies or even formal models (e.g. ontologies) in formulating these messages and requests, so they can be correctly interpreted. Thus, a Model-Driven Architecture for resolution of the interoperability requirements is foreseen. The conceptual view of involved models and dependencies between these models is illustrated on Figure 3.

The most difficult interoperability challenge of the extended clinical workflow is related to establishment of the correspondences between two, quite different domains of manufacturing and clinical practice. While the manufacturing domain knowledge is embedded in VBE and supply chain models and partially, in product model, the clinical practice is formalized by the EHR and procedure models.

Today's EHR records often suffer from the vendor-specific realizations of patient record data sets which rarely accommodate to the controlled terminologies [13]. However, the inefficiency of the clinical workflows which extend beyond the boundaries of a single medical centre is establishing EHR interoperability as one of the main requirements for health information systems. The issues of EHR interoperability are addressed by combining the standards for clinical vocabularies and healthcare message formats; with EHR ontologies (i.e., content and structure of the data entities, both from vocabularies and messages, in relation to each other).

Procedure model can be considered as a process model, as it is intended to formalize a set of actions in a linear or more complex flows, that could also include the equivalents of the error handler and compensation blocks from the workflow management.

4 Case Study – Extended Workflows for Custom Orthopedic Implants Manufacturing

The research of custom orthopedic implants manufacturing is typically focused to direct fabrication technologies [14]. Namely, direct manufacturing of high-strength materials provide far greater efficiency in one-of-a-kind runs for producing a finished custom implant than the conventional manufacturing technologies.

Depending on nature of the bone trauma, the custom orthopedic implant can be assembled of some of different types and designs of fixtures and scaffolds. In addition, some services may be associated to the product manufacturing and/or implementation, such as: pre-operation planning, reposition simulation, digital reconstruction, remodeling, analysis of biomechanical properties of the implant, sterilization, ethical review, product certification and others. For example, in case of bone cancer of tibia (larger of the two bones in the leg, below the knee), the missing part of the bone is replaced with the scaffold, which is enforced with the inner fixture. The scaffold is designed on the basis of bone geometry, which is digitally reconstructed from CT scans. Geometry and topology of inner fixture is designed on the basis of diagnosis and pre-operation plan, developed by surgeon. The process of manufacturing of the custom part is associated also with review of the design by the clinics ethical committee and analysis of biomechanical properties. Obviously, in above scenario, efficiency brought by the use of additive manufacturing is only a tip of the iceberg. It needs to be complemented by the effectiveness of the appropriate collaboration infrastructure which will facilitate all planning, sourcing, manufacturing and delivery aspects.

In our case, we propose to extend the clinical workflow for treatment of tibia bone cancer with the manufacturing of the custom implant parts and provision of the associated services. This is carried out within the VBE, which consists of the enterprises, capable, certified and competent to deliver a manufactured product and/or to provide associated services. VBE is organized as a cluster and technically coordinated by the brokering enterprise (broker). Each case of supply of the product and associated services is considered as a case of VE. In this case, the systems and models infrastructure, proposed in Section 3 is instantiated, as it is illustrated on Figure 4.

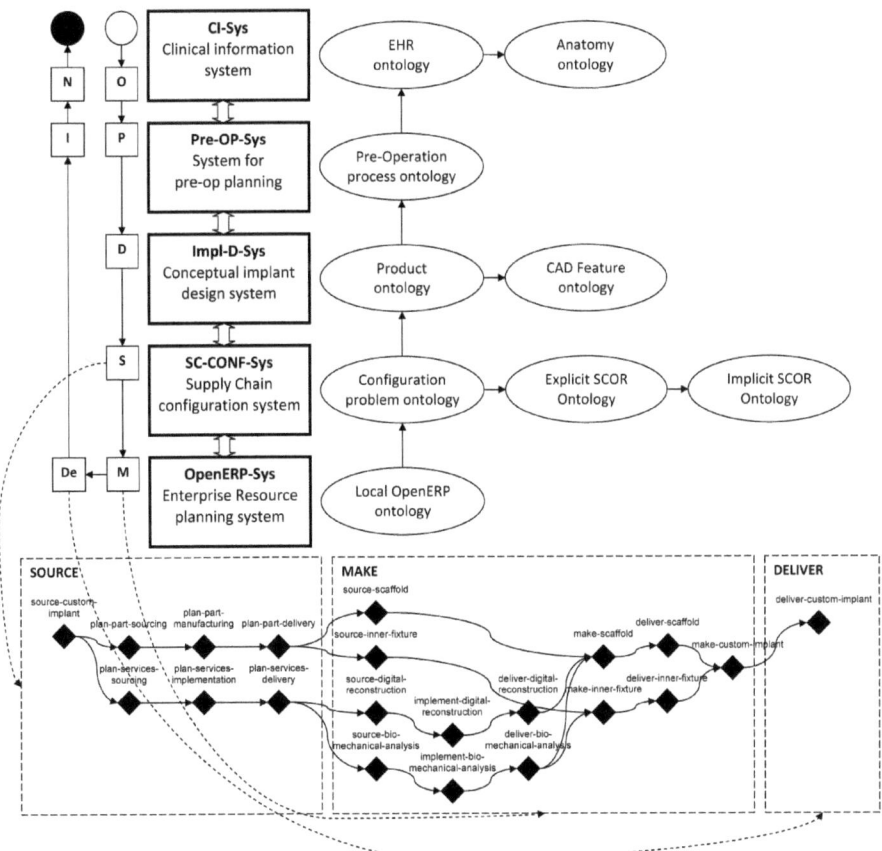

Fig. 4. Systems and models infrastructure for custom orthopedic implants manufacturing

The proposed infrastructure is implemented by using semantic applications and information systems which exploit the framework of inter related ontologies (models), that consist of the different domain (system) concepts and logical relationships between those [6]. The ontological framework corresponds to the assumed models infrastructure for extended clinical workflows and it is managed by the instances of the relevant assumed systems.

Clinical information system (CI-Sys) is used to create the order (O) for the custom implant manufacturing and to trigger the execution of the next (N) order of the extended clinical workflow, upon the installation of the implant.

System for pre-operation planning (Pre-OP-Sys) is used to plan (P) this installation (I). Pre-operation planning is based on the location and the arrangement of anatomical structure parts within the human body, expressed in quantitative or qualitative way (by using spatial orderings such as superior, anterior, lateral, etc). This arrangement can be formalized by appropriate anatomical ontology [15]. When operation is planned, the relevant spatial features are used to determine the features of the micro-steps which are carried out during the surgery, such as bone screw entry angles, fixture-bone assembly contact locations, etc. Hence, relevant properties of the spatial relations can be exploited for automated reasoning [16], which assists pre-operation planning process. In order to make this possible, Pre-OP-Sys need be capable to infer the spatial relations and corresponding micro-steps features, by exploiting previously established logical correspondences between anatomical ontology and pre-operation process ontology (model).

Above-mentioned spatial relations are also relevant for the custom implant design (D), which is facilitated by Impl-D-Sys system. These relations provide formal definitions of the geometry restrictions which are typically considered when design of the orthopedic implant is determined. For example, the angle between distal and proximal part of the inner fixture depends on the specific arrangement of bones and joints. Impl-D-Sys is a semantic application which formalizes parthood relationships of the product (Bill Of Material - BOM) and features of the respective parts and subassemblies. BOM also include relevant services.

Based on the product's topology and manufacturing or delivery strategies of each product part (including the services), a sourcing (S) strategy, namely the supply chain configuration is generated by SC-CONF-Sys application. SC-CONF-Sys is based on SCOR reference model for supply chain operations [17], a standard approach for analysis, design and implementation of core processes in supply chains. SC-CONF-Sys is semantic application which uses SCOR ontologies at two levels of conceptualization. While implicit SCOR ontology is used to enable interoperation of the SC-CONF-Sys with proprietary SCOR tools, explicit SCOR ontology is expressive domain ontology which defines the meanings of the implicit SCOR entities and thus, it facilitates interoperation of SC-CONF-Sys with other enterprise applications [18]. The supply chain configuration is based on the common rules related to the orderings of SCOR source, make and delivery processes in the different cases of the manufacturing strategies: make-to-stock, make-to-order and engineer-to-order; and a capacity of the supplier to deliver the desired part. At this moment, the capacity is evaluated only by checking the part production schedules of the suppliers through the semantic queries to the local ontologies of their information systems.

Exactly this last feature of the SC-CONF-Sys application demonstrates how the planning processes of custom orthopedic implants manufacturing could benefit from the semantic interoperability of the systems. Namely, during the process configuration, all local ontologies (representing their Enterprise Information Systems) of all registered manufacturing enterprises of the VBE, are queried by the SC-CONF-Sys for the production schedules of a given part. Then, based on the part availability at the calculated time, the selected enterprises are automatically assigned to specific process categories. Besides selection process, which is carried out on the basis of above criteria, corresponding semantic relationships between the SCOR ontologies and local ontologies of the EISs of the VBE partners can also facilitate planning of sourcing, manufacturing and delivery of custom product parts at all levels of BOM, as early as in the supply chain process configuration phase.

5 Conclusions

Extended clinical workflow aims at complementing the clinical practice with functions which are typically considered as external to the conventional clinical workflows. These functions extend the scope of the clinical practice and they are: procedure/treatment planning (in context of custom product implementation), conceptual custom product design, sourcing and implementation. In broader sense, even manufacturing and delivery can be considered in this extended scope. The main objective is to facilitate efficient application of custom medical products in daily practice. The interoperability challenges implied by the need to resolve many cross-domain issues are addressed by the high-level system and models infrastructure. This infrastructure is expected to enable execution of the processes that span the boundaries of the clinical centre and enterprises from the VBE.

The above assumptions are, to a certain extent validated in a case of manufacturing of custom orthopedic implants. Presented case confirms the hypothetical systems and models infrastructure and instantiates it by realizing the assumed functionality and purpose.

It is expected that the proposed infrastructure could reduce the lifecycle of the VE for custom orthopedic implant manufacturing to 4-8 days. This is considered as acceptable period for many cases of trauma, especially when having in mind that delivery lead time for custom orthopedic implants, even when manufactured by using additive technologies can reach up to 3 months [19]. The estimation of the saved time is based on the fact that integrated infrastructure practically automates the process configuration phase of VE lifecycle and exchange of information between relevant systems, by removing the need for complex technical preconditions so this exchange can occur and by minimizing the human effort in relevant knowledge and information exchanges. Thus, it significantly reduces the time typically needed for supply chain planning.

References

1. Fenner, J.W., Brook, B., Clapworthy, G., Coveney, P.V., Feipel, V., Gregersen, H., Hose, D.R., Kohl, P., Lawford, P., McCormack, K.M., Pinney, D., Thomas, S.R., Van Sint Jan, S., Waters, S., Viceconti, M.: The EuroPhysiome, STEP and a roadmap for the virtual physiological human. Philosophical Transactions of The Royal Society A Mathematical Physical and Engineering Sciences (July 2008)

2. Clapworthy, G., Viceconti, M., Coveney, P.V., Kohl, P.: The virtual physiological human: building a framework for computational biomedicine I. Editorial. Philos. Transact. A Math. Phys. Eng. Sci. 366(1878), 2975–2978 (2008)
3. Welsh, E., Jirotka, M., Gavaghan, D.: Post-genomic science: cross-disciplinary and largescale collaborative research and its organizational and technological challenges for the scientific research process. Phil. Trans. R. Soc. A. 364, 1533–1549 (2006)
4. VPH roadmap. Seeding the EuroPhysiome: a roadmap to the virtual physiological human (2008), http://www.europhysiome.org
5. Bentel, G.C., Marks, L.B., Sherouse, G.W., Spencer, D.P.: A customized head and neck support system. International Journal of Radiation Oncology, Biology and Physics 32(1), 245–248 (1995)
6. Zdravković. M., Trajanović, M., Stojković, M., Vitković, N., Mišić, D.: A case of using the Semantic Interoperability Framework for custom orthopedic implants manufacturing. Annual Reviews in Control 36(2) (2012)
7. Yassine, A., Kim, K.C., Roemer, T., Holweg, M.: Investigating the role of IT in customized product design. Production Planning & Control 15(4) (2004)
8. Hess, J.R., Holcomb, J.B., Hoyt, D.B.: Damage control resuscitation: the need for specific blood products to treat the coagulopathy of trauma. Transfusion 46(5), 685–686 (2006)
9. Puschmann, T.: Customer relationship management in the pharmaceutical industry. In: 34th Annual Hawaii International Conference on System Sciences, January 3-6 (2001)
10. Keenan, J., Chakrabarty, G., Newman, J.H.: Treatment of supracondylar femoral fracture above total knee replacement by custom made hinged prosthesis. Knee 7, 165–170 (2000)
11. Browne, J., Zhang, J.: Extended and virtual enterprises – similarities and differences. International Journal of Agile Management Systems 1(1), 30–36 (1999)
12. Sánchez, N.G., Apolinar, D., Zubiaga, G., Atahualpa, J., González, I., Molina, A: Virtual Breeding Environment: A First Approach to Understanding Working and Sharing Principles. In: Proceedings of the 1st International Conference on Interoperability of Enterprise Software and Applications, Geneva, Switzerland, February 23-25 (2005)
13. Harris, M.R., Ruggieri, A.P., Chute, C.G.: From Clinical Records to Regulatory Reporting: Formal Terminologies as Foundation. Health Care Financing Review 24(3), 118 (2003)
14. Gibson, I., Harrysson, O.L.A.: Direct Fabrication of Custom Orthopedic Implants Using Electron Beam Melting Technology. In: Advanced Manufacturing Technology for Medical Applications: Reverse Engineering, Software Conversion and Rapid Prototyping (2006)
15. Burger, A., Davidson, D., Baldock, R.: Anatomy Ontologies for Bioinformatics. Principles and Practice, 1st edn. Computational Biology, vol. 6, XVI, 356 p. (2008)
16. Schulz, S., Hahn, U.: Parts, Locations, and Holes – Formal Reasoning about Anatomical Structures. In: Quaglini, S., Barahona, P., Andreassen, S. (eds.) AIME 2001. LNCS (LNAI), vol. 2101, pp. 293–303. Springer, Heidelberg (2001)
17. Stewart, G.: Supply-chain operations reference model (SCOR): the first cross-industry framework for integrated supply-chain management. Logistics Information Management 10(2), 62–67 (1997)
18. Zdravković, M., Panetto, H., Trajanović, M., Aubrey, A.: An approach for formalising the supply chain operations. Enterprise Information Systems 5(4), 401–421 (2011)
19. Christensen, A., Chen, D.: Personalizing Orthopedic Implants, MDDI Online (2008), http://www.mddionline.com/article/personalizing-orthopedic-implants

Cross-Organizational Business Processes Modeling Using Design-by-Contract Approach

Malik Khalfallah, Nicolas Figay,
Parisa Ghodous, and Catarina Ferreira Da Silva

European Aeronautic Defence and Space Company (EADS), Paris, France
Lyon 1 University, Lyon, France
{malik.khalfallah,nicolas.figay}@eads.net,
{ghodous,catarina.ferreira-da-silva}@liris.cnrs.fr

Abstract. Reaching agreements between organizations in a collaborative environment is a way to ensure interoperability between these organizations at all levels. For business processes interoperability this agreement can be reached by well defining the cross-organizational process. However most BPM frameworks have used meta-models centered on flows of activities, with the data manipulated by these activities seen as second-class citizens. For business analysts (for example in complex product design collaborative environments) data plays a major role. In this paper, we propose a methodology backed by a conceptual framework to model the cross-organizational process relying on the product model. This framework defines the evolution of the product model through a finite number of states, and then automatically generates executable artifacts to support the collaboration during run-time phase. This approach is being implemented in the living laboratory provided by EADS in the context of the European project IMAGINE.

Keywords: design-by-contract, interoperability, product model, business process, model driven architecture, UML.

1 Introduction

The aeronautic and aerospace industries are seeing a rapid shift to the extended enterprise strategy. Companies specialized in this domain, including EADS, are increasingly externalizing activities for subcontractors while focusing on their core activities that are specific to their disciplines.

Ensuring interoperability between organizations in the extended enterprise is a complex problem and several studies have been conducted and reported in the literature. While many of these proposals focus on the static extended enterprise, where partners do not leave the network and are not replaced by new ones, ensuring sustainable interoperability for a dynamic extended enterprise has not been addressed well. We have recently seen the events of the volcano's eruption in Iceland and the nuclear disaster in Fukushima and their impact on enterprises. These events have reaffirmed the need for greater flexibility and maintaining organizations' interoperability and to cope with the dynamic nature of collaborative environments. To address this problem, the concept of Dynamic Manufacturing Network (DMN) has emerged [1].

In the context of product design collaborative environments, standards such as ISO-10303 (STEP) have been proposed in order to ensure partners' interoperability. The overall objective of STEP is to provide a mechanism that describes a complete and unambiguous product definition throughout the life cycle of a product. STEP provides both broadly useful data modeling methods and data models focused on specific industrial uses [2]. Even though STEP is an accepted standard in today's industry, it is still not sufficient to ensure a satisfactory level of interoperability in the extended enterprise. Indeed, relying on the classification of interoperability levels provided by Lewis et al. [3], we can say that STEP is limited to data interoperability of the first three levels (machine, syntactic, and semantic) but does not address data interoperability at the organizational level, as illustrated in figure 1, which remains the most complex one [3]. To fill this gap, EADS has participated to the European project CRESCENDO [4] that defined the concept of Behavioral Digital Aircraft Business Object Model (BOM). The BOM is a data model built with UML and defines high level concepts to be used by engineers pertaining to different organizations involved in the design and development of aircrafts. The BOM and its mapping to STEP concepts are the building blocks of the agreement necessary to ensure data interoperability at all levels.

In addition to data interoperability, another issue in the extended enterprise is the interoperability of organizations' business processes [5]. Cross-organizational processes aim to achieve an agreement between organizations at the process level. They specify what messages each organization should send and receive as well as their sequences. To model the cross-organizational process languages such as BPMN/XPDL (Business Process Modeling Notation/XML Process Definition Language) can be used. As illustrated in figure 1, XPDL covers the first three levels but not the fourth one. The reason is that when modeling the cross organizational process using XPDL, the business expert of each organization defines the exchanged messages based on their representation using STEP concepts (serialized in XML). Consequently, the high level concepts defined by the BOM are not usable and the business expert needs to understand the concepts defined by STEP. Moreover, the constructs provided by process modeling languages do not fit well for DMN processes due to the dynamic nature of DMN. They do not support well the changes on-the-fly that could occur [6]. This analysis raised the following challenges: (i) how to define an agreement between participants that will ensure their business processes interoperability at the organizational level while using the concepts defined by the BOM? (ii) How to make this agreement flexible enough to maintain a sustainable interoperability of the whole DMN?

Contributions. Since the BOM defines the concepts used to design the whole aircraft from different point of views (i.e. physical, functional, system), we start from this data model and then, define the evolution of the product model properties along the collaboration until reaching the final configuration. The evolution is modeled using temporal logic relations between product model states' specifications. Each state describes what constraints should the product model fulfill and which organizations should ensure these constraints.

Using the proposed framework to model the cross-organizational process is promising because it decreases the coupling between organizations' processes. In addition it provides the business expert the means to naturally define the cross-organizational process based on high-level concepts, since existing business process modeling approaches fail to capture the business intent underlying the interactions [7].

The rest of the paper is organized as follow: in section 2, we provide motivations regarding the proposed approach. In section 3 we give an overview of the methodology accompanied with an example. Section 4 elaborates on the conceptual framework that supports this methodology. Section 5 gives an overview of the implementation. Section 6 discusses the related work. Finally, section 7 concludes the paper and out-lines the perspectives of the current work.

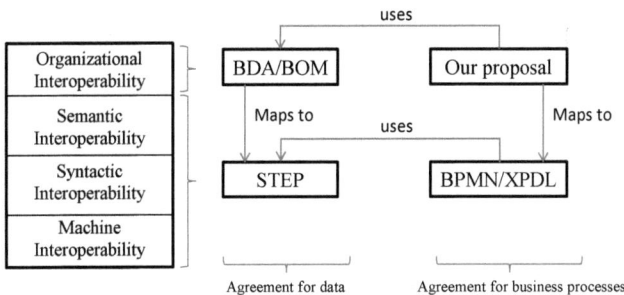

Fig. 1. Proposal overview

2 Background

In this section we give a brief description of the building blocks of the proposed framework.

2.1 Model Driven Architecture

At the conceptual level, MDA is a holistic approach to improving the entire IT life cycle specification, architecture, design, development, maintenance and integration based on formal modeling [8]. Today's MDA is less about generating code per se and much more about precisely capturing requirements, enforcing architectural standards, maintaining traceability, and facilitating effective communication between the business and IT.

From the analysis above, we figured out that we are facing the same issues that software developers faced in the domain of software engineering. One major issue is the lack of abstraction. Since MDA has proved to be successful as illustrated by industrial case studies demonstrated by [8], or even internally in EADS, where it has been used in multiple projects, we carry on in this direction by using it. Our aim is not limited to generate executable code but also to generate more complex artifacts as explained below. Such an approach provides engineers with high level concepts when modeling the cross-organizational process without caring how this process will be implemented using workflow engines.

3 Design By Contract

Design by Contract (DbC) is an approach to building reliable software that focuses on making the contract of a software module explicit and formal [9]. DbC is not limited to software design but can be used for high-level modeling [10]. DbC involves writing two kinds of formal constraints:

- Preconditions and post-conditions that are assertions about operations;
- Invariants that are assertions about the system state that must be true, except during the execution of an operation.

In this paper we extend the core idea of DbC - software development through elaboration of type signature with logical predicates - to the design and modeling of cross-organizational process by linking constraints' specifications on product model properties using temporal logic relationships. This approach allows us to formalize an agreement between all organizations involved in the collaboration based on the product model. This is an important element to ensure interoperability at organizational level as noticed by Lewis et al. [3].

3.1 Business Rules

A business rule is "a statement that defines or constrains some aspect of the business. It is attended to assert business structure or to control or influence the behavior of the business" [11].

Business rules are executable by rules engine, thus they bridge the gap between contract constraints expressed at the organizational level and their implementation in the execution platform. A typical pattern of business rules is the ECA (Event Condition Action) notation [12]:

- The event component specifies when the rule has to be executed;
- The condition component indicates a condition to be checked before any action is triggered;
- The action states what has to be done depending on the result of the evaluation of the condition component. In general an action terminates by raising one or more relevant events.

We elaborate on the usage of business rules in the implementation overview in section 5.

3.2 Problem Statement

The general problem addressed in this paper is the need to develop a product-based technique to improve the change management and maintainability of cross-organizational business processes for DMN. Such a method should allow the product architect to predict and manage the impact of change on the processes used to develop the product, while decreasing the time needed to implement changes.

4 Methodology of Design by Contract for DMN

In this section, we present a methodology that defines how our approach can be used to model the cross-organizational process. This is illustrated in figure 2.

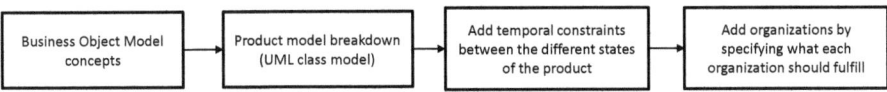

Fig. 2. Proposal overview

Step 1. The Business Object Model is an ontology that defines the concepts used by all organizations in the DMN. It ensures semantic interoperability between all participants. It defines the concepts used to develop all product components.

Step 2. The product model breakdown is a static model that defines the structure of the product. It structures the concepts defined in the BOM and establishes the relationships between these concepts. The product model is the building block of the contract, because all participants agree on this structure. However it remains not sufficient because it does not cover the behavior of the collaboration.

Step 3. Adding generic constraints to the classes' attributes of the product break-down allows the architects to formally define what values the properties should take. The objective of the collaboration is to iterate over the cross-organizational process until finding the optimal values of all product and sub products properties and defining the final configuration of the product. Relying on the classical relationships between constraints (e.g. and, or) is not sufficient to define the cross-organizational process. We need to add temporal relationships between constraints in order to define the succession of the product model states until reaching its final state.

Step 4. The logic-based model of the product model evolution is stable and it is in-dependent from: the organizations involved in the DMN, the processes enacted by these organizations and the IT systems that support the collaboration. Therefore, the last step adds organizations to the model and specifies what constraints each organization should fulfill.

4.1 Example

The following is an example of applying the proposed methodology using the results of the project CRESCENDO [4]:

Step 1. The concepts defined in the real BOM are complicated for non-aircraft engineers to understand. In this example we use usual concepts and simple attributes in order to demonstrate our solution.

Step 2. The product model of an aircraft is a tree-like structure. For a single aircraft, we can have several views that generate multiple decompositions (physical, functional, system etc.). Figure 3 illustrates this decomposition.

Step 3. Relying on the product model, the aircraft architect develops the cross-organizational process by defining the constraints on the aircraft functions (i.e. what functions the aircraft should fulfill). Additionally, he adds relationships between these constraints to indicate their dependencies as illustrated in figure 4. For this specific example, since a function is realized by physical components, the aircraft architect sets constraints on these components as well. This is illustrated in figure 5.

Step 4. Finally, each constraint is attached to two actors the requester, who sets the values of the attributes (the aircraft architect in our case) and the supplier (e.g. the wing designer) who tries to design the sub-product using these values.

At this stage the design of the contract is complete. The next step consists in iteratively running the collaboration between the involved partners until satisfying all constraints.

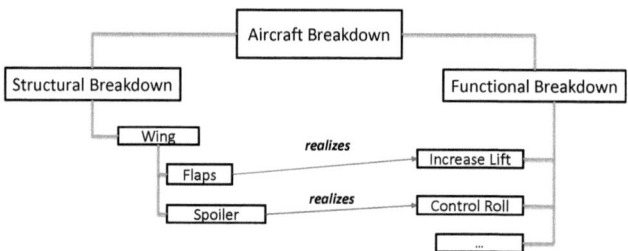

Fig. 3. Proposal overview

4.2 Handling Network Dynamicity

Using the proposed methodology, backed by a conceptual framework presented in the next section, reveals some advantages regarding the way of modeling the cross-organizational process and how to maintain interoperability between organizations.

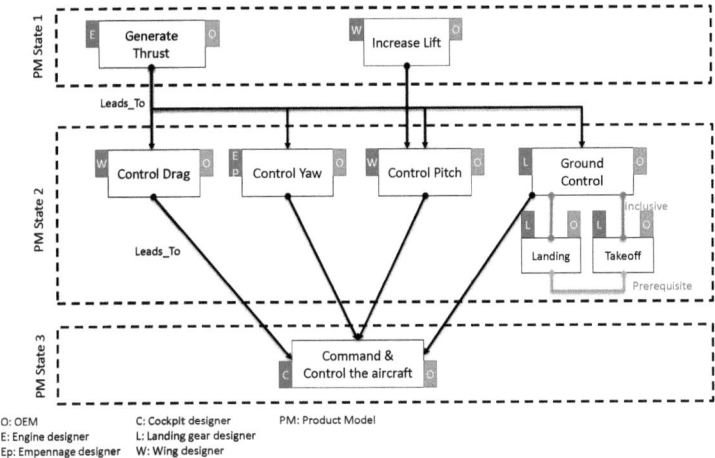

Fig. 4. Proposal overview

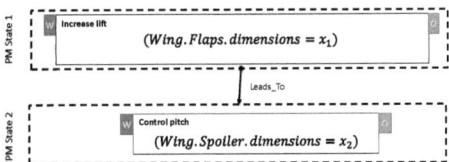

Fig. 5. Proposal overview

Product architects define the desired evolution of the product along the collaboration by defining constraints and their relationships. Consequently, the focus is put on the product model which remains stable even if some organizations quit the network. This decreases the coupling between organizations' processes which ensures a sustainable interoperability of the whole collaborative environment.

For example, in figure 5, if the wing designer quits the DMN and he should be replaced by two separate designers: one to design the spoiler and another to design the flaps. This will have no impact neither on the evolution of the product nor on the remaining organizations in the DMN.

5 A Conceptual Framework for DbC

The objective of this framework is to back the presented methodology by formal basis. For this purpose, we define the concept of *Obligation*.

Definition 1. *An obligation defines both what one party is obliged to guarantee and, dually, what other parties can rely on.*

More specifically, each product component designed by an external organization needs to respect predicates over attributes representing its properties. These predicates are obligations for the component designer and a guarantee for all other organizations (e.g. the aircraft architect decides that the length of the wing shall be 20m. This is a guarantee for the aircraft architect and an obligation for the wing designer).

5.1 Contract Formalization

It is essential to have a tractable and rigorous representation of obligations. Formal representation of obligations will provide accurate and unambiguous specifications. For this reason we use logic formulae to formalize obligations. Logic formulae are a general, rigorous and flexible tool to describe constraints. Indeed using logic formulae, the product architect specifies the properties of the subcomponents composing the product and the relationships between these properties.

Obligations are the building block of the cross-organizational process. Relationships between obligations are important as well. Using temporal logic provides the means to define how the collaboration should evolve through different product model states.

Definition 2. *A product model state is a set of obligations specifying constraints on a subset of objects defined in this model.*

Two states are interconnected by a temporal logic relationship *LeadsTo*, as illustrated in figure 4, to express the precedence relationship between these states.

In this framework we purposely use temporal logic relationships patterns to inter-connect obligations and states. For instance, the knowledge required to use formal models and their complexity remain a significant obstacle for their widely adoption by business experts (i.e. product architects) [13]. Using patterns supports shielding the complexity of formalisms from business experts and facilitate their specification in the abstract.

[14,15] already identified temporal logic patterns that we use to formalize the relationships between obligations and states. Given two obligations: O_1, O_2 and two states: S_1, S_2:

Table 1. A set of patterns to interconnect obligations and states

Pattern	Description
$O_1 inclusive O_2$	The fulfillment of O_1 mandates the fulfillment of O_2
$O_1 exclusive O_2$	The fulfillment of O_1 mandates the non-fulfillment of O_2
$O_1 prerequisite O_2$	The non-fulfillment of O_1 mandates the non-fulfillment of O_2
$O_1 mutexchoice O_2$	Either O_1 or O_2 are fulfilled but not any of them or both of them
$S_1 LeadsTo S_2$	State S_1 must always be followed by state S_2

Besides states and obligations, we add the concept of role. There are two types of roles:

- The requester: this is the partner who instantiate the obligations and waits to see whether the physical component can be designed under these obligations.
- The supplier: this is the partner who fulfills the obligations set by the requester.

5.2 Local Projections of the Contract

Modeling the cross-organizational process using obligations and product model states makes the local projections easy to generate. There are three kinds of artifacts to generate:

The Requester Process. The process of the organization that relies on obligations is illustrated in the right hand side of figure 6. For example, the aircraft architect and the wing designer collaborate in order to build an optimal model of the wing. The aircraft architect starts by giving a value to the flaps dimension. After that the wing designer executes its business process, the aircraft architect receives the value of the new flaps dimension. This value can be equal to the already set value in the constraint which means that the wing designer has fulfilled its obligation in this case the aircraft architect carries on the execution of his internal process. Otherwise, the aircraft architect may give a new value to the constraint and repeat the process.

The Supplier Process. The process of the organization that fulfills a particular obligation has the pattern illustrated in the left hand side of figure 6. For example, the wing designer and the aircraft architect collaborate in order to ensure state 1 in figure 5. The wing designer receives the value of the flaps dimension, carries out an internal process to design the flaps following the set conditions, and then he notifies the aircraft architect of the new value.

The Business Rules that Manage the Update of the Product Shared Model. Since in our implementation we are using a shared product model of the aircraft that is updated during the collaboration until reaching the final state, we decided to generate business rules that handle the updates of attributes' values and that generate notifications. Notice that even if this shared product model was absent, the generated artifacts would have been different but this remains an implementation detail and it has no impact on the way the cross-organizational process is modeled. processes interoperability issues in this case has been addressed in our previous paper [16]. Figure 7 gives an excerpt of the generated business rules of the given example. We rely on the business rules of type ECA as defined in [12].

6 Implementation

To illustrate our proposal, we have started to develop a prototype to test it with the results of the CRESCENDO project. The following steps illustrate how the proposed architecture (figure 8) implements the presented methodology with the conceptual framework. We should notice that there are two different phases: the design-time phase where the aircraft architect defines generic constraints and assigns them to organizations. This defines the cross-organizational process

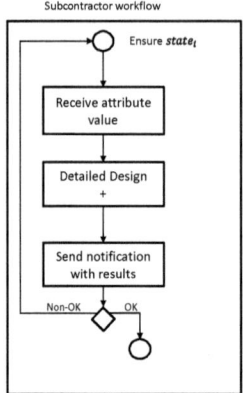 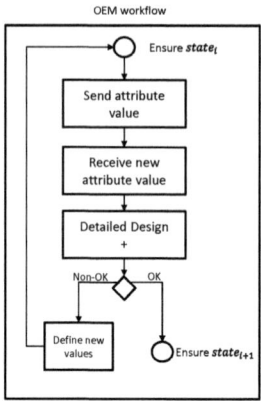

Fig. 6. Process Pattern for both sides of collaboration

```
ON Ensure_state1_event
IF State1 = true
RAISE Ensure_state2_event
ON Ensure_state2_event
IF State1 Leads_To State2 = true
RAISE Ensure_state3_event
```

Fig. 7. Generated business rules

(steps: 1, 2 and 3) and the run-time phase, where the cross-organizational process is executed until reaching the final configuration of the product model (step4):

Step 1. We assume that a product model is built and is being shared through a collaborative platform.

Step 2. The aircraft architect sets the (temporal) constraints on the shared product model through the collaborative platform. He uses an extension of the language OCL (Object Constraints Language) with temporal properties to define constraints on the classes in the UML model of the product. Additionally, he assigns corresponding organizations to each constraint. This step can be further enhanced by using advanced graphical user interfaces. At this stage we use an extension of OCL that supports temporal logic constructs and organizations assignment to constraints.

Step 3. Once the cross-organizational process is ready, the workflow generation module generates the workflows of the organizations and deploys them in their work-flow engines. Actually, a generated workflow is the public view on the complete organization's process. More specifically, it contains activities involved in the exchange of data with other organizations or with the collaborative platform. The detailed design sub-process (illustrated in figure 5) is the internal process of each organization that contains private activities and is not shared with the external world. Additionally, in this step, the workflow generation module generates the business rules that handle update events that occur on the shared product model and verify the fulfillment of every obligation of every state.

Step 4. The aircraft architect collaborates with the sub-products designer through an iterative process until reaching a satisfactory configuration of the product.

We can notice that in the cross-organizational process model illustrated in figure 4, there is no exception handling (i.e. it models only the nominal process). This is purposeful, because we noticed that it is very difficult for an aircraft architect to identify all possible exceptions that can occur during a product design at the design time phase of the cross-organizational process. These exceptions are handled during the run-time phase.

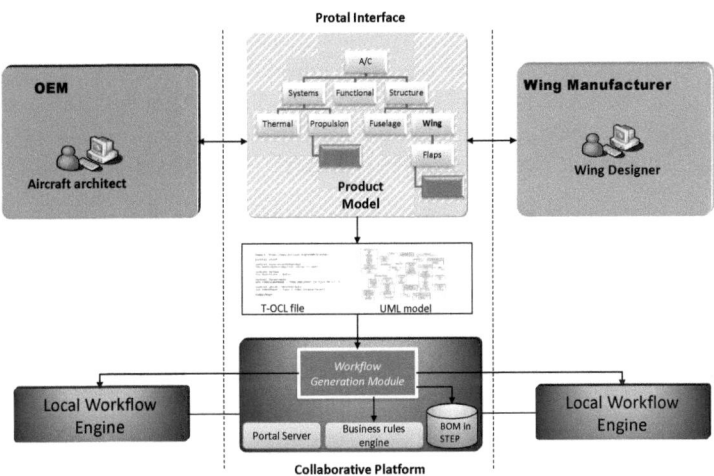

Fig. 8. Implementation overview

7 Related Work

Our objective in this paper is to provide a framework supported by a formal theory that allows product engineers to model the cross-organizational process (i.e. the con-tract) using business concepts that are more abstract than low-level concepts such as data and control flows modeling constructs.

Modeling cross-organizational processes and defining their local projections is a widely studied subject: standardized languages WS-CDL, BPMN as well as Decserflow for choreography [19], Scribble [20], and Bocchi et al. proposal [10] focus on formally defining the cross-organizational process and propose a formal definition of the projection to generate participating organizations processes' public and private views. The common limits of these proposals regarding our problematic are twofold:

- They still use constructs such as messages, activities, flows that were demonstrated to be low-level concepts Telang et al. [7].
- The coupling maintained between organizations that could be difficult to handle when an organization quits the network and be replaced by a new organization.

Business Rules and Business Processes. Eijndhoven et al, and Charfi et al. [11], [21] Work aims to increase the process flexibility by separating between the procedural flow of the process and the business rules. Their proposal is limited to a single enterprise process, because they assume that business rules are internal to an enterprise and not shared with the external world.

Product Model and Business Processes. Van der aalst et al. [22] proposed a method to design the optimal workflow based on the product model. The proposed methodology is limited to decision-making processes. They gave the example of a product decomposition of a candidate that wants to become a pilot. Relying on multiple criteria, they generated the optimal workflow that can decide whether a given candidate is able to become a pilot or not.

Declarative Modeling of Business Processes. Van der aalst et al. [23] already pointed out the limits and the rigidity of procedural modeling languages such as BPMN and proposed a declarative language to model business processes. This work was used by Montali et al. [19] in order to model the cross-organizational process. The limit of this proposal is the possible ambiguity when interpreting these models. While Van der aalst et al. [24] pointed out the mandatory nature of a process model to be unambiguous, these studies lack this property. Indeed, the modeled process is a temporal logic formula interconnecting activities. Inherently, they assume that the activity is true when it finishes, while there is a possibility to give a different interpretation: an activity is true when it starts. These two possible interpretations generate two different processes, the first one where two successive activities are executed in sequence and the second interpretation is that two successive activities are executed in parallel.

Business Processes and Web Services. The interoperability of services' processes is also a widely studied subject and several researches are conducted in the domain of web services. Basically, these approaches generate adapters either automatically or semi automatically that could resolve both structural and behavioral mismatches between two communicating business processes. We have already defined an ontology-based approach to resolve structural mismatches that could occur due to the difference of STEP application protocols used by two communicating organizations [25], [26]. For the behavioral mismatches we have decided to use the concept of DbC because mediation generation is an organization-dependent approach. If an organization quits the network we are obliged to regenerate a new mediator and redeploy it in the collaborative platform, which can be time consuming and expensive. Munusamy et al. [27] provide a thorough state of the art on the techniques that generate adapters to resolve mismatches between two communicating business processes.

8 Conclusion

Imperative languages have proven to be non-trivial to support changes of the pro-cesses on-the-fly [6]. This is a major obstacle to ensure business process interoperability in Dynamic Manufacturing Networks (DMN). In this paper we have presented a methodology backed by a conceptual framework to ensure business processes interoperability for DMN. We have used the Design by Contract (DbC) approach. DbC provides a declarative specification of what each organization in the DMN should accomplish (obligations) while maintaining this specification independent from organizations' specificities and the IT platform that supports the collaboration. Using the MDA architecture, we were able to project the DbC specification on the execution platforms and run the collaboration in order to fulfill the contract.

The results presented in this paper are being implemented in the living lab of EADS provided in the context of the European project IMAGINE [1].

References

1. Innovative end-to-end Management of Dynamic Manufacturing Networks (IMAGINE Project) (September 2012), http://www.imagine-futurefactory.eu/
2. Kramer, T., Xu, X.: STEP in a Nutshell. In: Xu, X., Nee, A.Y.C. (eds.) Advanced Design and Manufacturing Based on STEP, pp. 1–22. Springer, London (2009)
3. Lewis, G.A., Morris, E.J., Simanta, S., Wrage, L.: Why Standards Are Not Enough to Guarantee End-to-End Interoperability. In: ICCBSS, pp. 164–173 (2008)
4. Collaborative and Robust Engineering using Simulation Capability Enabling Next Design Optimization (CRESCENDO Project) (September 2012), http://www.crescendo-fp7.eu/
5. Papazoglou, M.P., van den Heuvel, W.-J.: Service oriented architectures: approaches, technologies and research issues. VLDB J. 16(3), 389–415 (2007)
6. van der Aalst, W.M.P., Jablonski, S.: Dealing with workflow change: identification of issues and solutions. International Journal of Computer Systems Science and Engineering 15(5), 267–276 (2000)
7. Telang, P.R., Singh, M.P.: Business Modeling via Commitments. In: Kowalczyk, R., Vo, Q.B., Maamar, Z., Huhns, M. (eds.) SOCASE 2009. LNCS, vol. 5907, pp. 111–125. Springer, Heidelberg (2009)
8. Guttman, M., Parodi, J.: Real-Life MDA: Solving Business Problems with Model Driven Architecture. Morgan Kaufmann Publishers Inc. (2007)
9. Frankel, D.: Model Driven Architecture: Applying MDA to Enterprise Computing. John Wiley and Sons, Inc. (2002)
10. Bocchi, L., Honda, K., Tuosto, E., Yoshida, N.: A Theory of Design-by-Contract for Distributed Multiparty Interactions. In: Gastin, P., Laroussinie, F. (eds.) CONCUR 2010. LNCS, vol. 6269, pp. 162–176. Springer, Heidelberg (2010)
11. van Eijndhoven, T., Iacob, M.-E., Ponisio, M.L.: Achieving Business Process Flexibility with Business Rules. In: EDOC, pp. 95–104 (2008)

12. Knolmayer, G., Endl, R., Pfahrer, M.: Modeling Processes and Workflows by Business Rules. In: van der Aalst, W.M.P., Desel, J., Oberweis, A. (eds.) Business Process Management. LNCS, vol. 1806, pp. 16–29. Springer, Heidelberg (2000)
13. Kharbili, M., Keil, T.: Bringing Agility to Business Process Management: Rules Deployment in an SOA. In: Binder, W., Dustdar, S. (eds.) Emerging Web Services Technology, vol. III, pp. 157–170. Birkhäuser, Basel (2010)
14. Dwyer, M.B., Avrunin, G.S., Corbett, J.C.: Property specification patterns for finite-state verification. In: Proceedings of the Second Workshop on Formal Methods in Software Practice, pp. 7–15. ACM (1998)
15. Türetken, O., Elgammal, A., van den Heuvel, W.-J., Papazoglou, M.P.: Enforcing compliance on business processes through the use of patterns. In: ECIS (2011)
16. Khalfallah, M., Figay, N., Barhamgi, M., Ghodous, P.: Product-based Business Processes Interoperability. In: ACM Symposium on Applied Computing (2013)
17. van der Aalst, W.M.P., Lohmann, N., Massuthe, P., Stahl, C., Wolf, K.: Multiparty Contracts: Agreeing and Implementing Interorganizational Processes. Comput. J. 53(1), 90–106 (2010)
18. Zaha, J.M., Barros, A., Dumas, M., ter Hofstede, A.: Let's Dance: A Language for Service Behavior Modeling. In: Meersman, R., Tari, Z. (eds.) OTM 2006. LNCS, vol. 4275, pp. 145–162. Springer, Heidelberg (2006)
19. Montali, M., Pesic, M., van der Aalst, W.M.P., Chesani, F., Mello, P., Storari, S.: Declarative specification and verification of service choreographiess. TWEB 4(1) (2010)
20. Honda, K., Mukhamedov, A., Brown, G., Chen, T.-C., Yoshida, N.: Scribbling Interactions with a Formal Foundation. In: Natarajan, R., Ojo, A. (eds.) ICDCIT 2011. LNCS, vol. 6536, pp. 55–75. Springer, Heidelberg (2011)
21. Charfi, A., Mezini, M.: Hybrid web service composition: business processes meet business rules. In: ICSOC, pp. 30–38 (2004)
22. Reijers, H.A., Limam, S., van der Aalst, W.M.P.: Product- Based Workflow Design. J. of Management Information Systems 20(1), 229–262 (2003)
23. van der Aalst, W.M.P., Pesic, M.: DecSerFlow: Towards a Truly Declarative Service Flow Language. In: Bravetti, M., Núñez, M., Zavattaro, G. (eds.) WS-FM 2006. LNCS, vol. 4184, pp. 1–23. Springer, Heidelberg (2006)
24. van der Aalst, W.M.P., ter Hofstede, A.H.M., Weske, M.: Business Process Management: A Survey. In: van der Aalst, W.M.P., ter Hofstede, A.H.M., Weske, M. (eds.) BPM 2003. LNCS, vol. 2678, pp. 1–12. Springer, Heidelberg (2003)
25. Khalfallah, M., Barhamgi, M., Figay, N., Ghodous, P.: A Novel Approach to Ensure Interoperability Based on a Cloud Infrastructure. In: ISPE CE, pp. 1143–1154 (2012)
26. Figay, N., Ghodous, P., Khalfallah, M., Barhamgi, M.: Interoperability framework for dynamic manufacturing networks. Computers in Industry 63(8), 749–755 (2012)
27. Munusamy, K., Selamat, H.B., Ibrahim, S., Baba, M.S.: A comparative study of process mediator components that support behavioral incompatibility. CoRR abs/1110.2258, volume abs/1110.2258 (2011)

Fit for Purpose: Toward an Engineering Basis for Data Exchange Standards

Arnon Rosenthal[1], Len Seligman[2], M. David Allen[2], and Adriane Chapman[2]

[1] The MITRE Corporation, Bedford, Massachusetts, USA
[2] The MITRE Corporation, McLean, Virginia, USA
{arnie,seligman,dmallen,achapman}@mitre.org

Abstract. Data standards are a powerful, real-world tool for enterprise interoperability, yet there exists no rigorous methodology for selecting among alternative standards approaches. This paper is a first step toward creating a detailed *engineering* basis for choosing among standards approaches. We define a specific sub-problem within a community's data sharing challenge, and focus on it in depth. We describe the major choices (*kinds* of standards) applied to that task, examining tradeoffs. We present characteristics of a data sharing community that one should consider in selecting a standards approach—such as relative power, motivation level, and technical sophistication of different participants—and illustrate with real-world examples. We then show that one can state *simple* decision rules (based on engineering experience) that system engineers without decades of data experience can apply. We also comment on the methodology used, extracting lessons (e.g., "negative rules are simpler") that can be used in similar analyses on other issues.

Keywords: Science basis for enterprise interoperability, experience reports on interoperability solutions, reference ontologies and mapping mechanisms, model-to-model transformations.

1 Introduction

Many of the biggest practical successes in data integration have been due to effective use of data standards [9]. In one survey, a substantial majority of participants in data standards development indicated that high quality data standards lead to improved interoperability [4]. The reason for this is straightforward: the right standard for a given community reduces the amount of data heterogeneity that must be bridged and therefore saves time and effort when new data exchanges must be built. Unfortunately, there are also many cases of failures, where standards failed to provide positive return on investment [9].

Despite the importance of good data standards, the research community to date has offered practitioners little help in selecting a standards strategy that will work for their particular data sharing community. This is perhaps not surprising, since researchers naturally focus on well-bounded problems suited to deep computational analysis (e.g., schema matching [8, 2, 12], mapping generation [3, 7]). This research has spawned some powerful and useful commercial and open source integration tools. *Yet researchers are mostly mute on the important strategic questions facing data integration professionals that must pick a standardization approach appropriate to their data sharing community. Addressing these strategic questions is a necessary precondition to establishing a scientific and engineering basis for enterprise interoperability.*

This paper identifies a key strategic question that must be addressed by a science or engineering process of enterprise interoperability—how to select a data exchange standardization approach that is fit for its intended purpose—and makes progress addressing it. Our contributions are:

- We describe characteristics of a data sharing community that one should consider in selecting a data standards approach and illustrate with real-world examples;
- We delineate the broad categories of data standards and present the relative strengths and weaknesses of each;
- We present an initial set of decision rules that help a data integration expert pick an appropriate type of standard for a particular data sharing community; and
- We describe important topics for future research on strategic help for data integration professionals.

Instead of presenting rigorous results on a narrow question, this paper presents a novel, strategic perspective on a familiar problem (data integration) on which novel perspectives are rare. The state of the practice is "Do a tradeoff analysis and apply engineering judgment, based on your knowledge of the various technologies". We hope that this paper will inspire other researchers to address problems of strategic importance that can truly be the basis of an engineering discipline of enterprise interoperability.

1.1 Scope

For this paper, we assume that a community is interested in creating many exchanges, covering similar data, such as might be described by a message standard. For example, among a region's medical offices, hospitals, labs, pharmacies, insurance companies, and relevant government agencies, there are many reasons different sets of partners would want to exchange basic medical information about patients. The goal of a data standard in such a community is to minimize the amount of development effort required to build and maintain all the required data exchanges. This paper examines several ways that data standards are expressed and used, discusses the pragmatic tradeoffs, and provides some easy to use decision rules to guide a selection for a particular data exchange problem.

Terminology in this area is diverse and conflicting. In this paper, an *exchange* concerns all work necessary to take data between data *producer* and *consumer* organizations. A *(full) transform* is the executable function that maps data from a producer's export interface to a consumer import interface. To permit direct comparisons of alternate approaches on a well-defined task, we seek specifically to minimize the effort to develop and maintain the transforms used by a set of exchanges.

A *message-based* transform is composed of two *sub-transforms*, from the producer's native interface to create a structure conforming to the *message standard*, and one onward to the consumer interface. The message standard is often described as an XML schema, supplemented by requirements captured in English or as code sets. Data typically flows point to point, being transformed en route, usually without a central server. The end points of any transform are called its *source* and *target*.

To write a transform, one needs to understand what differences between source and target need to be spanned. These differences may involve *meaning* (what is a patient, a testDate, a homeState, or a secondaryDiagnosis), *value domains* (what is meant by Date, State, or Diagnosis; what values are allowed for each?), *value format* (the coded value "54131-8" refers to Gender under LOINC; dates have many representations, such as "dd-mm-yyyy" or "yyyymmdd"), and *structure* (e.g., HL7 C32 message, as a tree). To make descriptions more concrete, we will assume system interfaces and the message standards use XML; the work still applies when alternatives to XML are used. A typical description is part *formal* (i.e., interpretable by tools; XML schemas are formal) and partly English. An alternative to full description is to identify *correspondences* – areas where the source conforms to the target interface and the transform need do nothing. Formal descriptions reduce ambiguity, and may drive automated tools, such as when multiple partners' data schemata are mapped to a common reference ontology.

1.2 Paper Roadmap

Section 2 describes characteristics of a data sharing community that affect the choice of an appropriate data standards strategy. Section 3 describes the major styles of data standards, along with examples. Following a discussion of pragmatics (Section 4), Section 5 presents decision rules for selecting among the major standardization strategies described. These rules consider factors described in all the previous sections. Section 6 concludes with topics for future research.

2 Characteristics of Data Sharing Communities

This section describes key characteristics of a data sharing community that affect the choice of an appropriate data standards strategy, illustrated with real-world examples. (The list of characteristics is not comprehensive, but emphasizes factors that have generally received less attention in prior research.[1])

First, *is this a community of peers with roughly equal power or is there is a dominant player* (a so-called "800 pound gorilla")? The Indiana Health Information Exchange[2] is an example of a community of peers, in which hospitals, rehabilitation

---

[1] [13] presents additional factors and offers a useful conceptual framework for standards communities, while [6] offers additional insights on the issues of motivation and technical sophistication of participants.

[2] http://www.ihie.com/

centers, long term care facilities, laboratories, imaging centers, clinics, community health centers and other healthcare organizations exchange health information. In contrast, the Centers for Medicare and Medicaid Services (CMS) have a dominant position in the U.S. healthcare marketplace, covering almost one third of the US population[3]; providers that wish to receive payment from this major player have strong incentives to support CMS' data submission requirements.

Second, even when there is a dominant player, *communities differ in the extent to which the dominant organization uses its power dictatorially or benevolently.* Using the former approach, financial regulators could simply threaten penalties or legal action against non-compliant companies. Benevolent financial regulators might also offer tools that ease compliance as well as benefits to data submitters (e.g., by selecting a standard and providing tools to minimize submitters' costs, or by allowing participating financial institutions to see industry-wide data and compare it to their own practices).

A third issue is the *motivation level of participants*. Information consumers are usually highly motivated, since they are the ones that derive value by using the exchanged data. Whether data producers are similarly motivated depends upon their perception of benefits vs. costs and risks. Producers can be motivated by legal mandates (e.g., taxpayers that fail to provide the government required information can face penalties or even jail), financial incentives (e.g., the U.S. government is offering payments to healthcare providers that demonstrate "meaningful use" of electronic health records technology), or a perception of benefit (e.g., U.S. airlines and other stakeholders voluntarily provide safety information to the Aviation Safety Information Analysis and Sharing[4] collaboration because of a shared desire to improve aviation safety). As another example, drug companies are highly motivated to comply with Food and Drug Administration data submission requirements, since they need FDA approval to be able to sell a new drug in the U.S. market. In contrast, for an application that analyzes a company's competitors' web-accessible price lists, the data producers (other companies) have no motivation to help.

Fourth, participants often vary greatly in terms of both *technical sophistication and financial resources*. In sharing emergency response information, U.S. state and local authorities generally have far fewer resources and less technical sophistication than U.S. federal government agencies. In contrast, in the financial regulatory environment, data producers (i.e., financial institutions) have ample resources and sophisticated IT capabilities. Healthcare information exchange varies greatly; some providers (large health maintenance organizations or hospital systems) are amply resourced, while others (individual doctors' offices) have little or no IT budget or capabilities. In such cases, it is often valuable for a government entity (such as the U.S. Office of the National Coordinator for Health IT), an industry consortium, or an open source community to offer tools and/or services that lower the barriers to data sharing for under-resourced players.

---

[3] http://cms.gov/
[4] http://www.asias.aero/

These issues are all important in considering the most appropriate data standards strategy. Much prior research fails to realistically consider participants' incentives [10]; this has also led to some catastrophic failures in real-world data integration efforts [9].

3 Standards Options

This section presents several flavors of data standards and usage. For each, we ask:

- Are standard messages generated, as an intermediate result? If so, how tightly does the standard constrain them? How much of that standard is expressed formally?
- Do the formal descriptions of data producer, consumer, and (if used) message standard suffice for developing transform code? Are all these interfaces described using the same formalism? Is that formalism standard or proprietary?
- Who needs to do what work to create a transformation? How many topics must a community resolve in order to create their descriptive standard?

Our biggest contribution lies in the nature of the analysis – a well-defined task within data exchange, and description of the alternative models. We expect the set of decision rules to be extended and refined by later researchers. While there are many discussions of strengths and weaknesses, we know of no systematic comparison and usable set of decision rules. [14] begins studying the area scientifically; we seek to create an engineering solution, usable by MITRE's system engineers (who are not all data experts).

Our assessments of the strengths and weaknesses of each standardization approach are based on over 50+ years' direct experience among the co-authors, consulting on U.S. government data integration efforts, plus many discussions with other data integration experts at MITRE.

3.1 "Nailed Down" Exchange Schemas That Specify a Single Physical Data Structure

Approach 1: Create a message-based transform, using a detailed, straightforward message standard that specifies a fixed meaning and format for each element. An XML schema often describes the structure, simple constraints on content, plus part of the syntax. Remaining message-standard details are described in English, in a proprietary tool, or as standard code sets (e.g., "`countryOfOrigin` uses FIPS Country Codes"). Transform developers must be aware of these details to ensure that the delivered content meets the needs of the consumer. A natural division of labor is that each producer/consumer creates *one* sub-transform between their own interface and the standard; these are composed automatically to create producer-to-consumer transforms. For example, if a community agrees to exchange patient information via a greenCDA[5] XML message, each participating data producer and consumer will have to develop the sub-transform from its electronic health record format to the standard.[6] Documentation for producer and consumer interfaces is typically left to each organization.

Most exchanges today take this approach. For example, the National Information Exchange Model (NIEM)[7] describes a process that employs reusable schema components to build message standards, which NIEM calls information exchange package descriptions (IEPD). Many IEPDs which are built fall into the category of "nailed down" exchange schemas. The web's Really Simple Syndication (RSS) is another important example.

Discussion: The popularity of approach 1 is based on real advantages. Only one sub-transform need be built for each producer or consumer. When development is manual, there are usually large savings over creating a separate data transform to each partner. It is often natural for each producer or consumer to build and host its own sub-transforms. Otherwise (e.g., for secondary uses), whoever benefits from the exchange can build and/or host the transforms.

There are still difficulties. Developing one sub-transform per interface is still a significant cost, and a real barrier to entry for technology-challenged organizations. Furthermore, if a community extends the standard, they face costs to create transforms that exploit the extensions. Depending on the design of the transform code, a later (extended) version of a standard may not be plug-compatible with an older version. Precision (numeric or in concept definitions) may be lost in conversion to the standard, even though the consumer could have accommodated it.

The community cost to develop a message standard can be high, depending on the complexity of the message standard and interface and the number of stakeholders with distinct points of view. Not only do they need to agree on data content, but they must also agree on a tree structure and value formats – what concepts are on the top of hierarchical structures and whose native representation to use.

3.2 Flexible Exchange Schemas That Permit Alternate Representations

Approach 2: Participants agree on a message structure but allow alternative formats for some of the individual properties and occasionally for overall message syntax. For example, they might allow different measurement units (feet vs. meters), value syntax and international codesets (National Drug Code or RxNorm to describe medications), and allow both XML and JSON to represent the tree.

With this approach, a producer chooses the most convenient supported format for each item in the standard message, and then creates a sub-transform to it. Just as in the previous section, consumers create transforms from the message, to the consumer's

---

[5] http://wiki.hl7.org/index.php?title=GreenCDA_Project
[6] In the event that the producer or consumer organization is using a vendor's electronic health record system, it be able to acquire the data transform code as a part of the software package or as an add-on.
[7] http://niem.gov

format, converting as necessary. The formalism is often XML schema, with certain elements being assigned a special meaning as descriptors of other elements.

The C32 and Clinical Document Architecture (CDA) standards are examples in this area. CDA permits the use of a number of different coding systems. For example, in a Continuity of Care (CCD) document, different codes might indicate the role of a physician, or the race of a patient. But the content of the code itself is not fixed; the standard may permit several coding systems, such as SNOMED or ICD-9 to describe medical conditions. As a different example, consider "message envelope" designs that contain a standard structure for the manifest of the contents, but leave the contents open to customization depending on the user; an example for health information is Restful Health Exchange (RHEx).[8]

Discussion: This approach is friendlier to data producers. By giving them alternate submission formats, it lowers the barrier for entry. This is especially important when producers have limited resources or a low motivation to contribute data. An additional advantage is that this approach can avoid gratuitous loss of data precision caused by a "least common denominator" interchange standard, in cases where the source and target may both use the same higher precision representation. No exchange standard can remedy a situation where the consumer requires information, or precision, that the producer does not possess.

The major drawback of permitting alternate representations within the standard is that to be interoperable with all producing systems, each consumer's sub-transform becomes much more complex; it must interpret descriptors of the representation choice selected and then invoke the correct format translation. Also, while XML schema can specify the message structure (Approach 1), no popular standard captures the special usage for format descriptor elements.

To see the advantage of flexible representations, a medical data exchange standard could allow producers to furnish `prescribedMedication` using either National Drug Code or RxNorm, given that straightforward conversions exist from NDC to RxNorm. The advantages are less clear cut when such conversions cannot be automated. For example, while ICD-9, ICD-10, and SNOMED could all be used for `diagnosis`, there is often no straightforward mapping among them. If a standard allowed all of those representations, then the consumer will only see diagnoses for which there is an unambiguous mapping to his chosen coding scheme.

A final consideration with this approach is the cost of obtaining the consensus necessary to develop the standard. While initially this cost may be less than approach 1, since supporting several popular formats can avoid some arguments, subsequent costs may be similar, as participants argue about whether to accept the next one alternate representation, and the next.

3.3 "Enriched" Exchange Schema (Schema Plus Formal Descriptions)

Approach 3: *This approach enhances approach 1, adding formal descriptions plus automated tools that compare descriptions and in some cases automatically generate sub-transforms to and from a standard message.*

---

[8] http://wiki.siframework.org/RHEx

Here, the community must choose a formalism for capturing semantic knowledge that XML Schema does not capture (e.g., that `hemogram` is a kind of `labTest` or `anesthesiologist` is a kind of `physician`); popular formalisms for capturing such a domain model include UML, the Resource Description Framework (RDF)[9] and Web Ontology Language (OWL).[10] Then, instead of just presenting the community with an exchange schema (as in approach 1), the elements of the exchange schema are described by correspondences to elements in the domain model.[11] (One could, more awkwardly and less expressively, use the XML exchange schema itself as a domain model). Whenever producers or consumers describe their systems in terms of the same domain model, data exchange is eased. First, there is the possibility of doing automated mediation using sophisticated tools that automatically generate some of the sub-transforms. Crucially, the descriptive tasks can be done by a domain analyst, or in less critical settings, a power user. When automated transform generation succeeds, there is much less need for programming. Costs are reduced, and more systems can be included in exchanges. In addition, even when fully automated mediation is not possible, the additional semantic richness of the descriptions can make the programmer's job substantially easier.

Discussion: This approach has the potential to reduce the cost and time required to create sub-transforms. Compared with approach 1, it adds formal capture of the knowledge that the developer needed for generating mappings. Major vendors' tools (e.g., IBM, Microsoft) have proprietary logic-based formalisms for expressing and exploiting correspondences to generate transforms. This represents a big advance over the current state of the practice of capturing correspondences in Excel or (even worse) Powerpoint followed by manual programming (e.g., in Java) of sub-transforms.[12] Another advantage of this approach is support for incremental adoption. Where automated transform generation is impossible or is incomplete, one can always fall back on the techniques of approach 1 to fill in the gaps.

A drawback of this approach is that while individual correspondence capture acts are simpler, the setup is not. The community (or some members) must invest in sophisticated tools, *and* the skills to apply them, when transforms cannot be generated automatically. This may be a challenge for communities in which key participants are poor in either resources or technical sophistication. In compensation, if the community can come up with a strategy to address these challenges (e.g., by providing free tools or putting the mediation burden primarily on better resourced partners), the approach has the potential to substantially reduce the effort required to build new data exchanges.

---

[9] http://www.w3.org/RDF/

[10] http://www.w3.org/OWL/

[11] There are two flavors of correspondence: a simple "is compatible with", and "is derivable by <formula>". From these fine grained correspondences, a tool can derive a transform between whole schemas. Correspondences can also include small sets of elements, e.g., M, D, Y → Date.

[12] One shortcoming of current tools is they have difficulty making very large schemas and the correspondences among them intelligible [1].

We considered a hybrid this approach with approach 2 (i.e., using a "semantically enriched" schema but with alternate acceptable representations), but none of the current standards provides for elements (i.e., meta-attributes) that describe the format of other elements.

3.4 Formal Descriptions without an Intermediate Message

Approach 4 rests on having a domain model, and formally describing all producer and consumer interfaces in terms of this model, all in the same formalism. Using these descriptions, one generates transforms for all desired exchanges, going <u>directly</u> from producer to consumer interface. The domain model acts as intermediary for descriptions, but not for physically creating messages.

Automation is essential because for each producer, one must generate direct mappings to all of its exchange partners, not just to a standard. Formal descriptions are essential to automation. The community must again acquire tools and skills, but will need fewer programmers. Then, the community creates its standard domain model, and some entities within it acquire the tools and skill to use them.

There are major risks with this approach. If the community is not new, organizations who have already built their sub-transforms will have little short term reason to create the needed formal descriptions. The tools are bleeding edge and not industrial strength; the techniques are unfamiliar to existing developers. And the larger number of transforms makes manual coding a less effective backup plan. Thus, its niche may be limited to new efforts, plus situations where translation to a fixed message format is not practical.

The Biomedical Informatics Research Network (BIRN) has begun to use this approach for real information exchanges [5]. Interestingly, BIRN mediates not just data transformation, but also queries. In addition, many models exist to describe portions of the health domain, including the Federal Health Information Models (FHIMS[13]), and the NIEM UML Profile[14] and the Health Level 7 Reference Information Model (HL7 RIM)[15], which is used to derive other standards like the Clinical Document Architecture (CDA). While these models by themselves do not constitute a "formal description" approach, they do provide useful building blocks for such an approach.

Discussion: This approach potentially makes interoperability, and especially extensibility, an order of magnitude cheaper, compared to standards plus hand-coded transforms (approaches 1 and 2). Also, since the tools convert values directly between producer and consumer representations without an intermediary, the standard does not cause unnecessary loss of precision. Extension is particularly easy – GUIs and wizards relate the new standard elements to elements in source and target, and a

---

[13] http://www.fhims.org/
[14] https://www.niem.gov/news/Pages/uml-profile.aspx
[15] http://www.hl7.org/implement/standards/rim.cfm

mediator generates updated transforms. No programmer and test organization will be involved, at least once the tools mature.

Unfortunately, present transform-generation tools are unsatisfactory. Without reliable automation, it is not feasible to generate a separate transform for each exchange. For long term planners such as CIOs and architects, it is worth pointing out that without formal descriptions of systems, it will not be possible to generate transforms automatically; as such, those descriptions will eventually be necessary if systems are to move beyond hand-coded transforms.

4 Pragmatics and Metrics

In selecting a data exchange standard, there are several aspects of the sharing problem that everyone needs to examine, whether or not they have additional specialized concerns (a few were touched on in Section 2):

- **Timeline:** how much time does the community have before a capability is needed?
- **Ambition level and risk tolerance:** Will managers accept some risk, in hope of transformative improvements, long term?
- **Legacy:** Are there significant legacy message standards? One or multiple?
- **Funding and incentive structure:** Are all players willing to invest? Will a central fund or major player support community needs? Will consumers fund descriptions and sub-transforms of producers? What is the time horizon for costs?
- **Technical skills:** which technologies are developers familiar with? Do all organizations have software developers?
- **Number of producers and consumers:** how many are there, both absolute and relative? What are their incentives (desire to exchange, who hosts, who funds)?
- **The rate of change of the domain:** How often are extensions requested, and with what timeline? Is there likely to be merger with another community?

We do not have a formal metric approach. It is easy to estimate the number of transforms to be programmed, semantic correspondences to be represented, and decisions of each type in defining a standard. However, many other issues are dealt with qualitatively, because there is no general means of estimating them. How much faster is it to describe an interface, rather than code transforms? Stakeholders will agree to an approach more quickly if multiple formats (including theirs) are supported, but that decision may have costs in terms of transforms required. Analysis and programming effort is also notoriously hard to estimate correctly. Finally, it is usually hard to trade political versus technical costs.

Rather than require decision makers to estimate all of these difficult parameters, our decision rules use qualitative terms (e.g., "many more producers than consumers") which decision makers must interpret in their program context.

5 Decision Rules – Exclusions

This work sought to simplify decisions for MITRE's front line engineers, few of whom are data researchers. For that reason, we tackled one narrow problem, and provide simple decision rules. The rules are based on the authors' engineering judgment, based on decades of experience supporting U.S. government interoperability efforts, observing both successes and failures.

We initially tried to formulate positive rules (i.e., "Use approach #1 under these circumstances") for selecting a standards approach but quickly ran into a problem: most rules had a long series of required conditions, making it difficult to specify modular rules. Even worse, a positive recommendation requires comparing with all

Table 1. Rules for Excluding Data Standardization Approaches

Situation	Excluded Approaches	Justification and Comments
Want to minimize the need for programmers in generating transforms	1: Fixed, 2: Flexible	These approaches require programmers, testers, and accreditors. They are not agile, nor suited for in-the-field improvisation.
Transform-generator tools cannot be effectively deployed *at all*. Either: • Tool purchase plus skill-center costs seem too high, and no organization will step up to support them • No transform-generator product is effective (e.g., on very large schemas) • Short term focus with little concern for long term support	4: Formal, 3: Enriched	Approach 4 depends completely on mediation, so must be ruled out entirely. Approach 3 is more amenable to incremental adoption, since less capable partners can map to the physical schema, as in Approach 1. Notes: • Open source avoids licensing, but sometimes has higher people costs • If a vendor's tool suite is already in use, skills and metadata may be available. Adding a transform-generation capability product may be less expensive.
Does the community already have many transform-based exchanges working?	4: Formal	Automated mediation involves both ends' being documented formally; systems that have satisfactory sub-transforms will not invest in formal descriptions
The burden on producers must be minimized.	1: Fixed	Approach 2 provides flexibility for producers to use different formats.
Producers will provide data in any case, and do not greatly outnumber consumers	2: Flexible	Approach 2 greatly increases consumers' costs.
Data resolution needs (numeric, concept specificity) differ; the community needs to: • Avoid "lossy" exchange; or • Avoid overhead of high resolution formats	1: Fixed	Permits certain exchange pairs to have finer qualitative categories (e.g. left ventricle valve failure, rather than heart attack) or finer granularity. Other approaches avoid the least common denominator problem of Approach 1.
A typical message has many consumers	4: Formal	Multicasting a standardized message to all consumers can save bandwidth.

alternatives – so it is almost impossible to be simple. Instead, we found it much more natural to formulate *negative rules*. These permit data integration experts to eliminate possibilities based on what they know of their situation, and narrow down the list of options. If all alternatives are excluded, then the community must change its stated requirements or assumed resources.

Table 1 shows rules for ruling out approaches, using the following labels as abbreviations for approaches 1 – 4:

- *1: Fixed*
- *2: Flexible*
- *3: Enriched*
- *4: Formal*

6   Conclusions and Future Research

We have presented important characteristics of data sharing communities with real-world examples, several approaches to data exchange standards, and some simple decision rules for how to select a data exchange approach based on the community's situation. The current popular approach (a simple standard XML schema) is the best low-risk, moderate-immediate-cost approach today, unless there are special situations of avoiding information loss or favoring producers over consumers. Even at one sub-transform per producer or consumer, programmers are needed, and coding, testing, and maintenance costs can be high ($millions/year, for USMTF systems working with the Air Tasking Order message).

For the long term, automated mediation offers hope of order of magnitude further improvements. Avoiding those costs will eventually require automated generation, driven by formal descriptions of participant systems' element semantics and representation. Automated generation is becoming practical today with approach 3; one can supplement the automatically generated transforms with manually coded ones wherever necessary.

This work opens several avenues for future research. First, our categories and rules are just a first-step and allow ample room for refinement. Second, there is a need for empirical research to test our engineering judgments; experimentation or surveys are needed to see how systems engineers are guided by such decision rules, and whether they are satisfied with the results. Third, there is a continuing need for progress on automated mediators that support approaches 3 and (especially) 4. One important area is how to handle situations where auto-generation of a sub-transform is only partially successful. How should tools present the remaining work that needs to be done to systems engineers to maximize their effectiveness? Will the resulting code be maintainable? How should this be handled in cases where the consumer has no development resources and is willing to accept "best effort" data, as for example in recent "pay as you go" data integration research [11]?

Additionally, one can apply a similar methodology to other problems involved in data sharing, such as populating the exchange message (we considered schema, not contents), access rights, or transport security. One can also dig deeper into how values or codesets are specified and converted. Finally, the general methodology—create a bounded problem important to practitioners and derive simple, modular decision rules—could be applied in other domains.

Acknowledgments. We thank Prof. Harry Zhu, Rob McCready, Mary Pulvermacher, and the anonymous referees for their helpful comments.

References

1. Bernstein, P.A., Melnik, S., Petropoulos, M., Quix, C.: Industrial-Strength Schema Matching. SIGMOD Record 33, 38–43 (2004)
2. Doan, A., Domingos, P., Halevy, A.Y.: Learning to Match the Schemas of Databases: A Multistrategy Approach. Machine Learning 50, 279–301 (2003)
3. Fagin, R., Kolaitis, P.G., Miller, R.J., Popa, L.: Data Exchange: Semantics and Query Answering. In: Calvanese, D., Lenzerini, M., Motwani, R. (eds.) ICDT 2003. LNCS, vol. 2572, pp. 207–224. Springer, Heidelberg (2002)
4. Folmer, E., Luttighuis, P.O., van Hillegersberg, J.: Do Semantic Standards Lack Quality? A survey among 34 semantic standards. Electronic Markets 21(2) (2011)
5. Helmer, K.G., Ambite, J.L., Ames, J., Ananthakrishnan, R., Burns, G., Chervenak, A.L., Foster, I., Liming, L., Keator, D., Macciardi, F., Madduri, R., Navarro, J.P., Potkin, S., Rosen, B., Ruffins, S., Schuler, R., Turner, J.A., Toga, A., Williams, C., Kesselman, C.: Enabling collaborative research using the Biomedical Informatics Research Network (BIRN). J. Am. Med. Inform. Assoc. (April 2011)
6. Markus, M.L., Steinfield, C.W., Wigand, R.T., Minton, G.: Industry-wide information systems standardization as collective action: the case of the U.S. residential mortgage industry. MIS Quarterly 30(1) (August 2006)
7. Miller, R., Hernández, M.A., Haas, L.M., Yan, L., Ho, C.T.H., Fagin, R., Popa, L.: The Clio Project: Managing Heterogeneity. SIGMOD Record 30, 78–83 (2001)
8. Rahm, E., Bernstein, P.A.: A Survey of Approaches to Automatic Schema Matching. The VDLB Journal 10, 334–350 (2001)
9. Rosenthal, A., Seligman, L., Renner, S.: From Semantic Integration to Semantics Management: Case Studies and a Way Forward. ACM SIGMOD Record, Special Issue on Semantic Integration (December 2004)
10. Rosenthal, A., Seligman, L., Blaustein, B.: Beyond the Sandbox: How Integration Researchers Can Actually Help Integration. In: Workshop on Information Integration, October 26-27. University of Pennsylvania, Philadelphia (2006)
11. Sarma, A.D., Dong, X., Halevy, A.Y.: Bootstrapping pay-as-you-go data integration systems. In: SIGMOD Conference, pp. 861–874 (2008)
12. Shvaiko, P., Euzenat, J.: A Survey of Schema-Based Matching Approaches. In: Spaccapietra, S. (ed.) Journal on Data Semantics IV. LNCS, vol. 3730, pp. 146–171. Springer, Heidelberg (2005)
13. Zhao, K., Xia, M., Shaw, M.J.: Vertical E-Business Standards and Standards Developing Organizations: A conceptual framework. Electronic Markets 15(4), 289–300 (2005)
14. Zhu, H., Wu, H.: Quality of Data Standards: Framework and Illustration using XBRL Taxonomy and Instances. Electronic Markets 21(2), 129–139 (2011)

P²AMF: Predictive, Probabilistic Architecture Modeling Framework

Pontus Johnson[1], Johan Ullberg[1], Markus Buschle[1], Ulrik Franke[1,2], and Khurram Shahzad[1]

[1] Industrial Information and Control Systems,
KTH Royal Institute of Technology,
Osquldas v. 12, SE-10044 Stockholm, Sweden
{pj101,johanu,markusb,khurrams}@ics.kth.se
[2] FOI - Swedish Defence Research Agency,
SE-16490 Stockholm, Sweden
ulrik.franke@foi.se

Abstract. In the design phase of business and software system development, it is desirable to predict the properties of the system-to-be. Existing prediction systems do, however, not allow the modeler to express *uncertainty* with respect to the design of the considered system. In this paper, we propose a formalism, the *Predictive, Probabilistic Architecture Modeling Framework* (P²AMF), capable of advanced and probabilistically sound reasoning about architecture models given in the form of UML class and object diagrams. The proposed formalism is based on the Object Constraint Language (OCL). To OCL, P²AMF adds a probabilistic inference mechanism. The paper introduces P²AMF, describes its use for system property prediction and assessment, and proposes an algorithm for probabilistic inference.

Keywords: probabilistic inference, system properties, prediction, Object Constraint Language, UML, class diagram, object diagram.

1 Introduction

As an alternative to business and software service development by trial-and-error, it is desirable to predict the properties of envisioned services already in the early phases of the lifecycle. Such predictions may guide developers, allowing them to explore and compare design alternatives at a low cost. Business and software developers routinely argue for or against alternative design choices based on the expected impact of those choices on, e.g., the future system's efficiency, availability, security or functional capabilities. However, experience-based predictions made by individual developers have drawbacks in terms of transparency, consistency, cost and availability. Therefore, formal approaches to such predictions are highly desirable. In addition to prediction, system property analysis methods may be employed to assess properties of existing systems that are difficult to measure directly, e.g. in the case of information security. From an enterprise interoperability perspective, one common approach to the field is the use of various forms of architecture models [1]. The abstraction in these models allows for quantitative reasoning about various issues. Incorporating the ability to perform quantitative analysis and prediction would further improve the reasoning. Most current system architecture frameworks, however, lack modeling languages that support interoperability analysis[2].

In this article, we present P^{2}AMF, a framework for generic business and software system analysis. P^{2}AMF is based on the Object Constraint Language (OCL), which is a formal language used to describe expressions on models in the Unified Modeling Language (UML) [3]. The most prominent difference between P^{2}AMF and OCL is the probabilistic nature of P^{2}AMF. P^{2}AMF allows the user to capture uncertainties in both attribute values and model structure.

1.1 OCL for System Property Predictions

In business and software development, many system qualities are worth predicting. These include theoretically well-established non-functional properties such as performance [4]. There are also properties where consensus on the theoretical base has yet to materialize, e.g. in the case of security [5], and interoperability [1]. Finally, there are many functional capabilities and non-functional properties that are so specific to a certain context that the analysis approach needs to be tailored for each instance, e.g. the coverage of the dictionary in a word processor application or the acoustic faithfulness of instruments in a music production application. The multitude of potentially interesting analyses prompts the need for generic languages and frameworks for system property analysis. An additional justification for such formalisms is the integrated analysis of multiple properties that they enable. Multi-attribute analysis provides a base for structured system quality trade-off, and the trade-off between different properties is a key element in any design activity.

To contain the analysis algorithms of multiple system properties, a framework needs to feature an appropriate and sufficiently flexible language. Many system property analysis approaches are based on logic, arithmetic operations and structural aspects of the system [6][7]. The dominating notation for software modeling today is the Unified Modeling Language (UML) [8]. Any generic framework for quality analysis therefore benefits from UML compatibility, allowing models to be shared between design and analysis.

The Object Constraint Language (OCL) [3], satisfies these requirements. OCL incorporates predicate logic, arithmetics and set theory, making it sufficiently expressive to contain most system property analysis needs. As a part of UML, OCL is also highly interoperable.

OCL was developed with *normative* purposes in mind, allowing the designer to constrain future implementation to conform not only to UML models, but also to OCL statements. However, OCL is also suitable for the *descriptive* (in particular *predictive*) purposes of system analysis, [5]. Still, one increasingly important characteristic of modern business and software systems is not captured by OCL: *uncertainty*.

As the business and IT-systems grows older, our knowledge of them becomes less certain. There are several reasons for this development. Firstly, business and software systems are rapidly increasing in complexity; they are growing in size as well as in the complexity of the underlying technologies. Secondly, as systems and components grow older, so do the people who developed them, and finally they will no longer be available. Combined with the poor state of documentation that plagues many projects, this adds to our uncertainty. Thirdly, the use of externally developed and maintained software is increasing.

To allow for explicit consideration of uncertainty in the analysis of non-functional properties, the framework presented in this paper, P^2AMF, is capable of expressing and comprehensively treating uncertainty in UML models. In P^2AMF, attributes are random variables. P^2AMF also allows the explicit modeling of structural uncertainty, i.e. uncertainty regarding the existence of objects and links. Indeed, as opposed to comparable formalisms (cf. Section 4 on related work), P^2AMF features probabilistic versions of logic, arithmetic and set operators, properly reflecting both structural uncertainty and the uncertainty of attribute values.

This article unfolds as follows: In Section 2, P^2AMF is described from the perspective of the user; in this section, the contribution of the article is provided in its most accessible form. The section also include references to some current applications, ranging from business aspects such as organizational structure to more IT related aspects. The most challenging part of the development of P^2AMF was the extension of OCL to a probabilistic context. The proposed inference approach is presented in Section 3. In Section 4, related work is considered. Finally, in Section 5 conclusions are described.

2 Introduction to P^2AMF

In this section, P^2AMF is described from the point of view of the user, i.e. an analyst evaluating a system property. In the first subsection, the differences between P^2AMF and the UML-OCL duo are explained. Then, an example class diagram is introduced and subsequently instantiated. This is followed by a subsection where the object diagram attribute values are predicted. The final two subsections describe the expressiveness and some current applications of P^2AMF.

2.1 Differences between P^2AMF and UML-OCL

The Object Constraint Language (OCL) is a formal language used to describe expressions on UML models. These expressions typically specify invariant conditions that must hold for the system being modeled, or queries over objects described in a model [3].

From the user perspective, P^2AMF has many similarities to UML-OCL; from a syntax perspective, every valid P^2AMF statement is also a valid OCL statement. There are, however, also significant differences. The first and most important difference is that while OCL mainly is employed in the design phase to specify constraints on a future implementation, P²AMF is used to reason about existing or potential systems. P²AMF may be employed to *predict* the uptime of a system while OCL is used to *pose requirements on the uptime* of the same system. While OCL is normative, mandating what *should* be, P²AMF is descriptive and predictive, calculating what *is* or *will be*.

A second difference between UML-OCL and P²AMF is the importance of the object diagram for P²AMF. As in standard UML, class diagrams with embedded expressions may be constructed that represent a whole class of systems. These diagrams may then be instantiated into object diagrams representing the actual systems considered. In P²AMF, however, the object diagrams become particularly significant as inference is performed on them.

Furthermore, P²AMF takes *uncertainty* into consideration. In particular, two kinds of uncertainty are introduced. Firstly, attributes may be stochastic. For instance, when classes are instantiated, the initial values of their attributes may be expressed as probability distributions. As will be described later, the values may subsequently be individualized for each instance.

Secondly, the existence of objects and links may be uncertain. It may, for instance, be the case that we no longer know whether a specific server is still in service or whether it has been retired. This is a case of object existence uncertainty. Such uncertainty is specified using an `existence` attribute that is mandatory for all classes. We may also be unsure of whether a server is still in the cluster servicing a specific application. This is an example of association uncertainty. Similarly, this is specified with an `existence` attribute on the association, implemented using association classes.

The introduction of two mandatory `existence` attributes and the specification of attribute values by means of probability distributions thus constitute the only changes to OCL as perceived by the user. These modest changes, however, allow for a comprehensive probabilistic treatment of the affected class and object diagrams, including both attribute uncertainty and structural uncertainty, enabling proper probabilistic inference over OCL expressions.

2.2 An Example Class Diagram

To illustrate the usage of P²AMF, consider the simple example of a cloud service. This is a case where the probabilistic nature of P²AMF is relevant; in cloud computing, the sheer complexity of the cloud mandate for an architecture, and architecture analysis, approach. Furthermore, there is a fundamental uncertainty about such things as the number of servers currently providing a given service, about the characteristics of these particular servers, etc. Nevertheless, these aspects influence the properties of the service at hand. From an interoperability perspective, properties such as response time and availability are important to consider. Although these are only a small part of aspects important for interoperability, they serve as an well-sized and self-contained example for illustrating P²AMF.

The class diagram for the example is given in Fig. 1. It contains three classes: `Service`, `Cloud` and `Server`. In the present example, we assume that the service

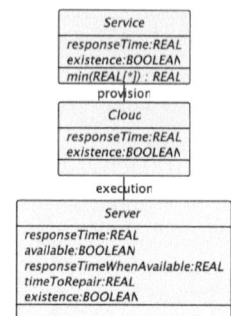

Fig. 1. An example class diagram

provider, in order to commit to a feasible service level agreement, would like to predict the future response time of the provided service. Thus, `responseTime` is an attribute of each of the three classes. Furthermore, every server can be up or down, thus prompting the attribute `available`. If a server is down, the time to repair is given by the attribute `timeToRepair`. Some of the attributes are given initial values while the rest are derived from other attributes. There is also a helper operation, `min`, returning the minimum of the provided values. Below, the model's P²AMF expressions are provided.

```
context Service :: responseTime : Real
derive: cloud.responseTime + min(cloud.server.responseTime)

context Service :: min(values : Bag(Real)): Real
body: values -> iterate (x : Real;
acc : Real=maxVal | x.min(acc))

context Service :: existence : Boolean
init : Bernoulli (0.98)

context Provision :: existence : Boolean
init : Bernoulli (0.98)

context Cloud :: responseTime : Real
init : Normal (0.05, 0.01)

context Cloud :: existence : Boolean
init : Bernoulli (1.0)

context Execution :: existence : Boolean
init : Bernoulli (0.70)

context Server :: responseTime : Real
derive:  if available
then responseTimeWA
else timeToRepair
endif

context Server :: responseTimeWA : Real
init : Normal (0.1, 0.02)

context Server :: timeToRepair : Real
init : Normal (3600, 900)

context Server :: available : Boolean
```

```
init: Bernoulli(0.95)
context Server::existence:Boolean
init: Bernoulli(0.97)
```

Going from the bottom and up in the P²AMF expressions above, first consider the Boolean server existence attribute. The probability that a given server exists is given by a Bernoulli distribution of 97%. Since the running example concerns a future state, this probability distribution represents the belief that a server will in fact be installed as planned, and will be dependent on the modeler's or other expert's knowledge . Continuing to the attribute `available`, the distribution specifies a 95% probability that a given server is up and running at any given moment. For the attributes `timeToRepair` and `responseTimeWA`, normal distributions specify the expected time (in seconds) before a server is up and running again after a failure and the response time for the case of a server that has not failed respectively. So far, we have considered four attributes assigned initial probability distributions on the class level. They thus represent the whole population of considered servers. Later, as the class diagram is instantiated, these estimates can be updated with system-specific data.

The top-most attribute of the `Server` class differs from the previously presented as it is *derived*. The derivation states that the response time of the server depends on whether it is available or not. If it is available, `responseTimeWA` gives the response time while `timeToRepair` returns the relevant value when the server is down. The `Execution` association connects the `Server` to the `Cloud` class. As there is uncertainty about whether a given server is connected to the Cloud, its `existence` attribute is assigned a probability of 70%.

The `Cloud` class has two attributes: its existence, which is similar to the existence attribute of the server class except that we are certain that the Cloud exists; and a real attribute with an initial probability distribution specifying the expected response time of the networking infrastructure. The `Provision` association class connects `Service` to the `Cloud`. Its features are similar to the `Execution` association class.

Finally, the class `Service` contains one derived attribute, `responseTime`, one operation, `min`, and the mandatory existence attribute. The service response time is given as a sum of the Cloud networking infrastructure response time on the one hand, and the minimum response time of the set of providing servers on the other. The `min` operation simply returns the minimum value of a set of values. The existence attribute is similar to those of the other classes.

2.3 An Example Object Diagram

The class diagram captures the general type of system and the causal effects that such systems are subject to. In order to make specific predictions, however, object diagrams detailing actual system instances are required. Instantiation follows the same rules as in object orientation in general. Classes are instantiated into objects, associations into links, multiplicities must be respected, and attributes may be assigned values (in the case of P²AMF, either deterministic values or probability distributions).

There is, however, one interesting and useful difference. In ordinary UML/OCL, values may not be assigned to derived attributes since those attributes are inferred from the derivation expression. Assignment of a different value than the one resulting from the derivation rule would lead to an inconsistent model. The probabilistic inference algorithm presented in Section 3, however, does allow the assignment of values to derived attributes, as long as attributes are assigned values within the ranges specified by the probability distributions, on the class level. The most useful consequence of this capability is the possibility to infer backwards in the causal chain. In our running example, we can therefore gain knowledge about the availability of the servers merely by observing the response time of the service. This capacity for backwards reasoning is not available in standard OCL/UML. As an example, consider a model where $x = y + z$. If x is assigned a value, OCL can tell us nothing of the value of y. P^2AMF, however, can. Therefore, in P^2AMF, all information that is provided in the object diagram is used to improve the predictions of attribute values.

Returning to the running example, consider the object diagram of Fig. 2. In this instance of the class diagram, the calculator – an instance of the Service class – uses theCloud, which is the single instance of the Cloud class. Three redundant Server instances are present in the Cloud, calcServA, calcServB and calcServC.

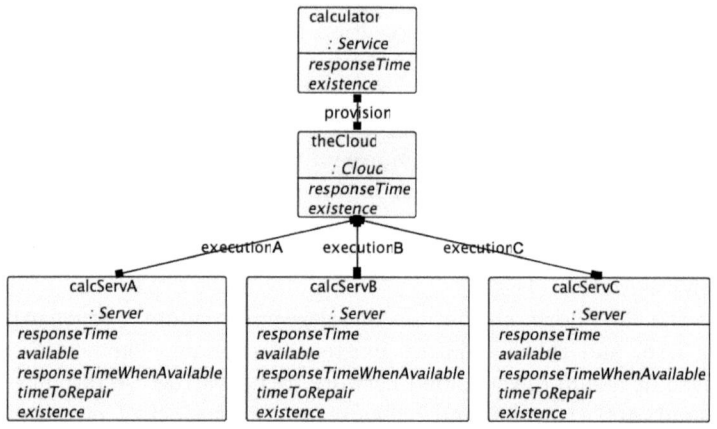

Fig. 2. Instantiation of the example class diagram

We assume that the service provider estimates the attribute values as presented in Table 1. Note that attributes may be assigned either deterministic values, as theCloud.existence, or stochastic ones, as e.g. calcServC.timeToRepair. Some are not assigned any values at all. These will instead be inferred as part of the prediction. Again, note that unlike standard UML/OCL, any attribute may be assigned a value and any attribute may be unassigned; inference will still be possible. A modeler can therefore obtain predictions based on the current state of knowledge, however poor that knowledge is. Of course, high uncertainties in the object diagram will generally lead to high uncertainties in the predictions.

Table 1. Attributes are assigned either probability distributions or deterministic values in the object diagram

Attribute type	Class.Attribute	Assigned value
Real	calculator.responseTime	
Boolean	calculator.existence	Bernoulli(0.997)
Boolean	provision.existence	True
Real	theCloud.responseTime	Normal(0.05, 0.005)
Boolean	theCloud.existence	True
Boolean	executionA.existence	Bernoulli(0.85)
Real	calcServA.responseTime	
Real	calcServA.responseTimeWA	Normal(0.08, 0.01)
Real	calcServA.timeToRepair	Normal(6000, 2000)
Boolean	calcServA.available	Bernoulli(0.94)
Boolean	calcServA.existence	Bernoulli(0.975)
Boolean	executionB.existence	Bernoulli(0.85)
Real	calcServB.responseTime	
Real	calcServB.responseTimeWA	Normal(0.03, 0.005)
Real	calcServB.timeToRepair	Normal(9000, 3000)
Boolean	calcServB.available	Bernoulli(0.91)
Boolean	calcServB.existence	Bernoulli(0.975)
Boolean	executionC.existence	Bernoulli(0.92)
Real	calcServC.responseTime	
Real	calcServC.responseTimeWA	Normal(0.12, 0.015)
Real	calcServC.timeToRepair	Normal(6000, 2000)
Boolean	calcServC.available	
Boolean	calcServC.existence	Bernoulli(0.975)

2.4 Inference in the Object Diagram

With support of a tool [9], the analyst can perform predictive inference on the object diagram described above with the click of a button. The details of the underlying algorithms are presented in Section 3. The results of the inference are new probability distributions assigned to the attributes. As these are typically non-parametric, they are most easily presented in the form of diagrams. Fig 3 displays the distribution of the most interesting attribute, calculator.responseTime. We note that the most probable response time is 80ms. This is the sum of the most probable response times of theCloud and calcServB, as calcServB is the fastest server and it is probably available. However, there is a certain probability (24%) that calcServB is down (i.e. that available is false) or that it is not in service (that existence is false). In this case, calcServA will most probably (83%) be available, and the response time will increase to 130 ms on average. If calcServA also fails or if it is not in service, calcServC will provide a mean response time of 170 ms. Despite the tripled redundancy, there is a small probability (1.2%) that none of the servers are available. In that case, the response time depends on the installed server with the shortest time to repair, i.e. either calcServA or calcServC, with a mean of 1:40h (6000 s) each. Finally, although quite unlikely, there is the risk (0,3%) that none of the servers will exist as modeled; they could have been taken out of service or were perhaps never installed in the first place. In this case, the response time will be so high that the exact value no longer matters.

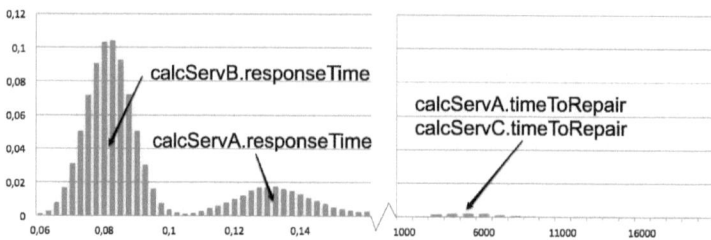

Fig. 3. `calculator.responseTime` probability distribution

As mentioned, backward inference is an important capability of probabilistic reasoning. As an example, suppose that when the system has been installed, an end user of the `calculator` service measures its response time to 130 ms. From this information, the prediction system automatically infers that both `calcServA` and `calcServB` must be either unavailable (90% probability) or non-existent (e.g. retired) (10% probability) while `calcServC` must be providing the service. This conclusion is reached automatically, but it can be understood intuitively as follows: Provided by redundant servers, the `calculator` service response time is given by the fastest available server. Since the measured service response time (taking the Cloud into account) is slower than those of `calcServA` and `calcServB`, they are surely down. Since the measured response time fits the probability distribution of `calcServC` when it is up and running, this must be the providing server.

2.5 Expressiveness of P²AMF

A set of expressive characteristics makes P²AMF particularly well suited for specifying predictive system property models. These include object orientation, support for first-order logic, arithmetics, set theory and support for expressing both class and instance level uncertainty, as described in this section.

P²AMF operates on class and object diagrams. The object-oriented features of such diagrams may therefore be leveraged by the predictive systems in P²AMF. These features are well known and include class instantiation, inheritance, polymorphism, etc. Secondly, P²AMF is able to express first-order logical relations. The predictive benefits of predicate logic are undisputed and used as a base for many deductive formalisms [10]. Furthermore, arithmetics, the oldest branch of mathematics, is used for prediction of properties ranging from hardware-related ones such as reliability [11] to organizational and economic ones, e.g. efficiency [12].

In order to efficiently make predictions on models such as the ones exemplified above, set theory is indispensable. The ability to speak of the number of components in a certain system, the qualities of a set of objects following a given navigation path in an object diagram, etc. are important for predictions on most systems with varying structure [10].

As previously discussed, for many real-world systems and situations, perfect information is rare. On the contrary, the available information is often incomplete or otherwise uncertain [13]. In P²AMF, attributes of objects may be expressed by probability distributions. For many systems, not only the attribute values are associated with uncertainty, but also the system structure, e.g. does cloud service Z have double servers as the specification claims, or was one retired last month? The introduction of the `existence` attribute on classes and associations allows the specification of structural uncertainty in P²AMF.

The object-oriented separation of theoretical prediction laws on the class level and the particulars about a specific system on the object level also pertains to the specification of uncertainty. The class-level modeler may need to express uncertainties about e.g. the strengths of attribute relations. For instance, to what extent a certain category of firewalls reduces the success rate of cyber attacks is rarely known precisely. Similarly as for the instance level, P²AMF allows for specification of attribute uncertainty as well as structural uncertainty on the class level.

2.6 Applications of P²AMF

P²AMF has been used in class diagrams predicting such diverse properties as interoperability [1], availability [14], and the effects of changes to the organizational structure of an enterprise [15]. It has also been used for multi-property analysis [16]. These applications can be seen as evaluations of P²AMF, in particular of the expressiveness of the formalism, as well as examples of the wide variety of properties that can be evaluated using P²AMF. Furthermore, a software tool supporting modeling and prediction using P²AMF has been developed, see [3] for a description of an early version of this tool.

3 Probabilistic Inference

In this section, we explain how inference is performed in P²AMF models. A Monte Carlo approach is employed, where the probabilistic P²AMF object diagram is sampled to create a set of deterministic UML/OCL object diagrams. For each of these sample diagrams, standard OCL inference is performed, thus generating sample values for all model attributes. For each attribute, the sample set collected from all sampled OCL models is used to characterize the posterior distribution.

Several Monte Carlo methods may be employed for probabilistic inference in P²AMF models, including forward sampling, rejection sampling and Metropolis-Hastings sampling [17]. Of these, rejection and Metropolis-Hastings sampling allow the specification of evidence on any attribute in the object models while forward sampling only allows evidence on root attributes[1].

In this section, we will only present rejection sampling as it is the simplest method that allows evidence on all attributes. Let O^p denote a P²AMF object

---

[1] Root attributes have no causal parents.

diagram, let $X_1, ..., X_m$ be the set of Boolean existence attributes $\mathbf{X}$ in such a diagram and let $Y_1, ..., Y_n$ be a topological ordering of the remaining attributes $\mathbf{Y}$ in the diagram. A topological ordering requires that causal parent attributes appear earlier in the sequence than their children[2]. The parents of Y_i, $\mathbf{Pa}_{Y_i}$, are those attributes that are independent variables in the OCL definition of the child attributes, $Y_i = f_{Y_i}(\mathbf{Pa}_{Y_i})$, where f_{Y_i} is the OCL expression defining Y_i. Furthermore, let $\mathbf{Y}^r$ represent the subset of $\mathbf{Y}$ that are root attributes, $\mathbf{Pa}_{Y_i^r} = \emptyset$, i.e. they are defined by probability distributions rather than by OCL expressions, $P(\mathbf{Y}^r)$. Let $\mathbf{Y}^{\bar{r}}$ represent the subset of $\mathbf{Y}$ that are not root attributes, $\mathbf{Y}^{\bar{r}} = \mathbf{Y} \setminus \mathbf{Y}^r$, i.e. that are defined by OCL statements rather than by probability distributions, $Y_i^{\bar{r}} = f_{Y_i^{\bar{r}}}(\mathbf{Pa}_{Y_i^{\bar{r}}})$.

The objective of the rejection sampling algorithm is to generate samples from the posterior probability distribution $P(\mathbf{X}, \mathbf{Y}|\mathbf{e})$, where $\mathbf{e} = \mathbf{e}^X \cup \mathbf{e}^Y$ denotes the evidence of existence attributes as well as the remaining attributes. The objective is thus to approximate the probability distributions of all attributes, given that we have observations on the actual values of some attributes, and prior probability distributions representing our beliefs about the values of all attributes prior to observing any evidence.

The first step in the algorithm is to generate random samples from the existence attributes' probability distribution $P(\mathbf{X})$: $\mathbf{x}[1], ..., \mathbf{x}[M]$. For each sample, $\mathbf{x}[i]$, and based on the P^{2}AMF object diagram O^p, a reduced object diagram, $N_i \in \mathbf{N}$, containing only those objects and links whose existence attributes, X_j, were assigned the value **true**, is created. Some object diagrams generated in this manner will not conform to the constraints of UML. In particular, object diagrams may appear where a link is connected to only one or even zero objects. Such samples are rejected. Other generated object diagrams will violate e.g. the multiplicity constraints of the class diagram. Such samples are also rejected. Finally, some OCL expressions are undefined for certain object diagrams, for instance a summation expression over an empty set of attributes. Remains a set of traditional UML/OCL object diagrams, $\Xi \subset \mathbf{N}$, whose structures vary but are syntactically correct, and whose attributes are not yet assigned values.

In the second step, for each of the remaining object diagrams, Ξ_i, the probability distribution of the root attributes, $P(\mathbf{Y}^r)$ is sampled, thus producing the sample set $\mathbf{y}^r[1], ..., \mathbf{y}^r[size(\Xi)]$. If there is evidence on a root attribute, the sample is assigned the evidence value. Based on the samples of the root attributes, the OCL expressions are calculated in topological order for each remaining attribute in the object diagram, $y_i^{\bar{r}} = f_{y_i^{\bar{r}}}(\mathbf{Pa}_{y_i^{\bar{r}}})$. The result is a set of deterministic UML/OCL object diagrams, $\Lambda \subset \Xi$, where in each diagram, all attributes are assigned values.

The third step of the sampling algorithm rejects those object diagrams that contain attributes which do not conform to the evidence. The sampling process ensures that root attributes always do conform, but this is not the case for OCL-defined attributes. The final set of object diagrams, $\mathbf{O} \subset \Lambda$, contains attribute

---

[2] That it is possible to order the attributes topologically requires the absence of cycles. Acyclicity is therefore a requirement for P^{2}AMF, just as for e.g. Bayesian networks.

samples from the posterior probability distribution $P(\mathbf{X},\mathbf{Y}|\mathbf{e})$. These samples may thus be used to approximate the posterior. The algorithm is presented in pseudo code below.

```
for(int i=1; i<M; i++) {
x = sampleExistenceAttributes();
  x = sampleExistenceAttributes();
  N = extractObjectDiagram(O^p, x);
  if (syntacticallyCorrect(N)) {
    y = sampleRemainingAttributes();
    Λ = assignAttributesToDiagram(y, N);
    if (conformsToEvidence(Λ)) {
      O.add(Λ);
    }
  }
}
```

4 Related Work

There are three categories of work that in different ways are similar to P²AMF. The first category includes variants of first-order probabilistic models. Among other proposals, these include Bayesian Logic (BLOG) [18] and Probabilistic Relational Models (PRM) [19]. These are similar to P²AMF in their use of object-based templates which may be instantiated into structures amenable to probabilistic inference. However, they do not consider how logic and arithmetic operators are affected by structural uncertainty.

The second category of related work comprises query and constraint languages such as SQL [20] and OCL [3]. Similarly to P²AMF, these languages allow logical and arithmetic queries of object or entity models. They are, however, deterministic rather than probabilistic.

The third and most important category of related work is work on stochastic quality prediction for software architecture. These include MARTE [4], KLAPER [21] and the Palladio component model for model-driven performance prediction [22], where two of them have opted for UML or MOF based modeling formalisms. However, common to all of these contributions is their focus on the analysis of particular properties. P²AMF differs from these, as it does not propose specific analyses but rather provides a general language for expressing them. The closest match is probably the work by Ferrer et al. on multiple non-functional property evaluation [23], using the Dempster-Shafer approach to probabilistic reasoning. However, P²AMF is more general still; aiming to offer not just a toolbox but a unified *language* where the best practice of e.g. reliability or performance modeling can be expressed. Within this third category, there are also generic frameworks for system quality analysis, such as ATAM [24]. These typically provide different support than P²AMF, and are not based on probabilistic foundations.

5 Conclusions

Prediction and assessment of the expected quality and behavior of business and software systems already in the design stage is a desirable capability. With the frequent re-configurations of services in a complex and uncertain environment, the need for such analyses to deal with uncertainty grows.

In this paper, we have reported on a language and tool for probabilistic prediction and assessment of system properties. The formalism, P^2AMF, supports automatic probabilistic reasoning based on set theory, first-order logic and algebra. With class and object diagrams as a base, P^2AMF is compatible with UML. This paper has introduced P^2AMF and exemplified it for a simple analysis case, pointed out other areas where P^2AMF is being employed and described the algorithm for performing the required probabilistic inference.

References

[1] Ullberg, J., Johnson, P., Buschle, M.: A language for interoperability modeling and prediction. Computers in Industry (2012)
[2] Chen, D., Doumeingts, G., Vernadat, F.: Architectures for enterprise integration and interoperability: Past, present and future. Computers in Industry 59(7), 647–659 (2008)
[3] Object Management Group: Object Constraint Language. Version 2.3 (2010)
[4] Object Management Group: UML Profile for MARTE: Modeling and Analysis of Real-Time Embedded Systems. Version 1.0 (2009)
[5] Lodderstedt, T., Basin, D., Doser, J.: SecureUML: A UML-Based Modeling Language for Model-Driven Security. In: Jézéquel, J.-M., Hussmann, H., Cook, S. (eds.) UML 2002. LNCS, vol. 2460, pp. 426–441. Springer, Heidelberg (2002)
[6] Hansson, H., Jonsson, B.: A Logic for Reasoning about Time and Reliability. Formal Aspects of Computing 6(5), 512–535 (1994)
[7] Ritchey, R., Ammann, P.: Using model checking to analyze network vulnerabilities. In: Proceedings of the 2000 IEEE Symposium on Security and Privacy, S & P 2000, pp. 156–165. IEEE (2000)
[8] Object Management Group: OMG Unified Modeling Language (OMG UML), Superstructure. Version 2.4 (2011)
[9] Ullberg, J., Franke, U., Buschle, M., Johnson, P.: A tool for interoperability analysis of enterprise architecture models using Pi-OCL. In: Enterprise Interoperability IV, pp. 81–90 (2010)
[10] Spivey, J.M.: The Z notation: a reference manual. Prentice Hall International (UK) Ltd. (1992)
[11] Lyu, M.R.: Handbook of Software Reliability Engineering. Mcgraw-Hill (1996)
[12] Mason-Jones, R., Towill, D.R.: Total cycle time compression and the agile supply chain. International Journal of Production Economics 62(1-2) (1999)
[13] Aier, S., Buckl, S., Franke, U., Gleichauf, B., Johnson, P., Närman, P., Schweda, C.M., Ullberg, J.: A survival analysis of application life spans based on enterprise architecture models. In: Proc. 3rd International Workshop on Enterprise Modelling and Information Systems Architectures, EMISA 2009. Lecture Notes in Informatics, pp. 141–154 (2009)

14. Franke, U., Johnson, P., König, J.: An architecture framework for enterprise IT service availability analysis. Software & Systems Modeling (2013)
15. Gustafsson, P., Höök, D., Franke, U., Johnson, P.: Modeling the IT impact on organizational structure. In: Proc. 13th IEEE International EDOC Conference, EDOC 2009 (2009)
16. Närman, P., Buschle, M., Ekstedt, M.: An enterprise architecture framework for multi-attribute information systems analysis. Software & Systems Modeling (2013)
17. Walsh, B.: Markov Chain Monte Carlo and Gibbs Sampling (2004)
18. Milch, B., Marthi, B., Russell, S., Sontag, D., Ong, D.L., Kolobov, A.: Blog: probabilistic models with unknown objects. In: Proceedings of the 19th International Joint Conference on Artificial Intelligence, IJCAI 2005, pp. 1352–1359. Morgan Kaufmann Publishers Inc. (2005)
19. Friedman, N., Getoor, L., Koller, D., Pfeffer, A.: Learning probabilistic relational models. In: Proceedings of the 16th International Joint Conference on Artificial Intelligence, vol. 2, pp. 1300–1307. Morgan Kaufmann Publishers Inc., San Francisco (1999)
20. Melton, J., Simon, A.: Understanding the new SQL: a complete guide. Morgan Kaufmann Publishers (1993)
21. Grassi, V., Mirandola, R., Randazzo, E., Sabetta, A.: **KLAPER**: An Intermediate Language for Model-Driven Predictive Analysis of Performance and Reliability. In: Rausch, A., Reussner, R., Mirandola, R., Plášil, F. (eds.) The Common Component Modeling Example. LNCS, vol. 5153, pp. 327–356. Springer, Heidelberg (2008)
22. Becker, S., Koziolek, H., Reussner, R.: The palladio component model for model-driven performance prediction. Journal of Systems and Software 82(1), 3–22 (2009)
23. Ferrer, A.J.: Optimis: A holistic approach to cloud service provisioning. Future Generation Computer Systems 28(1), 66–77 (2012)
24. Bass, L., Clements, P., Kazman, R.: Software Architecture in Practice, 2nd edn. Addison-Wesley Longman Publishing Co., Inc. (2003)

Business Model Risk Analysis: Predicting the Probability of Business Network Profitability

Pontus Johnson[1], Maria Eugenia Iacob[2], Margus Välja[1], Marten van Sinderen[2], Christer Magnusson[3], and Tobias Ladhe[3]

[1] Department of Industrial Information and Control Systems
Royal Institute of Technology (KTH), Stockholm, Sweden
[2] Centre for Telematics and Information Technology,
University of Twente, Enschede, The Netherlands
[3] Department of Computer and Systems Sciences
Stockholm University, Stockholm, Sweden
{pontusj,margus.valja}@ics.kth.se,
{m.e.iacob,m.j.vansinderen}@utwente.nl, {ladhe,cmagnus}@dsv.su.se

Abstract. In the design phase of business collaboration, it is desirable to be able to predict the profitability of the business-to-be. Therefore, techniques to assess qualities such as costs, revenues, risks, and profitability have been previously proposed. However, they do not allow the modeler to properly manage uncertainty with respect to the design of the considered business collaboration. In many real collaboration projects today, uncertainty regarding the business' present or future characteristics is so significant that ignoring it becomes problematic. In this paper, we propose an approach based on the Predictive, Probabilistic Architecture Modeling Framework (P^2AMF), capable of advanced and probabilistically sound reasoning about profitability risks. The P^2AMF-based approach for profitability risk prediction is also based on the e^3-value modeling language and on the Object Constraint Language (OCL). The paper introduces the prediction and modeling approach, and a supporting software tool. The use of the approach is illustrated by means of a case.

Keywords: value networks, profitability, risk analysis, probabilistic inference, goal interoperability.

1 Introduction

A business model is critical for any new business venture, and especially for those that involve multiple organizations, due to the complexity of their relationships. In the literature of the last decade several authors have proposed different frameworks aimed at identifying the main ingredients of a business model (e.g., [20,21]; for an overview, see [19,18]). An important motivation behind business modeling is its ability to provide an overview of the relationships between the actors involved in a business collaboration and of the way they all aim to benefit from it, financially or otherwise.

In the design phase of a business collaboration, it is desirable to be able to predict the risks concerning profitability associated with the "business-to-be". As an alternative to the rather costly trial-and-error approach, it is desirable to understand the properties of the envisioned collaboration already in its early phases. Therefore some of the existing business modeling approaches not only model the business, but also propose some techniques to assess qualities such as costs and revenues [20], and profitability [21]. However, they do not allow the modeler to properly express uncertainty with respect to the considered business collaboration. In many real collaboration projects today, uncertainty regarding the business' present or future characteristics is so significant that ignoring it becomes problematic.

Our main contribution in this paper is an approach capable of advanced and probabilistically sound reasoning about profitability risks of a given business model expressed in the e^3-value modeling language [21]. Such predictions may guide business managers, allowing them to explore and compare collaboration scenario alternatives at a low cost. Profitability predictions do, in fact, constitute an important element in the strategic decision making process, and a critical part of the assessment of risks associated with a new business venture. Managers routinely argue for or against alternative business opportunities based on those opportunities' expected impact on, e.g., the company's future financial and business performance. However, experience/intuition-based predictions made by individual managers have serious drawbacks in terms of transparency, consistency, and ability to correctly evaluate costs and risks. Therefore, formal approaches to business model quality prediction are required. They not only allow us to anticipate the business-to-be, but they are also a means to achieve pragmatic and, goal interoperability [30] in multi-actor business collaborations.

The proposed profitability prediction approach draws upon our earlier work concerning the Predictive, Probabilistic Architecture Modeling Framework (P^2AMF) [4] that, in turn, is based on the Object Constraint Language (OCL) [17]. The process we follow to develop our profitability prediction approach is as follows. In the first step, starting from the original definition of the e^3-value ontology, we define the e^3-value metamodel in the P^2AMF, expressed as an OCL-annotated class diagram. Consequently, any e^3-value model can be instantiated from the e^3-value class diagram metamodel in the form of an object diagram. Finally, we define and implement the underlying inference algorithm for the prediction of the attribute values associated with the model elements of the object model. Thus, the execution of the inference algorithm produces, for example, predictions about the net earnings attribute values for all actors participating in a business collaboration. Such profitability predictions of each of the actors involved, are determined taking into account given levels of uncertainty (expressed as probability distributions) at three levels: uncertainty regarding attribute values of objects in the object model, uncertainty related to objects (e.g., uncertainties regarding the actors' participation in the value network), and uncertainties regarding the (existence of) relationships between objects (e.g., uncertainties related to a value exchange). This represents an important advancement compared to Gordijn's work on profitability sheets and analysis [21], since Gordijn's approach only considers deterministic values for attributes, and value network models are fixed. Furthermore, due to the fact that the P2AMF and the EAAT allow us to incorporate uncertainty in e^3-value models, profitability predictions can be seen as risk assessments. To the best of our knowledge, this is the first time a formal business model-based profitability risk analysis method is proposed for business models. Work on how trust assumptions affect profitability in value networks has been reported (e.g., [24]). However, it should be noted that trust is just one specific source of risk.

The remainder of this paper is organized as follows. In Section 2 we briefly present the original e^3-value business model ontology [21]. Section 3 is devoted to the P^2AMF and tool. Section 4 describes the main contribution of this paper, the profitability prediction approach and illustrates the usage of this approach by means of the electric cars case study that has been defined in the scope of the Stockholm Royal Seaport Smart City project [29]. The papers ends with some conclusions and pointers to future work.

2   Business Modeling and the e^3-Value Ontology

In this section we motivate our choice for the e^3-value modeling formalism and briefly present the e^3-value ontology [21].

Many business model frameworks exist that aim at facilitating and guiding business modeling, e.g., *Activity system* [16], *e^3-value* [21], *VDML* [26], *REA* [27], *RCOV* [14], *The BM concept* [10], *Entrepreneur's BM* [13], *The social BM* [15], *The BM guide* [9], *4C* [11], *Internet BM* [12], and *BMO* [20]. Some of them have a strong link to information systems, others are closely related to strategic management or industrial organization. Most of the business model frameworks mentioned above have been published in the top 25 MIS journals. However, a systematic literature review we carried out recently [18] resulted in an initial set of 171 journal articles and conference papers relevant for the topic of business modeling. After filtering this set of publications, we ended up with 76 articles presenting some 43 different business model frameworks. Furthermore, five articles in the reviewed literature present a review of business model literature and aim to compare some existing frameworks: [19, 5, 7, 6, 8]. A common trait of most of these frameworks is that they lack the level of formality which is necessary to relate a business model to its supporting enterprise architecture at the model level. However, of the reviewed frameworks, two stand out as having, from the modeling point of view, a sufficient formal foundation: e^3-value [21] and BMO [20]. An extensive comparison of these two formalisms is presented in [5]. There are some significant differences between the two approaches. In terms of the scope covered, BMC is focused on a single element of a value chain and its direct relations with customers and suppliers, while e^3-value takes a network perspective in order to provide insight into value generation outside the formal boundary of a single organization. Also, at the conceptual level they are quite different: the BMO puts emphasis on resources needed to create a certain value proposition, while in e^3-value, the modeling of value streams in a business network is central. An approximate mapping between BMO and e^3-value concepts is proposed in [5], which clearly reveals these differences. When considering the level of formality, although both e^3-value and BMO have been found to be "light weight" ontologies [5], e^3-value is more formal than BMO since it comes with a metamodel [22] and a graphical notation, for which reason it is also a modeling language. The fact that BMC is widely accepted is partly due to its simplicity and ease of use, which come at the cost of formality. In this paper we choose for e^3-value because of its higher level of formalism and because it provides a network perspective on business collaborations which makes it suitable for capturing network effects regarding value propagation.

In the remainder of this section we briefly summarize the e^3-value modeling constructs (for more details we refer to [22, 21]). An e^3-value model essentially describes the value exchange relationships between two or more actors involved in a business collaboration, expressed as a value network model. The main concepts defined in the e^3-value business model ontology that capture these exchanges are: actor (with its specializations, market segment and composed actor), value exchange, value object, value port, and the value interface. Besides a structural specification of the elements of a business value network and of its value streams, an e^3-value model also captures behavioral aspects of such networks with respect to the flow of value. As such, concepts such as stimulus and end stimulus, dependency path and value exchange are used to define a so-called use case map describing the business behavior of actor in the collaboration modeled by the e^3-value model. In Table 1 below we summarize the definition of all these concepts, and their graphical notation. Furthermore, in Figure 2 an example of an e^3-value model can be seen.

3 The P²AMF

As mentioned before, we use the P²AMF framework [4] and the Enterprise Architecture Analysis Tool (EAAT) [3] tool to extend e^3-value to a probabilistic setting. P²AMF is based on the Object Constraint Language (OCL) [17], which is a formal language used to describe expressions on models in the Unified Modeling Language (UML). OCL expressions typically specify invariant conditions that must hold for the system being modeled or queries over objects described in a model. The most prominent difference between P²AMF and OCL is the probabilistic nature of P²AMF. P²AMF allows the user to capture uncertainties in both attribute values and model structure.

Table 1. e^3-value concepts

Concept	Definition	Notation
actor	"an economically independent (and often also legal) entity" [21]	actor
Market segment	Is a concept that breaks a market (consisting of actors) into segments that share common properties. It is often used to model that there is a large group of end-consumers who value objects similarly.	market segment
Value interface	Used to groups one or more value ports of one actor.	△▽
Value port	"An actor uses a value port to provide or request value objects to or from his/her environment, consisting of other actors. Thus, a value port is used to interconnect actors so that they are able to exchange value objects." [21]	▷

Table 1. (*continued*)

Value exchange	"Is used to connect two value ports with each other. It represents one or more potential trades of value object instances between value ports. As such, it is a prototype for actual trades between actors. [...] It does not model actual exchanges of value object instances." [21]	[Value Object] between actor 1 and actor 2
Value transaction	"Concept that aggregates all value exchanges, which define the value exchange instances that must occur as consequence of how value exchanges are connected, via value interfaces to actors." [21]	No distinct notation is defined in the tool.
Value object	"A service, a product, or even an experience, which is of economic value for at least one of the actors involved in a value model" [21]	Is represented as a label on a value exchange relationship.
Value activity	Collection of operational activities, which can be assigned as a whole to an actor and lead to creation of profit or economic value for the performing actor. [21]	value activity
And/Or fork and join	An AND fork connects a scenario element to one or more other elements, while the AND join connects one or more elements to one other element. An OR fork models a continuation of the scenario path into one direction, to be chosen from a number of alternatives. The OR join merges two or paths into one. [21]	
Start and end stimuli	"Use case maps start with one or more start stimuli. A start stimulus represents an event, possibly caused by an actor. [...] A use case map also has one or more end stimuli. They have no successors." [21]	

3.1 An Introduction to P²AMF

From the user perspective, P²AMF has many similarities to OCL applied to class and object diagrams. As can be seen in the derivations in Section 4, P²AMF statements generally appear identical to OCL statements. However, their interpretation differs because P²AMF takes uncertainty into consideration.

In P²AMF, two kinds of uncertainty are introduced. Firstly, attributes may be stochastic. For instance, when classes are instantiated, the initial values of their attributes may be expressed as probability distributions. To the attribute `Actor.expenses` in the following example,

```
context Actor::expenses:Real
init: Normal(3500,300)
```

a normal distribution with a mean of 3500 and a standard deviation of 300 is assigned. The above expression determines the initial value of attribute instances. In the corresponding object diagrams, the values may be further specified in the form of *evidence*. Evidence, a term borrowed from the Bayesian theory of probabilistic inference, determines the attribute value of the instance, and may be either deterministic (hard evidence) or probabilistic (soft evidence).

Secondly, the existence of objects and links may be uncertain. It may, for instance, be the case that we do not know whether we will be able to generate solar energy next week. This can be represented as a case of object existence uncertainty (i.e., whether the generation activity will exist next week is not certain). Such uncertainty is specified using an *existence* attribute that is mandatory for all classes:

```
context GenerationActivity::existence:Boolean
init: Bernoulli(0.8)
```

where the Bernoulli probability distribution states that there is an 80% chance that the activity in fact exists. Uncertainty with respect to the existence of links may be specified in a similar way.

The introduction of two mandatory existence attributes and the specification of attribute values by means of probability distributions thus constitute the only changes to OCL as perceived by the user. These changes, however, allow for a comprehensive probabilistic treatment of OCL-annotated class and object diagrams, including both attribute uncertainty and structural uncertainty. The mathematical approach and inference algorithms behind the approach are presented in [4]. In brief, object diagrams are subjected to Monte Carlo-based probabilistic inference with algorithms, e.g., Metropolis-Hastings [1] and Rejection Sampling [2]. Attributes with previously unknown values are assigned probability distributions. Those with known probability distributions are updated in the light of their relations to neighboring attributes as well as in the light of evidence assigned to various attributes.

With the tool support presented in Section 3.2, the analyst can perform predictive inference on object diagrams with the click of a button. The results of the inference are new probability distributions assigned to the attributes. As these are often non-parametric, they are most easily presented in the form of histograms.

3.2 The EAAT Tool

We have developed a software tool, the Enterprise Architecture Analysis Tool (EAAT), that allows both probabilistic class diagrams and probabilistic object diagrams to be modeled. It also performs inference as described in the previous subsection. The tool is presented in detail in [3] and can be downloaded from [32]. It is divided into two components, the CLASS MODELER, and the OBJECT MODELER, corresponding to two file types: class and object diagrams.

The CLASS MODELER is a graphical editing tool for probabilistic class diagrams. In addition to the basic editing functionality, the CLASS MODELER (i) allows attribute values to be defined either by probability distributions or by OCL expressions, (ii) requires a value for the mandatory existence attributes of classes and associations, and (iii) provides OCL syntax checking support.

The OBJECT MODELER has two components: 1) an editing tool for probabilistic object models, and 2) an inference engine. The editing tool (i) allows probabilistic attribute values, including the mandatory existence attributes, (ii) displays histograms for all attributes representing their probability distributions after inference, and (iii) offers an interface to different inference algorithms and parameters. With one click, the calculations described in Section 3.1 generate posterior probability distributions for all attributes.

4 Predicting Profitability Risks Using e³-Value Models and P²AMF

Due to the fact that the P²AMF and the EAAT allow us to incorporate uncertainty in e³-value models (at object, attribute and relationship levels), profitability predictions can be seen as risk assessments. Risk is generally defined as "the frequency and magnitude of loss that arises from a threat (whether human, animal, or natural event)" [25] and calculated as the threat's probability multiplied by the magnitude of its effect (i.e., the size of the value loss). Thus, our profitability calculation fits in the above definition (i.e., of profitability risk) as it takes into account both uncertainty and magnitude of the net earnings. In this section we present our approach for risk prediction.

4.1 The e³-Value Metamodel

As expressed in P²AMF (Figure 1), the e³-value metamodel is quite similar to the e³-value ontology presented in [21]. All metamodel entities and relations of the P²AMF version can be found in the e³-value ontology. For reasons of economy, a few concepts and relations in the e³-value ontology have been omitted in the P²AMF metamodel.

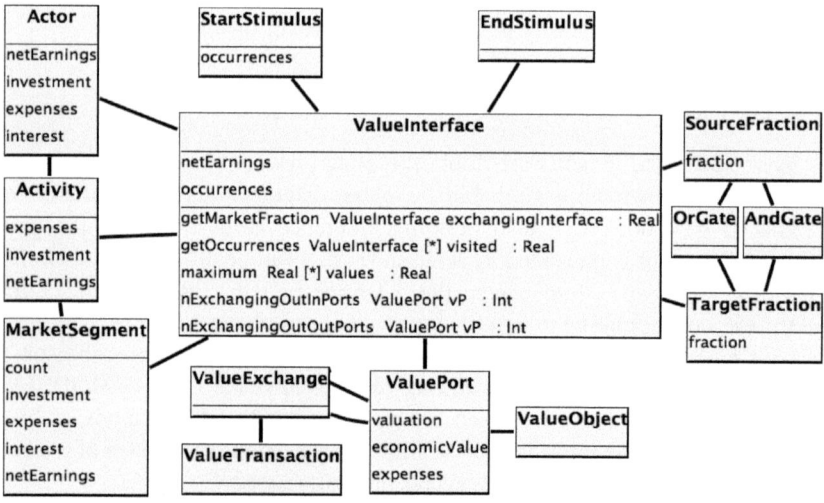

Fig. 1. e³-value metamodel

Currently, the P²AMF version does not feature composite actors. It was also possible to omit a few elements from the Use Case Maps of the e³-value ontology without affecting the profitability algorithms. A few attributes and several operations have also been added in the P²AMF-based metamodel. In this section, we will focus on these attributes and operations as these contain the OCL statements used to replicate the calculations of the e³-value profitability sheet.

4.2 The Risk Prediction Approach

The main goal of the profitability analysis is to calculate the net earnings of each actor. While this attribute is not explicit in the e^3-value ontology or tool, it is calculated in the Excel profitability sheet generated by the tool. In the P^2AMF-based metamodel, this attribute, Actor.netEarnings, is defined as follows:

```
context Actor::netEarnings: Real
derive: self.valueInterface.netEarnings->sum()
        - self.investment - self.expenses
        - self.activity.investment->sum()
        - self.activity.expenses->sum()
```

The net earnings are thus the sum of all net earnings of the actor's value interfaces minus the actor's direct investments and expenses and the investments and expenses of the actor's activities. As noted in [21], a proper net present value calculation requires a time series of e^3-value models. This is also the case for the P^2AMF-based version.

While investments and expenses are non-derived attributes, net earnings of value interfaces are derived.

```
context ValueInterface::netEarnings: Real
derive: self.valuePort.economicValue->sum()
```

The net earnings of a value interface are thus the sum of the economic values of the value ports.

```
context ValuePort::economicValue: Real
derive: if (self.valueExchangeIn->notEmpty())
        then self.valuation*self.valueInterface.getOccurrences(Set{})
        else                                                        -
self.valuation*self.valueInterface.getOccurrences(Set{})
        endif
```

Each value port has a valuation attribute, specifying the value of the exchanged value object. If the value port is incoming, net earnings are increased by the product of the valuation attribute and the number of transactions. If the value port is outgoing, the net earnings are decreased by the corresponding amount. The occurrences, or number of transactions, originate from the attribute occurrence in the start stimulus. The value port occurrences are also affected by the structure of the use case map. For instance, if the scenario path from the start stimulus to the considered value port contains an OR fork with two branches, then the occurrences of the value port will be a fraction of those of the start stimulus. In order to calculate the occurrences of a value port, a recursive algorithm is employed. The algorithm searches through the use case map in order to find the start stimulus. The occurrence value is then propagated and transformed from value interface to value interface by various mechanisms. In many cases, the occurrence value is simply copied. In other cases, such as for the OR fork, the occurrence value is diminished by a factor determined by the fraction attributes of the SourceFraction and TargetFraction classes.

4.3 The Electric Cars Case Study

The Stockholm Royal Seaport (SRS) smart city project has a vision of becoming a world class environmental city district [29]. This could include micro electricity generation by consumers and electric car usage. Our example includes both cases in one simplified scenario, in which we use pricing estimates from [28]. The scenario of the example is as follows. Electric cars used in the SRS area. The cars' owners want to maximize the usage of their resources and earn extra money with the cars when they are not in movement. They can do that by participating in the frequency control market, where electric car capacity is aggregated and sold as a resource to the transmission system operator [28]. In our scenario, the electric vehicle (EV) aggregator operates charging stations, where cars should be plugged in to the grid when idle. The micro-generators have long-term contracts with the aggregator. The example is presented as an e^3-value model in Figure 2.

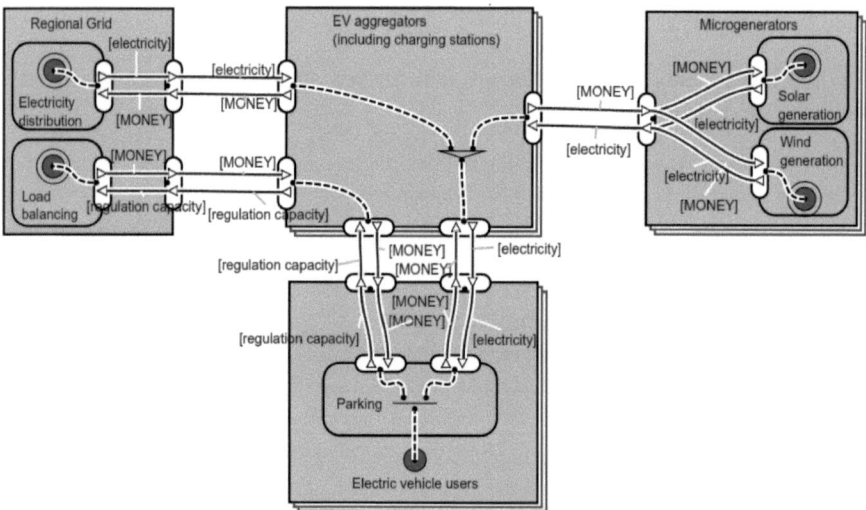

Fig. 2. The e^3-value model for the electric cars case

The models depict one day. It is assumed that there are B(20 000, 0.5) cars in the neighborhood, where B is the binomial distribution (in this case with a mean value of 10 000). They are assumed to have 10kWh batteries, needing to be charged once a day, which implies an occurrence attribute of the start stimulus with the value 1. We further estimate the number of micro generators to B(12, 0.5) and the number of EV aggregators to B(3, 0.75). There is only one regional grid. Since we are uncertain of the future price of electricity, we estimate that the car owner pays 0.98±0.1€ (where 0.98 is the mean and 0.1 is the standard deviation of a normal distribution) per charging, while the price of electricity for the EV aggregator from the regional grid is 0,81±0,1€. Due to its long-term contract, the EV aggregator purchases electricity from the local micro generators at a fixed price of 0.58€, when power is available. Considering the alternatives, customers on average value one battery charging at 1,2±0,2€. The regional grid buys electricity from producers, and thus values the electricity required for one charging at 0,6±0,1€. As the micro generators cannot sell their electricity elsewhere, it has no value to them outside of the transaction with the EV aggregator. The local grid operator is expected to value the capacity provided by one car battery at 0.4±0.05€/day, considering the available alternatives. Therefore, it makes sense to purchase that capacity for 0.32±0.05€ from the EV aggregator. The aggregator in turn, buys the capacity from each car owner for 0.25±0.05€. For the car owner, the cost of providing the regulation is low; the tapping and recharging cause some battery degradation, and there is an inconvenience finding the car with less than a full battery. Based on these considerations, the value of the capacity for the average car owner is estimated at 0.2±0.04€.

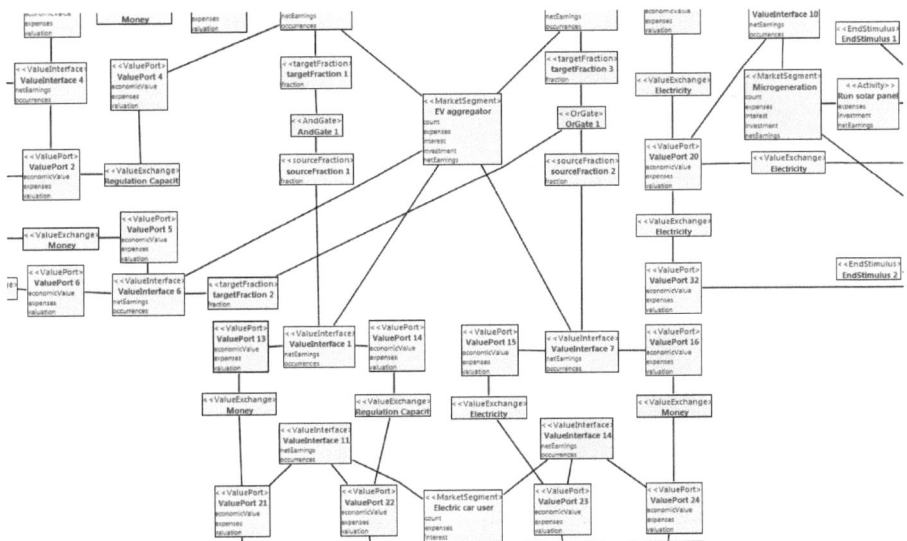

Fig. 3. The object models for the electric cars e^3-value model

Considering the investment costs and expenses, EV aggregators expect fixed costs of 600±200€/day, and running expenses of 500±200€/day. The micro generators' fixed costs are estimated to 110±20€/day with no running expenses. The regional grid has no extra costs in this business model, nor does the car owner. The e^3-value profitability sheet [21] sums up all the value generated in interfaces and subtracts investment and expense costs. The calculations are further based on the number of occurrences and market segment counts. As e^3-value does not consider uncertainty, mean values are utilized. According to the profitability sheet, the net earnings of each actor is the following: Regional Grid: 2 270 €/day; EV Aggregator: 445 €/day; Micro-generator: 180 €/day. As end-customers, the electric car owners' utility is calculated to be 0,27 €/day. Thus, according to the e^3-value model, the example is a sound business model that deserves investment from all parties. Let us now consider the P^2AMF-based version. In the EAAT tool, the graphical representation is a rather large object diagram, a fragment of which is shown in Figure 3. This is visually not as efficient as an e^3-value model, but the automated model transformation between the two notations is straightforward and could be implemented. In P^2AMF, the above uncertainties are easily accommodated. By the Monte-Carlo sampling approach, nonparametric probability distributions are generated for all attributes.

The distributions of the net earnings of the involved actors are presented in Figure 4, Figure 5, Figure 6, and Figure 7.

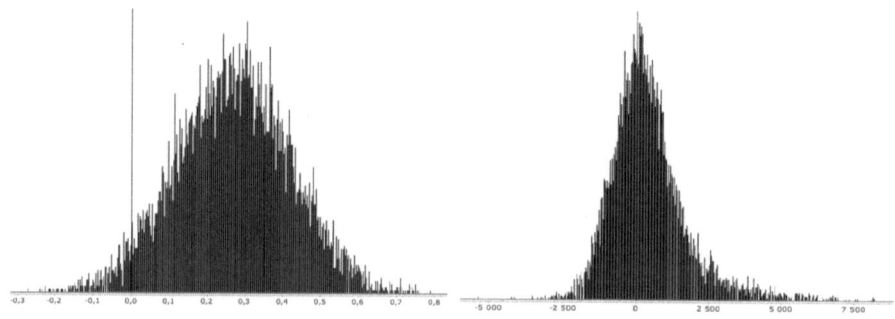

Fig. 4. Net earnings of electric car owner. Mean is 0.27€/day.

Fig. 5. Net earnings of EV Aggregator. Mean is 450€/day.

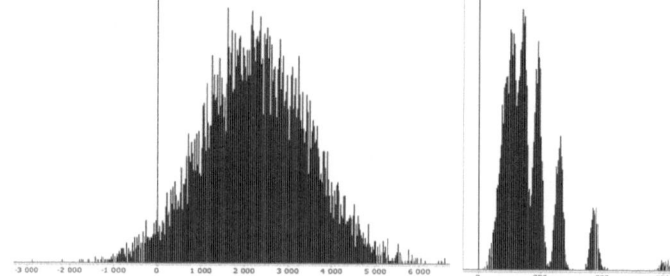
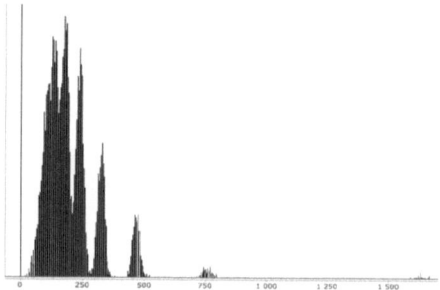

Fig. 6. Net earnings of Regional Grid. Mean is 2300 €/day.

Fig. 7. Net earnings of Micro-generators. Mean is 210 €/day. The irregular shape is due to the probability of competition.

Due to the replacement of the binomial distributions with the nearest integer, we find that the net earnings' mean values of the e^3-value model are slightly off. However, this error is marginal. In accordance with the e^3-value results, we find that there is good reason for the Regional Grid, the Micro-generators, and the electric car owners to sign up for this business model. However, the probability distribution of the EV Aggregator is alarming. Although the mean value is positive, the probability of economic loss is very high. There seems to be a 50% chance of losing money for the EV Aggregator. Any moderately risk-averse agent should be advised against this business model.

5 Conclusions

Prediction and assessment of the expected profitability and behavior of a new business venture already in the early planning phase is a desirable capability, especially in support of strategic decision making. As the business venture becomes more complex and involves more partners, the sources of risks also proliferate, which increases the criticality of analyses taking uncertainty into consideration. In this paper, we have reported on an approach and a tool for probabilistic prediction and assessment of profitability risks. The proposed formalism is based on the e^3-value business modeling language and the P^2AMF framework, and supports automated probabilistic reasoning based on set theory, first-order logic and algebra. Our approach allows us to anticipate profitability levels expressed as probability distributions assigned to the model elements' attributes.

The proposed approach assumes that the value network model is enriched with realistic probability distributions. However, in real situations the form of those distributions may be challenging to obtain. This lack of knowledge may have a negative impact on the quality of the analysis outcomes. To a very large extent this is due to the fact that value networks abstract from the internal details of the actors involved in the business collaboration. We argue that such quantitative input (of sufficient accuracy) can be obtained if one takes these internal details into account, and relates value network models to enterprise architecture models. Therefore, one direction in which we foresee a possible extension of our approach is that of chaining existing enterprise architecture cost analysis [31] and prediction techniques with the value network profitability prediction technique proposed in this study.

References

1. Koller, D., Friedman, N.: Probabilistic graphical models: principles and techniques (2009)
2. Walsh, B.: Markov chain monte carlo and gibbs sampling (2004)
3. Johnson, P., Johansson, E., Sommestad, T., Ullberg, J.: A Tool for Enterprise Architecture Analysis. In: Proceedings of the 11th IEEE International Enterprise Computing Conference, EDOC 2007, Annapolis, USA (2007)
4. Johnson, P., Ullberg, J., Buschle, M., Franke, U., Shahzad, K.: P^2 AMF: Predictive, Probabilistic Architecture Modeling Framework. In: van Sinderen, M., Luttighuis, P.O., Folmer, E., Bosems, S. (eds.) IWEI 2013. LNBIP, vol. 144, pp. 104–117. Springer, Heidelberg (2013)
5. Gordijn, J., Osterwalder, A., Pigneur, Y.: Comparing two Business Model Ontologies for Designing e-Business Models and Value Constellations. In: Proceedings of the 18th Bled eConference: eIntegration in Action, Slovenia (2005)
6. Al-Debei, M.M., Avison, A.: Developing a unified framework of the business model concept. European Journal of Information Systems 19, 359–376 (2010)
7. Lambert, S.: A Conceptual Framework for Business Model Research. In: Proceedings of the 21st Bled eConference: eIntegration in Action. 21st Bled eConference eCollaboration: Overcoming Boundaries through Multi-Channel Interaction, Slovenia, pp. 227–289 (2008)
8. Zott, C., Amit, R., Massa, L.: The Business Model: Recent Developments and Future Research. Journal of Management 37(4), 1019–1042 (2011)
9. Kim, W.C., Mauborgne, R.: Knowing a winning business idea when you see one. Harvard Business Review 78(5), 129–138 (2000)
10. Hedman, J., Kalling, T.: The business model concept: Theoretical underpinnings and empirical illustrations. European Journal of Information Systems 12(1), 49–59 (2003)

11. Wirtz, B.W., Schilke, O., Ullrich, S.: Strategic Development of Business Models. Implications of the Web 2.0 for Creating Value on the Internet. Long Range Planning 43, 272–290 (2010)
12. Lumpkin, G.T., Dess, G.G.: E-Business Strategies and Internet Business Models: How the Internet Adds Value. Organizational Dynamics 33(2), 161–173 (2004)
13. Morris, M., Schindehutte, M., Allen, J.: The entrepreneur's business model: toward a unified perspective. Journal of Business Research 58(6), 726–735 (2005)
14. Demil, B., Lecocq, X.: Business Model Evolution: In Search of Dynamic Consistency. Long Range Planning 43, 227–246 (2010)
15. Yunus, M., Moingeon, B., Lehmann-Ortega, L.: Building Social Business Models: Lessons from the Grameen Experience. Long Range Planning 43, 308–325 (2010)
16. Zott, C., Amit, R.: Business Model Design: An Activity System Perspective. Long Range Planning 43, 216–226 (2010)
17. OMG, Object Constraint Language, version 2.3 (2010)
18. Alberts, B.T., Meertens, L.O., Iacob, M.E., Nieuwenhuis, L.J.M.: The MOF Perspective on Business Modelling. In: Proceedings of the Second International Symposium on Business Modeling and Software Design 2012 (BMSD 2012), pp. 43–52 (2012)
19. Pateli, A.G., Giaglis, G.M.: A research framework for analysing eBusiness models. European Journal of Information Systems 13(4), 302–314 (2004)
20. Osterwalder, A.: The Business Model Ontology - a proposition in a design science approach, PhD Thesis, Université de Lausanne (2004)
21. Gordijn, J.: Value-based Requirements Engineering: Exploring Innovative e-Commerce Ideas. PhD Thesis. Vrije Universiteit Amsterdam (2002)
22. Gordijn, J., Akkermans, H.: Value based requirements engineering: Exploring innovative e-commerce idea. Requirements Engineering Journal 8(2), 114–134 (2003)
23. Iacob, M.E., Meertens, L.O., Jonkers, H., Quartel, D.A.C., Nieuwenhuis, L.J.M., van Sinderen, M.J.: From enterprise architecture to business models and back. Software & Systems Modeling (December 2012), doi:201210.1007/s10270-012-0304-6, Print ISSN1619-1366, Online ISSN1619-1374
24. Fatemi, H., Van Sinderen, M.J., Wieringa, R.J.: Trust and business webs. In: Proceedings of the 15th IEEE International Enterprise Distributed Object Computing Conference, EDOC 2011, Helsinki, Finland, August 29–September 02, pp. 119–128. IEEE Computer Society (2011)
25. The Open Group: Technical Standard Risk Taxonomy, January, Doc. No.: C08 (2009)
26. OMG, Value Delivery Modeling Language (VDML), Doc. No. bmi/2011-05-11 (2011)
27. Geerts, L.G., McCarthy, E.W.: An Ontological Analysis of the Primitives of the Extended-REA Enterprise Information Architecture. The International Journal of Accounting Information Systems 3, 1–16 (2002)
28. Andersson, S.-L., Elofsson, A.: Plug-in Hybrid Electric Vehicles as Control Power: Case studies of Sweden and Germany, Master Thesis, Report no: T-2008-317, Chalmers University of Technology, Göteborg, Sweden (2009)
29. Exploateringskontoret Stockholms Stad, Övergripande program för miljö och hållbar stadsutveckling i Norra Djurgårdsstaden, Stockholms Stad, Stockholm, Sweden (2010)
30. Asuncion, C.H., van Sinderen, M.J.: Pragmatic Interoperability: A Systematic Review of Published Definitions. In: Bernus, P., Doumeingts, G., Fox, M. (eds.) EAI2N 2010. IFIP AICT, vol. 326, pp. 164–175. Springer, Heidelberg (2010)
31. Iacob, M.-E., Jonkers, H.: Quantitative analysis of service-oriented architectures. International Journal of Enterprise Information Systems 3(1), 42–60 (2007)
32. EAAT tool download, http://www.kth.se/en/ees/omskolan/organisation/avdelningar/ics/research/eat/downloads-1.46631

Linked Services for Enabling Interoperability in the Sensing Enterprise

Matthias Thoma[1,2], Alexandru-Florian Antonescu[1,2], Theano Mintsi[1], and Torsten Braun[2]

[1] SAP (Switzerland) Inc.
SAP Research Zurich
Althardstrasse 80, 8105 Regensdorf, Switzerland
[2] University of Bern,
Institute of Computer Science and Applied Mathematics
Communication and Distributed Systems Research Group
Neubrueckstrasse 10, Bern, Switzerland

Abstract. In future, the so called "sensing enterprise", as part of the Future Internet, will play a crucial role in the success or the failure of an enterprise. We present our vision of an enterprise interacting with the physical world based on a retail scenario. One of the main challenges is the interoperability not only between the enterprise IT systems themselves, but also between these systems and the sensing devices. We will argue that semantically enriched service descriptions, the so called linked services will ease interoperability between two or more enterprises IT systems, and between enterprise systems and the physical environment.

Keywords: Linked services, enterprise integration, wireless sensor network, smart items, retail, sensing enterprise.

1 Introduction

One of the main challenges of future enterprise IT systems is the usage of data collected from the real world in real time, contextualizing it and providing the user of these systems with the best possible up to date information to base business decisions on. We will call the vision of context-aware and real-world aware enterprise IT systems the "Sensing Enterprise".

The emerging sensing enterprise makes cooperation and interoperability between enterprises, and more specifically, between heterogeneous enterprise IT systems on one hand more important than already today, but on the other hand also more complicated. It is a well known problem, that enterprises today have a need for collaboration, but because of interoperability issues between enterprise IT systems this is often not as successful as it would be desirable [1].

Traditionally enterprise IT vendors base their system on service oriented architectures (SOA). Furthermore they mainly use high-level, often proprietary, protocols. Unfortunately, this imposes a specific problem when implementing the sensing enterprise. The integration of sensing devices, which deliver the context information needed on the state of the physical world (like mobile phones, sensor networks, RFID readers and tags), is still performed manually and does not integrate well into SOA architectures of nowadays IT landscapes.

A recent approach to describe services in a SOA environment are semantically enriched service descriptions, based on RDF and semantic web technologies. In this paper we will present our vision of the sensing enterprise based on these next generation Linked Services. We use them to access sensor devices, which are able to describe themselves, thus enabling a sensing enterprise which seamlessly integrates into today's enterprise world. Furthermore, we will discuss an integration middleware which can be used to connect ERP systems to the physical world. We conclude by presenting a case study of applying the integration middleware, a reasoning system and data analysis to a real-world scenario.

2 Related Work

The idea of using Linked Data for service descriptions has received wider attention recently. There are approaches known as *linked service* (e. g. [2], [3] and [4]), which contribute to the web of data by applying ontologies for service descriptions and discovery. iServe [5], for example, aims to support service publishing and discovery in a better way. Service descriptions, on the other hand, have attracted a lot of attention in the context of the Internet of services. The most well known standard is the WS-* family, which centers around the Webservice Description language (WSDL) [6].

Many existing service description languages focus more or less on the description of technical interfaces, sometimes annotated with quality parameters. We currently use an RDF-based version of USDL (Unified Service Description Language), which addresses — in addition to the technical aspects — business-related properties, capabilities and non-functional characteristics [7].

The main difference between our approach and ontology-based linked service approaches, which try to contribute to the web of data, is that we focus purely on services, which do not necessarily have to be part of the web of data. This includes their capabilities and their integration into current enterprise IT systems.

The general problem of integrating smart items and data gathered from sensor networks is well known in the literature. Gomez et. al. [8] propose an additional layer called Enterprise Integration Component (EIC), which is a generic mediation layer between enterprise systems and the WSN middleware.

Two approaches which are also addressing some business aspects are from Glombitza et. al. [9] and from Carracas [10]. Glombitza et. al. propose the usage of standard web service technologies (SOAP, XML). They also target for using SOA principles aiming towards the integration with BPEL, nonetheless their approach is based on WSDL and covers only the pure technical aspects of SOA. Carracas [10] concentrates on WSN integration via BPMN and compiling corresponding code for running it on the mote.

Sensor description languages are used to model the characteristics, as well as the input and output parameters of sensing services. SensorML [11], for example, is an XML based modelling language, which allows specifying each sensor by its meta-data. It allows to model processes that are linked together through inputs and outputs.

3 Terminology

In this section we will properly define some terms we will use throughout this paper. Furthermore we provide some brief background informations on technologies used as this paper is combining ideas from different research areas (e. g. linked services, semantic web, business networks, enterprise systems, smart items, wireless sensor networks) and not ever reader might be fluent in all of these fields.

Enterprise System. We use the term enterprise system (often called ERP or Enterprise Resource planning system) as follows [8]: *An ERP is a set of business applications that allows large enterprises to run all phases of an enterprise's operations to facilitate cooperation and coordination of work across the enterprise. The ideal enterprise system could control all major business processes in real time.* Enterprise systems have in general high requirements concerning availability, scalability, reliability as well as security and interoperability.

Wireless Sensor Network. A wireless sensor network (WSN) is a network consisting of wirelessly connected small embedded devices (motes). The devices are equipped with one or more sensors, a microcontroller, radio transceiver, some memory and a power supply. Sensor nodes are often battery powered. Usually they are very restricted devices to reduce the cost per unit. They allow an enterprise to perceive the state of its environment in real-time at a low cost.

Interoperability. There has been a lot of research on enterprise interoperability in recent years. The term interoperability is defined by IEEE as "the ability of two or more systems or components to exchange information and to use the information that has been changed." [12]. More information on the theory behind enterprise interoperability can be found, for example, in [1] and [13].

OLTP (On Line Transaction Processing) and OLAP (On Line Analytic Processing) are two complementing technologies, which are used to facilitate business processes and enable business intelligence respectively. While OLTP focuses on serving the maximum possible number of short transactions as fast as possible and on maintaining vast, multi-access warehouses consistent, OLAP concentrates on complex, low-volume transactions over multi-dimensional data in order to support decision support and problem solving.

RDF and SPARQL. In search of a general method for interchanging data over the Web, W3C introduced Resource Description Framework (RDF). This simple semantic data model uses URIs to name things and the relationships between them, creating this way triples which can be conceptualized as directed, labeled graphs. RDF enables the easier integration of data in the web, an extension of existing schemas and a data consumption through the use of SPARQL queries. A more in-detail presentation can be found in [14].

4 Sensing Enterprise

The sensing enterprise is a catch phrase for the ongoing integration of physical data captured by sensors into ERP systems and the on-demand utilization (sometimes refereed to as *sense making*) of this data. This will allow a tight integration of events and processes in the physical world to be used in business processes. In the following two sections we will first present the key drivers of our current research, and then go on with explaining how semantically enriched linked services help solving the problems we identified.

4.1 Key Drivers

We see three key drivers in the sensing enterprise context, which motivates our current research. In section 5.1 we will show that the linked service paradigm is an ideal candidate for fulfilling these requirements. The three key drivers are:

Interoperability. In the past (and even nowadays, but at a lower level) ERP vendors used to base their system on proprietary protocols. Interoperability, as a result, meant implementing custom connectors to these services. To some degree this was caused by historical, technical reasons and the lack of agreed-on standards. Nowadays, in the days of coopetition interoperability has become more important. Thinking further in the future, especially in the sensing enterprise, where we might deal with all kinds of smart items from several vendors, which have to integrate into various backend systems, flexible and smart interoperability is a must. Furthermore, even nowadays, when we talk about enterprise interoperability there is specific knowledge of the used protocol and the data necessary. Future Enterprise systems need to target interoperability at a semantic level as well.

Enablement of Sense-Making. Future Enterprise backend systems will have to do reasoning on data coming from various sources. The description of these services should therefore allow semantic annotations, which are to be understood and processed by enterprise IT systems. As we will describe later, we are following a very pragmatic approach here, without the need of being fully reasonable in a theoretical sense.

Enablement of Real-Time Business Decision Support. In many industries the backend systems are still rather disconnected from what is actually happening. Often, the information is gathered a-posteriori and deviations from the planned state are detected late. Integrating real-time decision support into these systems will enable a business to run more efficient, react timely on changes in the business process and allow a proper exception handling. While this closely related to sense-making, real-time business decision support does not only rely on sense-making, it would be even possible without semantic (ontological) reasoning by utilizing domain knowledge and complex event processing, as it is already done today.

There are two recent emerging technologies which enables the sensing enterprise become a reality:

Real Time Big Data Analytics. A typical enterprise generates very large and diverse data sets coming from its distributed business locations. Besides OLAP data, the enterprise might also record data produced in social networks, surveillance devices or by third party systems owned by business partners. These massive amounts of detailed data can be combined and analyzed by predictive analytics, data mining or statistics. Doing this process in real-time, for example, by using in-memory data processing, creates a business advantage for the company by giving insight into the real-world dynamics of their business.

Sensor Networks and Near Field Communication. Sensor networks are starting to complement the already existing RFID (Auto ID) technologies that are already available on the market.

4.2 The Sensing Enterprise from a Retailer's Point of View

As the authors have the most proficient background in retail, we will illustrate the application and usefulness of the above-mentioned concepts in the retail domain. We will therefore just have a brief look on the transportation of goods from the producer to the retailer and, of course, finally to the consumer. Furthermore, we will focus on the data that can be gathered in the stores. An exemplary integration into enterprise IT systems is then discussed in section 6.

The spirit of the sensing enterprise will be everywhere in the stores of the future. In the retail store and in the supporting supply chain physical and social realities change at a high pace. In the stores themselves this includes different exceptional situations, such as out-of-shelve situations, technical problems or congestions at the point of sell. As an example, monitoring the freeing systems would help to prevent loss. If one freezing machine failed then the ERP would suggest shuffling them to other freezers and/or starting immediate discounts. In such a case the discount could be determined by checking the product validity ranges (e.g. temperature) associated with a product description, located in the manufacturer ERP system. The store's ERP would combine the sensor data with the remote descriptions in order to trigger the discount decision.

Furthermore, there are a magnitude of forecasts possible to avoid out-of-shelve situations or to detect unexpected high or low demand and to react on real-time, including sending the personnel to the right spot or to suggest changes in the product placement. This of course, does not apply to a single store only. Most stores are part of enormous, sometimes multi-national corporations, where predictions and forecasts based on information gathered from all stores contribute to one huge knowledge base.

An important and competitive requirement in the retail world is to deliver products according to a predefined agreement. A Service Level Agreement (SLA) defines the conditions under which a product is expected to get transported and delivered to the stores. Sensing comes into play to detect the conditions, that when deviating from the SLA, cause an internal system change and demand or even bring changes in the whole retail process. Through enriching this part of the retail procedure with sensing technologies and SLAs, every involved enterprise can benefit by reducing risks, saving time, reducing cost and increasing sales and earnings.

In our scenario, a sensor-equipped "intelligent container" is responsible for monitoring the goods. The monitoring process is driven by a device-constrained SLA, which would determine which sensors are used and how the information is processed. Upon arriving at a distribution point, such as a harbor or an airport, edge sensors of the transporter share their SLAs with the ERP of the distributor, while they also communicate their collected information to the central enterprise system of the receiving retailer. As the sensors are resource-constrained, the SLAs are not actually stored on them, but only a link is provided to the complete SLA description which resides in the transporter's ERP. An extra benefit is that this procedure creates an accurate track of the products transportation in terms of localization and transportation conditions. The entire tracking history would be recorded as ERP transactions in the intermediary ERP systems. Such information can prove vital to the retailer in terms of tracking back problems, deciding on its collaborators and defining the transportation costs.

At the next stage of the supply chain goods are at the selling point available for the customers. Following the same logic as in the transportation phase, there are wireless sensors on the shelves measuring all crucial parameters, carrying the SLAs and sending collected data to edge sensors, which in turn forward them to the store ERP. Upon arriving at the store, the SLA of every product is loaded on the local ERP, so that it is aware of the characteristics and maintenance conditions of each of them.

Sensing the conditions, under which products are maintained, and making decisions on the sensor level facilitates and expedites finding a solution. Analyzing the sensed data at real-time serves the retailers as a useful source of information for further investments and re-arranging the supply chain. In the retail world all that translates to time, successful collaborations, building a strong brand name and earnings.

Moving from the actual store, its supply chain and personnel to the consumers: The sensing enterprise will enable new ways of interacting with the consumers. Interactions with the consumer via mobile devices are then possible based on the consumers context. The smartphone use would also help track the user and then combining data from in-store video cameras and location processing would produce some dynamic price changes or voucher generation which would be then sent to the buyers smartphones, published on store's website, advertised in store, etc.

5 Linked Services and the Sensing Enterprise

As part of an enterprise level SOA platform, service descriptions are used to describe the functional and non-functional properties of a service, including but not limited to its technical interface. We follow the idea of using linked services which we will describe in detail in section 5.1 and then go on showing how they can be used in a sensing enterprise context in section 5.2. In this context we will present an enterprise architecture, which allows interacting with smart items based on linked services.

When talking about service descriptions it is important to distinguish between the actual deployed (and running) service and the description of the service. A linked service therefore describes a technical or non-technical service, it is not the service itself and thus does not have, for example, a technical service endpoint. It can describe one though, if the service described has one. A thorough classification and taxonomy of services and the difference to a service description can be found in [15]. Furthermore, as service is a term which can have many meanings. One wide-spread use of service is, especially in computer science, to use it as a synonym for a *technical interface*. We are following the approach of Barros et. al., where in [16] a service is defined as a "commercial transaction where one party grants temporary access to the resources of another party (...)".

A more thorough discussion of linked services can be found in [17] and [5]. In this work we do not dive deep into the realm of service science. We present enough background information for the reader to understand our contribution, but we limit ourselves to the sensing enterprise and more specifically the points were linked services contribute to that vision. A good and comprehensive overview can be found in [16].

5.1 Linked Services

In a nutshell the idea of linked services is to base service descriptions on standard technologies known from the semantic web (e. g. Ontologies, OWL and RDF). Furthermore, these semantically enriched service descriptions are following the linked data idea as outlined by Berners-Lee [18]. He suggested the following four simple rules for publishing data on the web, thus creating one single data space — the web of data:

1. Use URIs as names for things
2. Use HTTP so that people can look up those names
3. When someone looks up a URI, provide useful information, using the standards (RDF, SPARQL)
4. Include links to other URIs, so that they can discover more things

Compared to the very ambitious idea of the *web of data* our vision is way more focused on the interoperability between enterprise systems, and enterprise systems and end-user devices. We currently see reasoning applicable on a domain level only. In contrast to many research as it is going on today in the semantic web, we do not want to model or understand the whole world. Our mid-term goal is semantic interoperability in very specific domains (for example in retail). For this, we foresee the use of light-weight ontologies. Furthermore, we would even allow manual steps, like hard-coded rules by domain experts, in the processing of this services. Research on interoperability has shown the need of *semantic interoperability*, this is sometimes complemented by the need of *pragmatic interoperability*. Our approach does not solve all the problems that can arise from wrong assumptions on either the semantic or the pragmatic level, but the use of semantic technologies and the restriction on a domain-level should reduce the risk of making wrong assumptions on both sides of the communication channel.

Linked Services do not apply only to the description of one single service provided by one service provider. Linking services together will allow an even tighter integration of business partners, thus contributing to the idea of service networks [16].

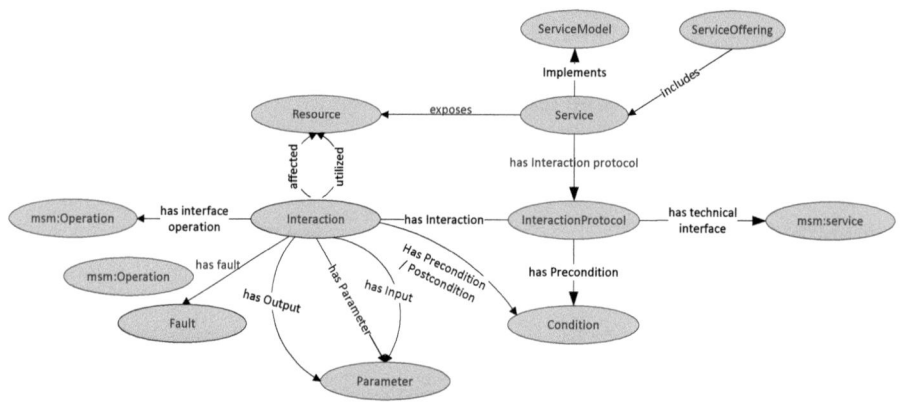

Fig. 1. Excerpt from the Linked USDL ontology

We use a specific implementation of Linked Services for expressing functional and non-functional properties, namely Linked USDL [2]. To maximize interoperability Linked USDL adopts, whenever possible, existing RDF(S) vocabularies such as the Minimal Service Model and FOAF. Linked USDLs objective is to develop an ontology to represent services. It therefore creates explicit ontological links to domain specific ontologies. While this is the origin of the name linked services, the authors see a lot of potential also in actually linking one part of the service description to more detailed information defining the very same service. An excerpt of the Linked USDL ontology is shown in figure 1.

To our knowledge Linked USDL is the only standardization effort driven by large corporations with the goal of expressing not only purely functional aspects of a service, but also the business and operational aspects. A comprehensive introduction into each can be found in [16].

A very concrete service description for a smart item, in this case a simple temperature sensor as it could be used in a shops freezers, looks as follows:

```
<> rdf:type usdl:ServiceDescription ;
   dcterms:title "USDL service description for Freezer";
   dcterms:creator :Matthias_Thoma ;
   owl:versionInfo "0.1";
   dcterms:contributor [
     a foaf:Person ;
     foaf:name "Matthias Thoma";
     foaf:firstName "Matthias";
     foaf:lastName "Thoma" ] ;
   dcterms:created "2011-09-29"^^xsd:date .

:FreezerTemperatureService a usdl:Service, msm:Service;
   usdl:hasNature usdl:Automated;
   usdl:hasServiceModel <http://research.sap.com/svc/sensors> ;
   dcterms:title "Temperature sensor service"@en;
   usdl:hasProvider :SAP_SENSOR_GROUP;
   usdl:hasInteractionProtocol :ip_1;
   usdl:hasImplementation <http://research.sap.com/bin/tsen.bin>;
   usdl:hasDocumentation <http://research.sap.com/doc/techspec.pdf> ;
   usdl:hasLegalCondition :termsAndConditions .

:termsAndConditions a legal:TermsAndConditions;
   dcterms:title "Terms and Conditions"@en;
   dcterms:description "Defines terms of use,liability,safety and so on."@en;
   legal:hasClause [ a legal:Clause;
     legal:name "Liability";
     legal:text "Legal, Warrenties etc."@en ] .

<http://research.sap.com/bin/tsen.bin> a usdl:Artifact;
   usdl:artifactType usdl:Software;
   dcterms:title "Binary for the sensor sofware" .

:SAP_SENSOR_GROUP a gr:BusinessEntity;
   foaf:name "SAP Sensors Service";
   foaf:homepage <http://www.sap.com>;
   usdl:legalForm "AG" .

:ip_1 a usdl:InteractionProtocol;
   dcterms:title "Read sensor value";
   dcterms:description "Read sensor data"@en;
   usdl:hasTechnicalInterface :SAPDataInterface_1 ;
   usdl:hasInteraction [
     a usdl:Interaction;
     dcterms:title "Get sensor data"@en ;
     usdl:hasOutput [ a usdl:Parameter;
                      gr:unitOfMeasurement "kelvin";
                      rdfs:label "temperature"@en ],
   ] .
```

In this simple example one can already see the advantages of Linked Services. The interaction protocol describes how to access the service in a technical way and provides semantics on the parameters. These can be used in a reasoning engine of an ERP system. The whole service description is based upon standard technologies. It can be queried using SPARQL and information that can be found elsewhere can be directly linked to the service description. There is no need for any additional layer.

Linked services is a very powerful concept, which goes way beyond our usage as an ERP interoperability and service exchange platform. For example, there already exists an marketplace for tradeable services, service repositories and registries based on Linked USDL.

5.2 Extending Linked Services to Sensors and Smart Items

In this section we will provide an overview of how linked services can be used to enable the sensing enterprise. We will present the architecture of a next-generation linked services enterprise platform and describe how we apply lightweight service descriptions to smart items and sensor networks. We are not going into too many details on how linked services integration is done in regular enterprise networks and service marketplaces, but present our extension to the concept. For more information on that we need refer to the already existing literature (e. g. [17] or [5]).

As shown in [19] a basic, shrunk to the essentials, version of the service description on the smart item which links to other parts of the service description (like comprehensive SLAs) is enough to enable interactions with sensor motes. Our platform, as shown in Fig. 1 enables an enterprise IT system to access and evaluate linked services.

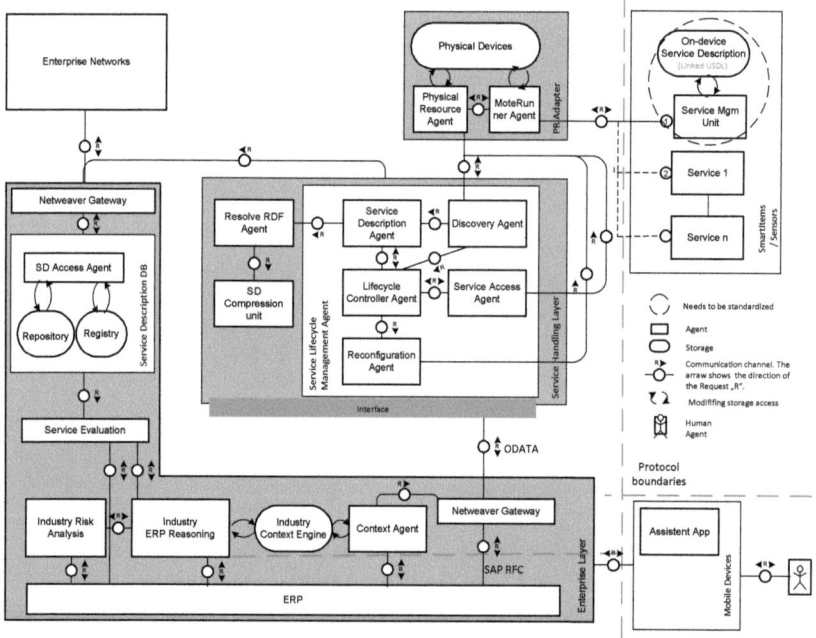

Fig. 2. High level block diagram of the linked service enterprise platform. (We are following the TAM standard for modeling the architecture)

As we consider smart items (sensor motes) as first-class entities in our SOA architecture, they are able to describe themselves through *linked services descriptions*. The actual *services* are accessed via the *service management unit*. Interoperability is achieved via a standardization of the interface to the management unit and of the service description language. Currently, CoAP seems to be a good candidate in addition to linked services. This allows different ERP vendors to implement their own integration platform without loosing interoperability. These self-description capabilities allow the smart items joining the realm of an ERP backend system to automatically integrate into the system based on the semantic information found in the *service description*, trigger backend actions and access the *services* on the smart item.

The *Service Handling Layer* is taking care of the actual handling of services on smart devices. It is exposed to the Enterprise Layer through a SOA compatible interface and is thus integrating into an enterprise' SOA environment. Within the Service Handling Layer there are several agents which we will describe briefly: The Discovery Agent (DA) is interacting with the Physical Resource Adapter (PRA) and discovers new services available on new smart items. Communication with and monitoring of smart items is done by the PRA. New service descriptions are first completed by the *Resolve RDF Agent* and (in case of compression) uncompressed by the *Service Description Compression* unit. The Service Description agent is then responsible for adding the service to the ERPs service registry and repository, thus making it available to the enterprise.

Having a closer look into the enterprise layer, the service descriptions are exposed to other ERP systems via a gateway using a standardized protocol. In addition to what already exists today in business intelligence (e. g. demand forecasting, campaing management, price calculations), we make use of context acquired by sensors. Based on this information, combined with historical data it is possible to do reasoning and real-time risk analysis. We currently see the short-term to mid-term applicability of this approach at a domain-specific or industry specific level.

The communication between the enterprise backend system and the SOA integration platform is commonly done via a *gateway component* (for example SAP Netweaver Gateway separating the *ERP* and auxiliary services. As the integration platform is for the ERP system also just a service, communication is done through a standard interface known to the enterprise SOA environment. Nowadays, ERP systems still use a lot of heavy-weight proprietary protocols, e. g. BAPI or SAP RFC, while the communication with the SOA platform can be done via a standardized protocol. The industry is currently moving towards the Open Data Protocol (OData) [20].

6 Applying Linked Services to the Sensing Enterprise

In this section we will present how our integration platform as described in the previous section and the concept of linked services enable realizing the sensing retailer as presented in section 4.2. We will assume that all enterprises involved are already linked services enabled.

Looking at the ERP systems of collaborating enterprises or cooperating ERPs withing one enterprise, there are usually many service invocations involved. They grant each other (restricted) access to their service repositories. The fact that they are semantically enriched allows reasoning even between systems. The retail sector is an ideal candidate for being used as pioneering industry, as there are already exchange formats (e. g. EDI) and identification systems for goods (e. g. EPCglobal) available. Furthermore, the retail industry already uses some sensing technologies like RFID tags and AutoID quite heavily. On the business side, existing business analytics are already working with these information, which allows incremental, non-disruptive, innovations to be performed.

We foresee a wide-spread use of sensing technologies used in the retail industry, e. g. within the supply chain as intelligent containers, for tracking of goods and their conditions or for tracking customers and personnel. Thanks to the self-description capabilities of these smart items the ERP system can communicate with them and exchange, for example, the SLAs and the corresponding sensed condition of goods.

In the following we will present a SLA document, which could be used for monitoring the temperature of goods. The *TransportationProfile* would then be referred from the sensor as residing in a remote ERP system.

```
<http://www.sap.com/research/2012/10/retail.owl> rdf:type owl:Ontology ;
    owl:imports <http://www.linked-usdl.org/ns/usdl-sla> .

:TemperatureServiceLevelExpression rdf:type <http://www.linked-usdl.org/ns/
        usdl-sla#ServiceLevelExpression> , owl:NamedIndividual ;
    owl:topDataProperty "temperature > 4 && temperature < 10" ;
    <http://www.linked-usdl.org/ns/usdl-sla#hasVariable> :temperature .
    <http://www.linked-usdl.org/ns/usdl-sla#hasUnit> :Celsius .

:TransportationProfile rdf:type <http://www.linked-usdl.org/ns/usdl-sla#
        ServiceLevelProfile> , owl:NamedIndividual ;
    <http://www.linked-usdl.org/ns/usdl-sla#hasServiceLevel> :
        temeratureServiceLevel .

:temeratureServiceLevel rdf:type <http://www.linked-usdl.org/ns/usdl-sla#
        GuaranteedState> , owl:NamedIndividual ;
    <http://www.linked-usdl.org/ns/usdl-sla#serviceLevelExpression> :
        TemperatureServiceLevelExpression .

:temperature rdf:type <http://www.linked-usdl.org/ns/usdl-sla#Variable> , owl
        :NamedIndividual ;
    <http://purl.oclc.org/NET/ssnx/qu/qu#referenceUnit> <http://purl.oclc.org/
        NET/ssnx/qu/unit#degreeCelsius> .
```

The temperate here would have to be within an temperate range of [4,10] degrees Celsius.

Within business analytics there are already many solutions available which work with near-realtime information. This can be transformed to real-time by leveraging big data technologies. The granularity of the results can be increased by using sensing technologies. Exception management, today a manual tasks as the ERP systems are often unaware of the real conditions the goods are in, will become easier. The store itself collects data about goods and customers, contextuilzes it and thus improves the business analytics process. Furthermore, a direct interaction with personel (e. g. sending them directly to out-of-shelve situations, or to supreme cusomers) and customers will be possible.

7 Further Work

In this paper we focused on the interoperability part and the vision of semanticaly enriched service descriptions for business intelligence systems. We will continue our work and integrate mobile devices also as first class entities in our platform and utilize data gathered from them. Furthermore, we are working on extending real systems, which are already using some kind of structured data, to use semantic technologies and to improve the quality of the results by using context information.

8 Conclusion

In this paper we extended the scope of Linked Services to the Sensing Enterprise. We specifically addressed the integration of semantically enriched Service Descriptions, which additionally follow the Linked Data principles, and of real-time sensed data into distributed Enterprise Systems and the involved business processes. The final goal is on one hand to enable decision-making at the low-level embedded devices supporting business processes and reduce thereby the time response in critical situations, while on the other hand to allow both low-level devices and backend of different enterprises to communicate independently and efficiently empowering the inter- operation of the involved enterprises. We presented all necessary concepts and the way we make use and elaborate on them, a motivating scenario in the retail world, whereas we also illustrated our suggested integration platform for applying the Linked Services in the Sensing Enterprise.

Acknowledgment. This research received funding from the European Commission under grant 257521 (IoT-A) and grant 285248 (FIWARE). The authors want to thank the Mote Runner team at IBM Research for their support.

References

1. van Sinderen, M.: Challenges and solutions in enterprise computing. Enterprise Information Systems 2(4), 341–346 (2008)
2. Leidig, T., Pedrinaci, C.: Linked usdl (2012)
3. Dietze, S., Yu, H.Q., Pedrinaci, C., Liu, D., Domingue, J.: SmartLink: A Web-Based Editor and Search Environment for Linked Services. In: Antoniou, G., Grobelnik, M., Simperl, E., Parsia, B., Plexousakis, D., De Leenheer, P., Pan, J. (eds.) ESWC 2011, Part II. LNCS, vol. 6644, pp. 436–440. Springer, Heidelberg (2011)
4. Speiser, S., Harth, A.: Taking the lids off data silos. In: Proceedings of the 6th International Conference on Semantic Systems, I-SEMANTICS 2010, pp. 44:1–44:4. ACM, New York (2010)
5. Pedrinaci, C., Liu, D., Maleshkova, M., Lambert, D., Kopecky, J., Domingue, J.: iServe: a linked services publishing platform. In: Workshop on Ontology Repositories and Editors for the Semantic Web, ORES 2010 (2010)
6. Christensen, E., Curbera, F., Meredith, G., Weerawarana, S.: Web services description language (wsdl). Technical report (March)

7. Charfi, A., Schmeling, B., Novelli, F., Witteborg, H., Kylau, U.: An overview of the unified service description language. In: 2010 IEEE 8th European Conference on Web Services, ECOWS (December 2010)
8. Gomez, L., Laube, A., Sorniotti, A.: Design guidelines for integration of wireless sensor networks with enterprise systems. In: Proceedings of the 1st International Conference on MOBILe Wireless MiddleWARE, Operating Systems, and Applications, MOBILWARE 2008, pp. 12:1–12:7. ICST, Brussels (2007)
9. Glombitza, N., Pfisterer, D., Fischer, S.: Integrating wireless sensor networks into web service-based business processes. In: Proceedings of the 4th International Workshop on Middleware Tools, Services and Run-Time Support for Sensor Networks, MidSens 2009, pp. 25–30. ACM, New York (2009)
10. Caracaş, A., Kramp, T.: On the Expressiveness of BPMN for Modeling Wireless Sensor Networks Applications. In: Dijkman, R., Hofstetter, J., Koehler, J. (eds.) BPMN 2011. LNBIP, vol. 95, pp. 16–30. Springer, Heidelberg (2011)
11. Open Geospatial Consortium. Technical report
12. Institute of Electrical and Electronics Engineers: IEEE standard computer dictionary: A compilation of IEEE standard computer glossaries, New York, NY (1990)
13. Chen, D., Doumeingts, G., Vernadat, F.: Architectures for enterprise integration and interoperability: Past, present and future. Computers in Industry 59(7), 647–659 (2008); Enterprise Integration and Interoperability in Manufacturing Systems
14. Klyne, G., Carroll, J.J., McBride, B.: Resource Description Framework (RDF): Concepts and Abstract Syntax. W3C Recommendation, W3C (February 2004)
15. Thoma, M., Meyer, S., Sperner, K., Meissner, S., Braun, T.: On iot-services: Survey, classification and enterprise integration. In: 2012 International Conference on and 5th International Conference on Cyber, Physical and Social Computing Internet of Things, iThings/CPSCom (November 2012)
16. Barros, A., Oberle, D.: Handbook of service description USDL and its methods. Springer, New York (2012)
17. Pedrinaci, C., Domingue, J.: Toward the next wave of services: Linked services for the web of data 16(3) (2010)
18. Berners-Lee, T.: Linked data - design issues (2006)
19. Thoma, M., Sperner, K., Braun, T.: Service descriptions and linked data for integrating wsns into enterprise. In: 2012 Third International Workshop on Software Engineering for Sensor Network Applications, SESENA (June 2012)
20. OData Technical Committee: Open data protocol (2012)

Business Rules Management Solutions: Added Value by Effective Means of Business Interoperability

Martijn Zoet and Johan Versendaal

HU University of Applied Sciences, Utrecht, The Netherlands
{martijn.zoet,johan.versendaal}@hu.nl

Abstract. Interoperability research, to date, primarily focuses on data, processes and technology and not explicitly on business rules. The core problem of interoperability from an organisation's perspective is the added value generated from collaborating with other parties. The added value from a data, process and technology perspective has been widely researched. Therefore it is the aim of this study to provide insights into the added value for organisations to collaborate when executing business rules management solutions. Explanations of possibilities, opportunities and challenges can help to increase the understanding of business rules interoperability value creation. Presented results provide a grounded basis from which empirical and practical investigation can be further explored.

Keywords: Business Rules Management, Interoperability, BRM, Business Interoperability.

1 Introduction

Many business services nowadays heavily rely on business rules to express business entities, coordination, constraints and decisions [1-3]. A business rule is [4] "a statement that defines or constrains some aspect of the business intending to assert business structure or to control the behaviour of the business." The field of business rules management knows various research streams. Examples are business rules authoring, business rules engines, application in expert systems, business rules architecture, business rules ontology's, data mining and artificial intelligence [3]. However, the research topics within each stream are technology driven [5, 6]. Yet, it is not the technology and software applications that are of interest to an organisation; it is the value proposition they deliver. Nevertheless research focusing on improving business rules management practices and its value proposition is nascent [5, 7].

An important design factor to increase an organisation's value proposition in general is cooperation [8]. To achieve effective cooperation organisations have to resolve interoperability issues. In this study business interoperability is defined as [9] "the organisational and operational ability of an enterprise to cooperate with its business partners and to efficiently establish, conduct and develop IT-supported business relationships with the objective to create value." An example from the airline industry can demonstrate business interoperability of business rules expressing decisions. A global airline alliance has 10 members. Each member has different business rules to decide whether customers are allowed into their business lounge. Airline X states that a customer must have acquired the silver status while airline Y states that the customer must have acquired the gold status. When a customer of airline Y arrives at a lounge managed by airline X carrying the silver status he will not be allowed access. Airline Y will not pay Airline X to take care of the customer. Two events change the business rules with regards to lounge access. First an airline changes its business rules or secondly an additional airline is allowed into the alliance. If the business rules are hard coded or stored locally all systems at all airports have to be altered. When each member offers a decision service containing their specific business rules only the specific decision service has to be altered improving the business interoperability of the entire alliance.

However, current interoperability research primarily focuses on data, services, processes, business and interaction and not explicitly on business rules [10]. For each previously mentioned concept three categories of interoperability research can be distinguished: conceptual, technological and organisational [11]. Conceptual research focuses on barriers related to syntactic and semantics', technological research focuses on information system technology while organisational research focuses on responsibility, organisational structure and business value. All research streams have the same purpose: to develop knowledge and solutions to remove barriers and enable effective business interoperability [11]. Since interoperability research related to business rules is nascent research needs to focus on the inquiry of the phenomenon itself [12].

This article extends understanding of business rules interoperability by addressing the underlying value proposition for organisations. Based on previous research, we will consider a business rules management solution (hence BRMS) as consisting of eleven different service systems. With these premises, the specific research question addressed is: "*What is the relation between forms of business interoperability and the* organisation's business rules management service systems in the perspective of value propositions?" Answering this question will help organizations better understand the value proposition behind collaborating with organisations in order to deliver business rules.

The paper is organised as follows. First we describe the individual business services of a BRMS. Then we present the various forms of interoperability and stages of service design. After which we present our analysis of BRMS interoperability. We conclude with a discussion of these findings, focusing on the implications for practice and for the study of business rules based services.

2 Literature

A *business service* is defined as [9]: "a coherent piece of functionality that offers added value to the environment, independent of the way this functionality is realized."

To deliver a business service a value-coproduction of resources, skills, knowledge and competences has to be configured [9]. This configuration is called a *service system*. A BRMS is a co-production of various resources, skills, knowledge and competences [7, 13, 14]: i.e. a co-production of service systems. Nelson [7] proposed a very rudimentary service system for business rules containing three elements a service provider, a service client and a service target. A more detailed classification has been proposed Zoet and Versendaal [14]. This classification scheme, existing of eleven service systems, classifies the processes, guidance elements, actors, input and output per service system. A detailed explanation of the BRMS can be found in [14]. However to ground our method and research a summary is provided.

Deployed business rules are monitored for proper execution. The 1) monitoring service system collects information from executed business rules and generates alerts when specific events occur. This information in turn can be used to improve existing or design new rule models. Execution of business rules is guided by a separate service system: 2) the execution service system. It transforms a platform specific rule model into the value proposition it must deliver. A platform specific rule model can be source code, handbooks or procedures. The execution in turn can be automated or performed by humans. To execute a platform specific rule model it needs to be created. A platform specific rule model is created from a non-platform specific rule model by the 3) deployment service system. Before deploying business rule models they have to be checked for two error types 1) semantic / syntax errors and errors in its intended behaviour. The first type of errors are removed from the business model by the 4) verification service system; the latter by the 5) validation service system. The business rule model itself is created within the 6) design service system. In addition an 7) improvement system exists. The improvement system contains among others functionality to execute impact analysis. To design business rules models data sources need to be mined; the 8) mining service system contains, processes, techniques and tools to extract information from various data sources, human or automated. Before mining can commence in some cases explicit data sources need to 9) cleansed. The cleansing service system removes all additional information intervening with proper mining or design activities. Each previous mentioned service systems provide output to two management service systems: 10) the version service system and 11) the audit service system. Changes made to the data source, platform specific rule models, non-platform specific rule models and all other input and output are registered by the version service. All data collected about realising changes to specific input, output and other service system elements are registered by the audit service system. Examples of registered elements are: execution dates, rule model use, rule model editing, verification and validation. All service systems described in this paragraph need to be designed developed and executed. Service design is the process of requirements analysis and service discovery. After requirements are analysed the service system needs to be configured. For this interaction, roles, functions, processes, knowledge and products need to be defined. After the service system is configured the service itself needs to be executed.

From literature four levels of collaboration can be recognized: 1) no collaboration, 2) bilateral collaboration, 3) multilateral collaboration and 4) extended collaboration [15]. Two organisations within the same industry or value chain working together is defined as a bilateral collaboration. Multilateral collaborations have the same characteristics as bilateral collaborations with the slight difference that more than two parties are involved. Extended collaboration describes many-to-many and 'n-tier' relationships between organisations. Two examples are consultative bodies and network orchestrators. We assume that the type of collaboration (X) implies different design, development and execution of the BRMS (Y). Fig. 1 schematically illustrates these dependencies.

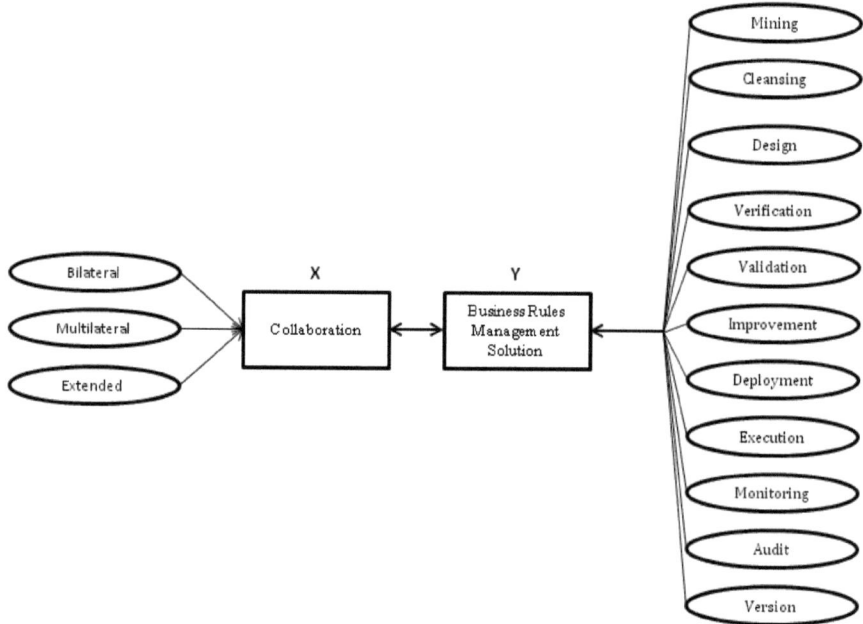

Fig. 1. Schematic Overview researched relations between Concepts

Nelson [7] classifies inter departmental collaboration for a specific BRMS along five dimensions organisation scope, ownership, structure, development responsibility and implementation responsibility. We adopt three dimensions in our analysis 1) ownership, 2) development responsibility and 3) implementation responsibility. However, to fit inter organisational collaboration they must be adapted. Ownership in our model is divided into two dimensions ownership of the input and output of a service system. Development responsibility is defined as the organisation that executes the service system process and implementation responsibility is defined as the organisation that implements the output of the service system. Organisation scope in our research is one of the variables of conceptual model namely: collaboration.

3 BRMS Analysis

Data gathering consisted of three phases. First the effect of the collaboration types on each business rules management service system has been evaluated by means of a workshop. Participants to the workshop were six business rules experts. During the second phase 12 projects have been surveyed to identify potential elements to which third parties could supply added value. During the last phase data sources such as press and analyst reports have been evaluated to indentify collaboration possibilities. The results are discussed in the remainder of this section. Per service system indentified additional variables and the characteristics of the dimensions are discussed.

3.1 Cleansing Service System and Mining Service System Interoperability

Explicit and tacit data sources are input for the business rules mining service system, cleansing service system, and design service system. Cleansing and mining are discussed in this section; the design service system in the next. The business interoperability question with regards to data sources is: can data from multiple organisations add additional value compared to data from a single organisation? Multiple organisations create and execute very similar or identical rule models. Examples of such rule models are medical treatment rules within the healthcare industry [16] and fraud detection rules used by banks and insurers [17]. Improvement of such rule sets is based on execution data of a single organisation. By means of collaboration larger and more accurate data sources can be created. Overall characteristics of the interoperability design issues for the cleansing and mining system are depicted in Table 1 and Table 2. Both tables show an additional variable influencing the development responsibility: privacy.

Table 1. Characteristics Dimensions Interoperability in relation to the Mining Service System

	Bilateral	Multilateral	Extended
Ownership Input	Providing Org.	Providing Org.	Providing Org.
Ownership Output	Providing Org. / Receiving Org.	Providing Org. / Receiving Org.	Consortium
Development Responsibility	*Privacy:* Receiving Org. *Non-Privacy:* Receiving or Providing Org.	*Privacy:* Receiving Org. *Non-Privacy:* Receiving or Providing Org.	*Privacy:* Receiving Org. *Non-Privacy:* Receiving or Providing Org.
Implementation Responsibility	Receiving Org.	Receiving Org.	Receiving Org.

Privacy influences the question which organisation is responsible for cleansing? If the data source contains sensitive information cleansing should occur at the providing organisation in the case of bilateral or multilateral collaboration. Cleansing in this case can also mean sanitising or anonymizing data [17]. Extended collaboration implies the same question. However, when data is collected and integrated by an independent consultative body this question may be easier to solve from a political viewpoint [18]. After the data source is created it can be used to mine rules. When an extended collaboration is realized the consultative body can mine the data sources after which the proposed business rules are shared with all partners e.g. the healthcare industry [16]. Other forms of collaboration have two choices 1) each party mines the data source itself or they appoint a partner to do so thus factually creating an extended collaboration.

Table 2. Characteristics Dimensions Interoperability in relation to the Cleansing Service System

	Bilateral	Multilateral	Extended
Ownership Input	Providing Org.	Providing Org.	Providing Org.
Ownership Output	Providing Org. / Receiving Org.	Providing Org. / Receiving Org.	Consortium
Development Responsibility	*Privacy:* Receiving Org. *Non-Privacy:* Receiving or Providing Org.	*Privacy:* Receiving Org. *Non-Privacy:* Receiving or Providing Org.	*Privacy:* Receiving Org. *Non-Privacy:* Receiving or Providing Org.
Implementation Responsibility	Receiving Org.	Receiving Org.	Receiving Org.

3.2 Design Service System Interoperability

The design of a rule model is based on a specific data source or on proposed business rules model by the mining service system. An additional variable has been indentified influencing the design service system: type of partners, see Table 3. A partner can be either a rule chain partner or a competitive/alliance partner. Competitive partners are defined as organizational entities from the same industry realizing an identical value proposition. A rule chain partner is an organizational entity that either formulates data sources or business rules that must be implemented by the organisation or an organizational entity that should implement business rules or data sources defined by the organisation. Interoperability between competitive / alliance partners deal with the same questions as the data source interoperability. Either organisations design rule model together or do so by providing input to a consultative body. Examples are organizations that together formulate business rules for risk management [3].

Interoperability between rule chain partners adds an extra dimension to designing the rule model. An example from the public sector will demonstrate this. The ministry of finance formulates tax laws that are analysed by the tax and customers administration to formulate business rules models. These business rules model are deployed into software and forms which are then sent to the citizens. In addition to the tax and customers administration multiple commercial and non-commercial organisations also formulate business rules based on the same tax laws. The same applies to other laws like for example the Sarbanes-Oxley Act (SOX) or the Fair and Accurate Credit Transaction Act (FACTA). All commercial organisations governed by specific laws are building rule models based on the text provided by the United States Government. Expending on the question at the beginning of this paragraph: who should translate the tax laws, SOX and FACTA to business rules models? The government or the individual commercial and non-commercial organisations governed by the rules? To answers this question first the difference between internal business rules and external business rules has to be explained.

Table 3. Characteristics Dimensions Interoperability in relation to the Design Service System

	Bilateral	Multilateral	Extended
Ownership Input	*Rule-Chain:* 1st order party *Non Rule-Chain:* Providing Org.	*Rule-Chain:* 1st order party *Non Rule-Chain:* Providing Org.	*Rule-Chain:* 1st order party *Non Rule-Chain:* Consortium
Ownership Output	*Rule-Chain:* 1st order party *Non Rule-Chain:* Providing Org. / Receiving Org.	*Rule-Chain:* 1st order party *Non Rule-Chain:* Individual Org./ Receiving Org.	*Rule-Chain:* 1st order party *Non Rule-Chain:* Consortium
Development Responsibility	*Rule-Chain:* 1st order party *Non Rule-Chain:* Receiving Org.	*Rule-Chain:* 1st order party *Non Rule-Chain:* Receiving Org.	*Rule-Chain:* 1st order party *Non Rule-Chain:* Consortium
Implementation Responsibility	*Rule-Chain:* Receiving Org. *Non Rule-Chain:* Receiving Org.	*Rule-Chain:* Receiving Org. *Non Rule-Chain:* Receiving Org.	*Rule-Chain:* Receiving Org. *Non Rule-Chain:* Receiving Org.

Two main sources of business rules can be distinguished, namely internal business rules sources and external business rules sources [3]. This adheres to the principle within risk management where a distinction exists between operational risk and compliance [19]. External business rules are specified by external parties through the creation of regulations stating which rules an organization needs to comply to. Internal business rules sources are specified by the organization itself; they decide which rules they want to enforce [11]. With external business rules organizations have to prove, based on externally imposed criteria, that they have established a sufficient system to control the business rules. For internal business rules there are no externally applied criteria or need to prove sufficient control; in this case organizations can implement their own criteria and create a system for measuring this. Expanding on the difference in enforceability indicates a mismatch in the power/knowledge nexus [20]. In practice organisation will translate laws and regulations to business rules in one of two ways: or they transform the laws themselves or they will hire a vendor, system integrator or consultancy firm to translate for them. In all previous mentioned cases the organisation that performs the translation is not the organisation that enforces the regulation. The number of parties between the enforcer and/or creator of the law and the actual implementation by means of business rule models we define as *n-order compliant*, see Fig. 2. If government agency X states law Z and organisation Y hires a consultancy firm to translate and implement the law by means of business rules they are 3rd order compliant. If they translate and implement the law directly they are 2nd order compliant. Only one organisation has the power (/knowledge) to provide 1st order compliancy, the organisation that defines the regulation, government agency X. They can achieve this by translating the law into a business rule model and distribute this model to the organisations. The same situation can be recognized within individual organisations. One department specifies strategy or internal policies. A second department translates the strategy to operational business rules. In turn the operational business rules are distributed to the information technology department achieving 2nd or 3rd order compliancy.

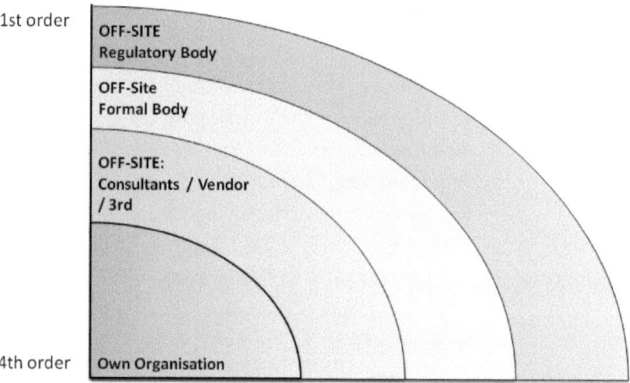

Fig. 2. Schematic Overview N-Order Compliancy

With respect to organisational collaboration in a rule chain the preferable solutions would be that 1st order compliancy is achieved. Thus that the regulatory body who defines the legislation also creates and distributes the business rule model. However, currently only one example of this is known to the authors the Australian Taxation Office [21]. In all other cases it is recommended to keep the n-order compliancy as low as possible.

3.3 Validation Service System Interoperability

Validation is the service system that explores errors in the intended behaviour of business rule models by means of test cases containing real life data. Likewise to design service system the partner type also influences validation, see Table 4. First order compliancy can still be achieved within the validation service system when the enforceable party is not responsible for the business rule model design however they need to validate the designed model and declare it compliant. The respondents and authors have no knowledge about a public body officially validating external rule models. Examples can be found within commercial rule chains. Authorised insurance brokers review, accept, administer, collect premiums and execute claim settlement for insurance agencies. They define rule models to support the previous mentioned tasks. Before deploying the actual rule models insurance organisations apply their test set to test if product business rules are properly deployed. If so, they consent on deploying the service to the live environment. In these cases an extended collaboration is established with the authorised insurance broker as consultative body. Other examples can be found in the healthcare industry where various consultative bodies have test cases for diagnoses rules sets. Bilateral or multilateral collaborations between two organisations can also apply validation in the same manner. Another possibility is sharing test cases between collaboration partners instead of 'outsourcing' the validation process.

Table 4. Characteristics Dimensions Interoperability in relation to the Validation Service System

	Bilateral	Multilateral	Extended
Ownership Input	Providing Org.	Providing Org.	Providing Org.
Ownership Output	Providing Org.	Providing Org.	Providing Org.
Development Responsibility	*Rule-Chain:* 1st order party	*Rule-Chain:* 1st order party	*Rule-Chain:* 1st order party
	Non Rule-Chain: Receiving Org.	*Non Rule-Chain:* Receiving Org.	*Non Rule-Chain:* Consortium
Implementation Responsibility	*Rule-Chain:* Providing Org.	*Rule-Chain:* Providing Org.	*Rule-Chain:* Providing Org.
	Non Rule-Chain: Providing Org.	*Non Rule-Chain:* Providing Org.	*Non Rule-Chain:* Providing Org.

3.4 Deployment, Execution and Monitoring Service System Interoperability

Within three projects information system deployment and maintenance to another organisational are outsourced to a third party, e.g. system integrator. Non-platform specific rule models are transformed to platform-specific rule models by the third party. The implementation and development responsibility in all collaboration forms lies with the receiving organisation (system integrator). Ownership of the input and output in most cases lies by the providing organisation.

Table 5. Characteristics Dimensions Interoperability in relation to the Deployment Service System

	Bilateral	Multilateral	Extended
Ownership Input	Providing Org.	Providing Org.	Providing Org.
Ownership Output	Providing Org.	Providing Org.	Consortium
Development Responsibility	Receiving Org.	Receiving Org.	Receiving Org.
Implementation Responsibility	Receiving Org.	Receiving Org.	Receiving Org.

Execution service interoperability occurs when one or more organisation(s) offer(s) a value proposition realized by means of a platform specific rule model to one or more organisation(s). The airline alliance example described in the introduction section is an example of this type of collaboration, which can be classified as business rules as a service. Another example can be found in the healthcare sector where specific hospital offer decisions service to multiple of its pears. No additional variables impacting the characteristics have been found, see Table. 6.

Table 6. Characteristics Dimensions Interoperability in relation to the Execution Service System

	Bilateral	Multilateral	Extended
Ownership Input	Providing Org.	Providing Org.	Providing Org.
Ownership Output	Receiving Org.	Receiving Org.	Receiving Org.
Development Responsibility	Providing Org.	Providing Org.	Providing Org.
Implementation Responsibility	Receiving Org.	Receiving Org.	Receiving Org.

Monitoring service system collaboration mainly will occur in rule-value chains since most organisations will not provide monitoring services to competitors. A possible exception might be extended collaboration with a consultative body. However, the output of the monitoring service system: performance data can be input for the cleansing service system, mining service system or design service system collaboration. An example of rule-value chains within the insurance industry is that an inspector applies a rule model to determine if a vehicle is either repairable or total loss. Based on the result of the rule model the insurance companies start different processes. Although not a collaboration between two organizations; another pattern instantiation is indentified in the business-to-consumer industry: telemedical care for patients [22]. The patient has physical equipment at home that contains the platform specific rule model. The execution of this model is monitored at the hospital or medical centre. All types of collaboration have the same dimensions characteristics, see Table 7.

Table 7. Characteristics Dimensions Interoperability in relation to the Monitoring Service System

	Bilateral	Multilateral	Extended
Ownership Input	Providing Org.	Providing Org.	Providing Org.
Ownership Output	Receiving Org./ Providing Org.	Receiving Org./ Providing Org.	Consortium
Development Responsibility	Receiving Org./ Providing Org.	Receiving Org./ Providing Org.	Receiving Org. / Providing Org.
Implementation Responsibility	Receiving Org./ Providing Org.	Receiving Org./ Providing Org.	Receiving Org. / Providing Org.

Regarding the audit service system and version service system no advantages can be distinguished regarding bilateral and multilateral collaborations. In extended collaboration consultative bodies and individual organisations need to determine how to manage local and network versions of the various business rules concepts. However, one can argue this can be considered overhead instead of added value.

4 Discussion

The analysis of our initial model revealed two additional variables 1) type of partners and 2) privacy. The latter indicates that sanitising and/or anonymizing should be taken into account when sharing input data among organisations. Research addressing sanitising and/or anonymizing data already has been conducted in various fields. Solutions can be adopted and adapted from these fields.

Our research revealed rule value chains and more specific the n-order compliance concept. N-order compliance raises questions in terms of organisational, social, cultural, political and economical effects and consequences [23]. Research indicates that 3rd and 4th order compliancy is a common grade of compliance. Are both levels the optimal form of interoperability from a political or economic viewpoint? From a political viewpoint most countries distinguish between policy makers (ministries) and a central government responsible for translating and executing policies. What effects would 1st order compliancy have on the political relationship? From an economic viewpoint an interesting question is: which savings can be achieved when realising 1st order compliance? Although limited, research on economic assessment of business interoperability shows improvements in throughput, cycle time and reduction of transaction cost [23]. How do these concepts relate to the various forms of n-order compliance?

Analysing the four dimensions for underlying trends reveals that both development and implementation responsibility vary per individual service system per organisation. The ownership of the input for a specific service system in all cases, except for the design service system, is at the providing organisation. This comes as no surprise. For organisations to derive value from the collaborated service systems the information needs to be contextualized for their specific information they own. This can only be achieved by contextualizing the input. The ownership of the output of the individual service systems follows the conceptual lifecycle of the four high-level business rules subjects 1) data, 2) non-platform specific rule model, 3) platform specific rule model and 4) value proposition [14]. Neglecting the design service system from a rule-chain perspective the input ownership changes at each of the four lifecycle points. When the output is data, the ownership is shared. The providing party has ownership of the non-platform specific and platform-specific rule models, while the value proposition ownership is at the receiving party. The reason the rule chain perspective deviates from the pattern is because 1st order compliance is considered to be preferable. To realize 1st order compliance the ownership of the output lies at the organisation that has the knowledge and power to do so.

5   Conclusion

Business rules are a key denominator for an organizations success. Likewise the ability to collaborate is important. Therefore we set out to answer the research question: *"What is the relation between forms of business interoperability and the* organisation's business rules management service systems in the perspective of value proposition?" In order to answer this question we first indentified the different types of interorganisational collaboration. After which the collaboration types have been combined with the eleven service systems of a BRMS. Explanatory research further operationalized the relation: we used data collected from a workshop and secondary data sources such as press reports, analyst reports and business rules management project documentation.

The aim of this study was to provide insights into different forms of interoperability that are related to an organisation's BRMS. The results have limitations. Insights are derived from a limited set of data and the existing knowledge base in the area of business rules management. Building on the results from this explorative research further research should be performed. Main subject of future work will be the further validation of the indentified interoperability possibilities in order to assess the practical relevance besides establishing its theoretical foundation. Another direction for future work is creating business, technical and process building blocks to realize interoperability.

References

[1] Shao, J., Pound, C.J.: Extracting business rules from information systems. BT Technology Journal, 179–186 (1999)
[2] Bajec, M., Krisper, M.: A methodology and tool support for managing business rules in organisations. Information Systems 30, 423–443 (2005)
[3] Zoet, M., Welke, R., Versendaal, J., Ravesteyn, P.: Aligning Risk Management and Compliance Considerations with Business Process Development. In: Di Noia, T., Buccafurri, F. (eds.) EC-Web 2009. LNCS, vol. 5692, pp. 157–168. Springer, Heidelberg (2009)
[4] Morgan, T.: Business rules and information systems: aligning IT with business goals. Addision-Wesley, London (2002)
[5] Arnott, D., Pervan, G.: A critical analysis of decision support systems research. Journal of Information Technology 20, 67–87 (2005)
[6] Rosca, D., Wild, C.: Towards a flexible deployment of business rules. Expert Systems with Applications 23, 385–394 (2002)
[7] Nelson, M.L., Peterson, J., Rariden, R.L., Sen, R.: Transitioning to a business rule management service model: Case studies from the property and casualty insurance industry. Information & Management 47, 30–41 (2010)
[8] Hammer, M., Champy, J.: Reengineering the Corporation: A Manifesto for Business Revolution. HarperBusiness, New York (2003)
[9] Lankhorst, M., Janssen, W., Proper, H., Steen, M.: Introducing Agile Service Development. In: Lankhorst, M. (ed.) Agile Service Development. Springer, Berlin (2012)

[10] Molina, A., Panetto, H., Chen, D., Whitman, L., Chapurlat, V., Vernadat, F.: Enterprise Integration and Networking: Challenges and Trends. Studies in Informatics and Control, vol. 16, pp. 353–368. Informatics and Control Publications (2007)

[11] Chen, D., Vallespir, B., Daclin, N.: An Approach for Enterprise Interoperability Measurement. In: Ebersold, S., Front, A., Lopistéguy, P., Nurcan, S., Franch, X., Hunt, E., Coletta, R. (eds.) International Workshop on Model Driven Information Systems Engineering: Enterprise, User and System Models, Montpellier, France. CEUR Workshop Proceedings, pp. 1–12 (2008)

[12] Edmondson, A., McManus, S.: Methodological Fit in Management Field Research. Academy of Management Review 32, 1155–1179 (2007)

[13] Nelson, M.L., Rariden, R.L., Sen, R.: A Lifecycle Approach towards Business Rules Management. In: 41st Hawaii International Conference on System Sciences, Hawaii, pp. 113–123 (2008)

[14] Zoet, M., Versendaal, J.: Business Rules Based Perspective on Services: A Mixed Method Analysis (2012) (manuscript submitted for publication)

[15] Plomp, M., Batenburg, R.: Measuring Chain Digitisation Maturity: An assessment of Dutch Retail Branches. Supply Chain Management 15, 227–237 (2010)

[16] Ferlie, E., McGivern, G., FitzGerald, L.: A new mode of organizing in healthcare? Governmentality and managed networks in cancers service in England. Social Science & Medicine 74, 340–347 (2012)

[17] Chiu, C., Tsai, C.: A Web Services-Based Collaborative Scheme for Credit Card Fraud Detection. In: Proceedings of the 2004 IEEE International Conference on e-Technology, e-Commerce and e-Service, pp. 177–181. IEEE (2004)

[18] Monsieur, G., De Rore, L., Snoeck, M., Lemahieu, W.: Handling Atomic Business Services. In: 15th Conference on Pattern Languages of Programs, PLOP Conference, pp. 1–12 (2008)

[19] Zoet, M., Versendaal, J., Ravesteyn, P., Welke, R.: Alignment of Business Process Management and Business Rules. In: Proceedings of the European Conference on Information Systems, ECIS 2011 (2011)

[20] Foucault, M.: Security, territoty, population - lectures at the college of france 1977 - 1987. Picador, New York (2007)

[21] Office, A.T., Legal Database Australian Taxation Office (2012), http://law.ato.gov.au/atolaw/index.html

[22] Fifer, S., Everett, W., Adams, M., Vincequere, J.: Critical Care, Critical Choices: The Case for Tele-ICUs in Intensive Care. In: King, N., Coffmann, G., Handt, J., Melissinos, D. (eds.) New England Healthcare Institute (2010)

[23] Legner, C., Lebreton, B.: Business Interoperability Research: Present Achievements and Upcoming Challenges. Electronic Markets 17, 176–186 (2007)

Behavioural Evaluation of Reputation-Based Trust Systems

Sini Ruohomaa and Lea Kutvonen

University of Helsinki, Department of Computer Science,
P.O. Box 68, FI-00014 University of Helsinki, Finland
{sini.ruohomaa,lea.kutvonen}@cs.helsinki.fi
http://cinco.cs.helsinki.fi/

Abstract. In the field of trust and reputation systems research, there is a need for common and more mature evaluation metrics for the purpose of producing meaningful comparisons of system proposals. In the state of the art, evaluations are based on simulated comparisons of how quickly negative reputation reports spread in the network or which decision policy gains more points against others in a specific gamelike setting, for example. We propose a next step in identifying criteria for a maturity model on the behavioural analysis of reputation-based trust systems.

Keywords: Trust management, reputation systems, inter-enterprise collaboration, simulation-based benchmarking, attack models.

1 Introduction

The goal of this methodological work is to advance the state of the art of evaluating reputation-based trust management systems. We find that the field currently suffers from a confusion of what kind of evidence simulation experiments can provide exactly, and there is a need for credibly evaluating the attack resistance and robustness of proposed systems [1]. We acknowledge that other attributes such as usability [2,3], viability [4], deployability [5] and adjustability to different business situations [6] require attention as well. Instead of a complete maturity model addressing all these aspects, our focus here is on trying to advance behavioural evaluation of reputation-based trust systems specifically.

We first summarize the problem setting of the field from the point of view of inter-enterprise collaborations, which are the context of our work [3]. Collaborations take place between autonomous business services operating in an open service ecosystem. New previously unknown or little known actors can join the ecosystem, and old ones may leave. In this environment, each actor has different goals, which change over time, and it must protect its own integrity by making decisions on whether it trusts another service enough to collaborate with it.

Trust management is the activity of upkeeping and processing information which trust decisions are based on, and a trust management system is an automation tool for the purpose. A trust decision is made by a trustor, gauging its willingness to engage in a given action with a given trustee, given the risks and incentives involved. The key input to a trust decision is reputation information, which is commonly used to evaluate the subjective probability that the trustee will either behave according to the collaboration contract (cooperate), or break the collaboration contract (defect).

Reputation information is divided into two categories: First-hand experiences are gained from the trustor monitoring the outcomes of actions it has engaged in itself, and are generally considered to be error-free within the limits of observability. External experiences are gained from third-party recommenders based on their own first-hand experiences; these actors may have an incentive to provide incorrect information deliberately or can simply disagree based on having observed different kinds of behaviour.

The aim of evaluating reputation-based trust systems in research is often phrased in terms of quantifying an improvement to existing work. The prevalent approach of evaluating trust and reputation systems relies on using simulations to produce evidence that a given trust or reputation system is able to correctly identify well- and misbehaved actors of specific kinds (e.g. [7]). These simulations are typically based on fixed stereotypical behaviour patterns (e.g. [8]), which falls under the field of reliability rather than security [1].

When scoring policy behaviour, it is tempting to set up a benchmark of measuring "correct" and "incorrect" decisions given specific evidence. Unfortunately, this is an oversimplification that relies on a set of quite fragile assumptions: that reputation information captures reality accurately, service providers act predictably enough to follow stereotypical patterns, and actors in the marketplace, especially the attackers, are not particularly resourceful. None of these assumptions can be said to be true in an ecosystem of inter-enterprise collaboration. This discrepancy causes a real danger that by introducing reputation measures into the market with inadequate analysis of their relevant behaviour we end up inviting rampant reputation fraud, and advance ecosystem deterioration by introducing a metric that does not serve its purpose. Farmer and Glass have analyzed the effects of deployed web reputation systems in the real world [9, ch. 5], while deployability and market acceptance analysis of system proposals also gain increasing attention in the field of security [4,5].

The main overarching goal of behavioural analysis of policies of any kind is to support policy selection, but this choice reflects the actors' different goals. There are no objectively correct answers. Summarizing policy behaviour given specific input patterns helps this comparison, even if there is no universal correct behaviour. As a special case, the purpose of a reputation-based trust management system is to detect and deter misbehaviour, so we should learn what its vulnerabilities and other costs are. These cannot be benchmarked by fixed loads, but have to be analyzed per system; from a security perspective, it is obviously not enough to conclude that a system is robust against the most popular attack of last year. Higher-level classifications of attacks may support vulnerability analysis in the form of a checklist.

Our research question is: what kinds of tools can we apply to evaluate whether a reputation-based trust management system fulfills its behavioural requirements, and particularly, what metrics could be organized as a reusable benchmark between systems and how?

Section 2 provides background on reputation-based trust management, how trust management systems are directed by policy, and summarizes our simulation experiments and attack resistance evaluation from earlier work. Section 3 presents the state of the art on evaluation methods in the field. Section 4 discusses the possibilities and limitations of different methods, such as simulation experiments in analyzing trust and reputation systems, and the ways to evaluate attack resistance based on methods adopted from computer security. Section 5 concludes.

2 Studying the Behaviour of Trust Management Systems

To support the discussion on development of evaluation methods, we use our own earlier work on trust management as an illustrative example in Section 2.1. During our simulation work summarized in Section 2.2 we learned the current evaluation methods could benefit from the steps we propose in Section 4.

2.1 Reputation-Based Trust Management

The purpose of a trust management system is to handle routine trust decisions on behalf of a human user and to collect and manage the relevant input needed for them, most notably first-hand and third-party reputation information. Third-party experiences must be evaluated for credibility and incorporated into the local body of reputation information with care, as they may include low-quality or intentionallly fraudulent data. Non-routine decisions, which for example involve high risks or cannot be automatically decided on due to insufficient information, must be forwarded to a human user to decide on. This division is explicitly configured.

In order for a deterministic automation system to adjust to different business situations, we must separate policy from implementation in the system and make the former modifiable during runtime. A sufficiently flexible information model allows the automated rules to handle quite complex contexts, such as a situation where the reputation of a minor actor in the collaboration is not spotless, but the monetary losses of any errors it may make are covered by insurance and the collaboration as a whole needs someone to fulfil the role in order to happen. The establishment of metapolicy which determines when a situation is routine and when it requires human intervention, in turn, will pick out cases that are not suitable to be handled automatically. This improves the trustworthiness of the decision-making system itself [6].

The two main policies of a reputation-based trust management system are the trust decision policy and the reputation update policy. The trust decision policy determines, based on input such as reputation information, whether we are willing to collaborate with an actor or not. The reputation update policy, on the other hand, establishes how to handle new reputation information; among other things, it must determine how much weight information from external sources is given over local observations [6]. A trust decision policy must balance the number of possible partners and requirement for positive evidence, while a reputation update policy must weigh information quality and credibilty against the amount of information that is available to support decision-making.

As reputation influences trust decisions and through that collaboration opportunities, it attracts manipulation attempts on competitors' and one's own reputation. This causes challenges for finding a robust reputation update policy that can still utilize the information available to support trust decisions. Example attacks on reputation systems [10] include undeserved negative feedback, collusions of multiple actors to skew a specific actor's reputation up- or downwards, or an actor stuffing the ballot by creating multiple seemingly independent identities in a Sybil attack [11].

When selecting a reputation update policy to protect the trustor from being mislead by external reputation information, we can roughly divide the trustees into four categories:

- Well-reputed actors recommended as trustworthy by high-credibility sources,
- Promising actors recommended as trustworthy by low-credibility sources, but generally unknown by high-credibility sources,
- Shunned actors warned to be untrustworthy either by high-credibility sources or by unanimous low-credibility sources, and
- Mysterious actors receiving either very few or contradictory recommendations.

While all of these categories are more or less subjective perceptions rather than proof of the trustees' actual behaviour and trustworthiness, a good reputation system should generally promote the well-reputed actors and weed out the shunned actors. The two other classes require more careful balancing.

A very risk-averse trustor will prefer not to collaborate with the mysterious actors, independent of whether they offer better terms of service. Should everyone adopt this approach, though, newcomers will have no chance of proving themselves, targets of defamation cannot clear their name, and the service ecosystem will begin to deteriorate. The promising actors face a problem similar to newcomers in that they have not proven themselves enough, but at least they have some recommendations supporting them. On the other hand, it is also easier for a malicious attacker to appear as one of the promising actors rather than a well-reputed one, or to claim that any negative recommendations about it result from reputation attacks rather than honest feedback.

2.2 Evaluating Reputation-Based Trust Management Systems

When evaluating the behaviour of a reputation-based trust management system, the usual interest is in studying whether a given trust decision or reputation update policy responds to a specific requirement, such as identifying actors that follow a specific type of misbehaviour as misbehaving. For trust decision policies, the usual appropriate reaction is then to not engage in collaboration with the actor, while for reputation update policies, it is to reject the likely fraudulent information.

In earlier work, we have summarized the simulations and analysis of example trust decision policies [6]; below, we summarize a reputation update policy experiment, where we have compared the effects that four reputation update policies have on trust decisions when the trust decision policy remains fixed [3, ch. 6.3]. Both experiments share a similar structure: the policies under scrutiny are applied to a set of different simulated experience streams as the sole input. Some of the streams have been optimized against each policy for the simulated attacker to defect as efficiently as possible.

Our experiments make two contributions [3]: The behaviour of a given decision or reputation update policy is illustrated through exposing it to different representative experience streams and plotting the resulting trust decision score. Second, the limitations of each policy are demonstrated by defining the behaviour of an optimal attacker, and calculating how much it is possible for it to benefit by defecting while it maintains its reputation above the level of positive trust decisions.

A reputation update policy determines both whether a new experience is incorporated into an agent's private reputation information storage, and how much weight it should be given in future decision-making. A key input to this decision is the source-dependent credibility of the experience. The studied reputation update policies have been selected to represent different types of solutions to this choice, and we have visualized how effectively they discriminate against ill-behaved actors.

The baseline policy for comparison is "Accepting", which simply incorporates all experiences independent of their credibility. The "Weighted" policy offsets the impact of dubious experiences by weighing them by their credibility: as we consider source credibility to be represented by a real number $c \in [0, 1]$, instead of incrementing the counter for the matching type of experiences with 1 per experience, this policy would increment it by c instead. The "Fixed-cutoff" policy ignores all experiences below a minimal credibility limit C_1, and the "Variable-cutoff" policy compared the so far amassed external experiences' average credibility C_2 to the new item's source-based credibility c and accepts the experience if $c \geq C_2$. This is to ensure that the trustor is open to new experiences when it has nothing better, but does not dilute its reputation storage by low-quality information when it has access to more credible experiences. The policies in question were selected to be understandable to a projected end user, and to take advantage of different features of the information model of the system in order to illustrate its advantages.

We matched our experience streams to the previously discussed well-reputed actors, promising actors with positive but low-credibility reputations, and mysterious actors who receive contradictory recommendations: positive reports from high-credibility sources, and negative from low-credibility sources. Shunned actors were covered in the first simulation [6,3]. Additional streams demonstrated optimal attacker behaviours.

Optimal attackers were designed to keep their reputation high enough to always ensure a positive trust decision, and the actions they could choose from were cooperating, faking a positive low-credibility experience to boost their reputation, and defecting. Each action was assigned a cost based on its impact [6]. The agent's task was to maximize its score per action taken [12] against each target policy separately. For example, the attacker defecting with a major negative monetary effect to the trustor would gain the attacker +6 points, a minor negative effect +2 points, generating a low-credibility fake experience would be a 0-cost action independent of whether it implied a major or minor positive experience, and actually cooperating would cost -1 or -3 points depending on whether the effect to the trustor was minor or major positive, respectively.

For example, the optimal attacker could generate fake experiences and then defect with major negative effect against the Accepting and Weighted policies, but it would require more fake experiences per defection against the Weighted policy. Both policies mainly suit environments where the vast majority of information is truthful, and the impact of the occasional error is low; they do not work against quickly mass-produced fake experiences. The Fixed-cutoff policy refused all suspicious experiences, but is left with fewer experiences and will not be able to take advantage of promising actors with low-credibility positive experiences only. The Variable-cutoff policy, in turn, could be circumvented with a large number of low-credibility reports before the first defection. We have discussed prompt reaction to notable changes in behaviour in other work [13], and proposed other extensions to the example policies in the thesis [3, 6.3].

3 State of the Art in Evaluation Metrics for Reputation-Based Trust Systems

A reputation-based trust management system implements the preferences of its user, and as such there is no objective "correct" result that could be validated. To discuss the state of the art in simulation experiments, we present experimentation approaches from two categories: simulating marketplace resistance against attackers following given behaviour patterns, and simulating a single actor's competitiveness in a marketplace. The first category corresponds to mechanism design. It sets all actors to use the same decision policies and measures how well the marketplace as a whole resists different kinds of misbehaviour. The second category represents agent design, pitting different decision policies against each other in the same marketplace. It measures an agent's competitiveness on the marketplace, given an existing mechanism it needs to adjust to.

3.1 Reputation Systems in Electronic Marketplaces

Related work presents simulation experiments on the behaviour of different accumulative and probabilistic reputation systems in an electronic marketplace

[8,14,15]. In such a marketplace, intelligent agents, which correspond to our service providers, perform pairwise brief transactions of buying and selling goods. The marketplace is given a distribution of agents with different behaviour profiles, and each agent type has a decision policy; typically the reputation update policy is equal between all agents, and all experience information is shared. The simulation then measures for example the average number of transactions taken with a given type of agent (honest, malicious, etc).

The basic behaviour profiles of agents are typically very straightforward, such as "honest agents always carry out transactions honestly and give fair ratings", while "malicious agents act honestly or dishonestly by chance, and always give negative ratings" [14]. More complex behaviour can be tied to the marketplace as a whole; for example, a "spamming" agent can otherwise act honestly, but always rate other agents negatively in order to make itself more attractive in comparison [14], or an agent may be an opportunistic defector, adjusting its behaviour based on whether there is anyone in the marketplace who will transact with it [15]. Schlosser et al. define a behaviour profile for a "disturbing" agent as one who first builds a high reputation with good transactions, and then uses up the reputation so gained by defection [8].

Honest agents all use the same decision algorithm, and if they transact frequently with malicious agents, the reputation system has failed to protect the marketplace. Based on this definition, few reputation systems are resistant to the optimal attacker model — even the "disturbing" behaviour model [8] turns out to be aptly named, when in fact it is nothing more than a model for a selfish agent behaving rationally within the limitations set by the environment.

To be able to give conclusive results, the tools of game theory require strict formal abstraction of the environment and agent behaviour; the core problem then becomes how to formulate a question within this vocabulary so that it is "solvable", while ensuring that the result still gives some useful information about real marketplaces.

One of the aspects left out by this simplification is the social control or deterrence effect of these reputation-based sanctioning mechanisms. In other words, the simulations do not measure how much the reputation system cuts down the expected gains from optimized misbehaviour, although they may show that a specific fixed negative behaviour pattern gains less in one system than another. The reputation system will inevitably be one step behind a rational attacker, so in the *prediction* of attacks our systems inevitably fail; the goal is therefore damage control and reducing the payoff of attacks. It should be noted that reputation loss can only ever deter an actor who plans to remain on the market in the future, so final sanctioning should come from the slower but generally effective judicial system.

Our own simulations have studied how a given agent survives against rational selfish agents. They simplify the interaction with other actors into experience input streams. We then specify policies that drop optimal attacker gains below a certain level to reflect the deterrence effect. The difference between fixed and optimal attackers is that within the same cost model, all attacks will bring equal or less gain than the optimal one. This allows policy comparisons. The challenge is finding a sufficiently realistic cost model.

As further examples of analysis against a given attack type, Margolin and Levine have measured the cost of successfully executing a Sybil attack [16], or the cost of extra "votes" gained through the attack in different schemes, and Srivatsa et al. have aimed to minimize attacker gains from fixed oscillatory behaviour such as the aforementioned "disturbing" agent model [17].

3.2 Competitive Agent Simulations

In competitive agent simulations, agents and policies are pitted against each other in a fixed environment. Each actor aims to maximize its own gains. The format of shared reputation information is fixed, but agents can choose their internal data representation themselves.

The Agent Reputation and Trust (ART) testbed [18] has attracted notable attention, but is no longer maintained. The Trust and Reputation Experimentation and Evaluation Testbed (TREET) [19] is a more recent proposal. It is a more flexible comparison tool, but does not include the yearly competition forum that helped ART attract wider research attention. Convincing the research community to adopt a specific testbed or a benchmark is a nontrivial task, and the differences in domain requirements make this even more difficult.

The ART testbed simulates a marketplace of service providers competing to sell their services [18]. The provided service is art evaluation for a customer: producing a real number as close to the unknown correct answer as possible. There are a number of limitations and costs related to providing the service: the agent can evaluate some art correctly, or get incorrect results and ask for help from others to validate its results. A reputation system is included to support requesting the help of other actors. The number of actors is low, 10-20, so in practice collecting direct experience on all of them is reasonably easy.

The learning agents in the testbed should maximize their own measured gains. The testbed specifies fixed prices for how much customers pay for an evaluation ($100), the cost of asking for an evaluation from another actor ($10), and the cost of asking for a reputation value (a real number between 0 and 1) from another actor ($1) [20]. In addition, the agent can spend an arbitrary amount of money for its own evaluation, with the quality of information depending on the money spent. Teacy et al. provide further analysis of the ART testbed [20].

There are a few factors that limit ART's usability as a benchmark environment. Besides limitations of the information model of the testbed itself [3,19], the design of the testbed has misdirected attention towards secondary features of the game: the winning strategy focused its effort on determining the most profitable amount of money to invest in generating its own opinion, and in general, very little reputation was exchanged between any of the agents [20]. As noted in the evaluations of ART [20], we cannot conclude that an agent's competitiveness in the simulated marketplace necessarily has anything to do with the policy performing well for a real enterprise operating in a real marketplace.

The benefit of competitive testbeds to fixed, deterministic benchmark scoring is that the evaluation system is adaptive: instead of optimizing policies against a fixed setup, researchers must prepare for tradeoffs in a more uncontrolled environment, which brings in new aspects of realism from the point of view of the system adapting to its environment. Contests attract researcher attention for psychological reasons as well, and the feedback and fame for winning can help motivate adjusting one's work to a given common framework of evaluation. This sets high demands for the evaluation framework, which must iteratively aim for a relevant abstraction of the marketplace.

There are limitations to the rational self-interested agent design approach as well: When agent fitness is observed in isolation, ecosystem-wide benefits of the reputation system, such as altruistic punishment [21] and social pressure to follow contracts [22], can easily become eliminated from the scope of the simulation. While online business is no doubt competitive, a market for inter-enterprise collaboration cannot sustain itself on short-term self-interest alone [22]. This may become a notable blind spot for the metric.

4 Benchmarking Trust Management Systems

Like most measurement at its core, simulation experiments are illustrative. They reflect their setup, first and foremost, and the results require validation even for reasonably objective measures such as raw performance. Fixed simulations do not test the system's resistance against anything else than the chosen specialized behaviour patterns. As the ART testbed competition shows, even pitting algorithms against each other in a tesbed may teach us very little about their relative fitness in the world outside the testbed. Test loads from actual ecosystems, once available, will also be selected illustrative datasets.

The behavioural requirements of a system should consider four key questions: 1) What kind of normal, constructive behaviour is expected in the system, 2) how effectively does the system recover from expected problems that are not calculated attacks, such as temporary malfunctions, 3) are the incentives the system creates in line with its role in the domain, and 4) how effectively does the system detect and deter both direct misbehaviour in the domain, and misbehaviour towards the system itself, such as reputation fraud?

The first two categories can be addressed with fixed-input simulations suitable for automated benchmarking. The latter two measure the success of the system in promoting desired behaviour and weeding out misbehaviour; as both incentives and attacks must assume a rational actor, they are not possible to capture by fixed behaviour patterns.

4.1 Repeatable Simulations with Fixed Loads

Like reputation itself, simulated experience about reputation-based trust management systems is a subjective, simplified tool for comparison which only gains meaning when coupled with a purpose-driven valuation. A fitting purpose for applying the same test case across multiple systems would then be to provide classifications to aid policy comparison. While benchmarks cannot capture notable differences in the information models of different systems, they can be used to summarize policies built on compatible information models.

The first, often inexplicit test done by a simulation is whether the core system is feasible to implement and run. Related to this, benchmark loads can be used to test the *efficiency and scalability* of a system that has non-trivial complexity, in terms of processing, communications and storage load caused by the decision-making and reputation processes. A well-argued mathematical model of the system complexity can be accepted as proof by itself, but a simulation result requires validation, as the implementation and the selection of loads adds a layer of possible measurement error.

If the system is implementable, the main question becomes whether it supports the intended activities of the user. In order to define a valuation of what is expected as normal behaviour, the *domain-specific requirements* must be made explicit. A set of metrics (cf. [5]) allows a categorization, and the domain-specific requirements guide metric selection. Metrics should reflect the goals of the system so that its success in fulfilling them can be evaluated. The subjective goals of a system designer can be very specific, however, while comparison across multiple systems should leave space for different policy adopter preferences within the domain as well. As an example of the importance of explicit assumptions, Kerr and Cohen measured that the reactivity of systems that assume truthful reports is better than of those who evaluate and weigh incoming experiences for credibility [7]; on the other hand, in a typical competitive environment, not being able to resist fraudulent reports would instead be a critical failure that renders the system unusable.

Once a domain model has been established, we can use it to define test patterns of *constructive behaviour*; this requirement is often taken for granted in systems concentrating on foiling a specific attack, which may lead to an unusable system in practice. Examples of interesting behaviour to simulate include how the system treats cooperative service providers with different capabilities for service provision, or how a newcomer with no reputation data entering the system is able to get started. On the level of reputation and recommender credibility, the system should be able to take advantage of the reputation reports of new actors besides the old ones, and serve cooperative reporters, also if their observations genuinely differ from those of the majority. There are no objectively correct solutions even for constructive behaviour: for example the goal of supporting newcomers is often in conflict with the goal of defending against re-entry attacks.

As a reliability test, a set of test patterns can be defined to illustrate *recovery from problems* as well, as long as they can be modelled statistically for benchmarking. Examples include reactivity to relevant changes in behaviour, how a service can recover its reputation after a temporary malfunction causes it to become unreliable for a while, a well-behaved user suffering and recovering from a defamation attack of fraudulent negative reports against it, or even load balancing for a service whose high reputation makes it too attractive to other actors in the ecosystem.[1]

Reputation-related problems can occur on two levels as well: the above examples represent the interaction of service provision and reputation, while on the second level actors' credibility as recommenders can suffer a disruption and need recovery. Like newcomer support, recovery support conflicts somewhat with robustness against malicious actors, but is important as a use case because the system is always designed for its non-malicious users. To be accepted by the market and serve its purpose, it must benefit the well-behaved actors enough to offset their cost of participation; otherwise it will not be used.

4.2 Robustness Analysis

When deploying a system that promotes good behaviour and sanctions misbehaviour, we must analyze its effects on rational actors who can adjust their behaviour to maximize their gains. The measurement system creates incentives that affect the behaviour of both benevolent and rational actors aiming to subvert the system. For example, if the actor with the highest number of positive transaction reports has a higher chance of being selected as a collaboration partner, the system provides an incentive to engage in many small transactions rather than a few large ones. These secondary incentives are not necessarily intentional or desired, but they should be included in the analysis of the system.

In the field of security, attacks and defenses form a continuous reactive loop, where new attacks are met with new defenses. When we analyze reputation as a sanctioning mechanism, the threat of reputation loss should hopefully deter deliberate attacks by making them more costly. The assumption is therefore that attackers aim to maximize their gains and to minimize costs, which renders them suitable for game-theoretic minimax analysis [12].

Rational attacker models should always be optimized against a specific policy setting. We should generally not depend on security through obscurity, so the attacker should have knowledge of the policy in use and its current reputation. It should have a set of reasonable strategies to choose from, with costs and values assigned according to the resources needed and what we want to defend against.

In our attacker model, we allowed optional ways to reach the goal of fraudulently making money off other actors: defection from many small transactions or a few large ones, and boosting reputation through fraudulent sources or by cooperating. We assigned a cost to cooperation, because while in a general market setting collaboration does pay off, we primarily wanted to ensure that defection does not, and selected the measurement accordingly.

To support attacker analysis, high-level *attack classifications* may act as a reusable checklist. Relevant attack categories include misbehaviour in service provisioning, deliberate omissions and misreporting, conspiracy with other malicious actors to increase own reputation, conspiracy to decrease a competitor's

---
[1] Load balancing through reputation is more relevant for e.g. routing services in mobile ad hoc networks than heterogeneous environments where all actors use their own policies. In marketplaces, pricing can be used to balance against overload.

reputation, coercion, replay and forgery to influence non-malicious actors' reports, and privacy violations against other actors e.g. through traffic analysis. In addition, the checklist can include rational but non-malicious grievances such as freeriding, i.e. not constructively participating in the aspects of the system that do not benefit the actor directly. One vulnerability grouping based on a review of existing systems has been presented in earlier work [10]; for an expansion to a checklist kind of design tool, a tree-structured categorization providing additional levels of detail may provide better usability.

Robustness analysis results should be approached with a similar curious scepticism as research prototypes when it comes to evaluating a system's deployability: rather than providing positivistic evidence of specific desirable attributes of the system, the analysis acts as a feedback-collection step in a design science process. In other words, while not coming up with a vulnerability does not prove that it does not exist, going through the exercise of systematically looking for holes in the design is a valuable step in improving system design itself, and a part of good research practice that leads to more mature systems.

4.3 Methods

A benchmark serves best as a summarizing tool that simplifies comparisons. While system designers cannot use a benchmark load to prove the absence of a vulnerability or the objective superiority of a scheme, deployers may well benefit from more standardized comparison frameworks that provide an overview of the tradeoffs made in any specific systems. Towards this goal, we are also working on a first prototype of a simulation-based comparison tool for reputation update policies in order to identify useful patterns for benchmarking.

A categorization framework would help in better capturing the fact that different policies represent different tradeoffs between partially conflicting goals, and as a result suit different environments and business needs. What the specific needs of a given environment are can only be determined by the actors in it [23]. Focusing too intently on specific behaviour patterns carries the risk of overly technology-centric evaluation of the proposed systems, so a balance must be sought between different methods of collecting feedback on a system.

Our own simulation experiments represent an initial step in more generally summarizing policy behaviour given a specific input, such as identifying policies that produce positive trust decisions for trustees who are only known through low-credibility sources but have only positive experiences within them ("accepts promising actors"). This could be used as a basis to develop a more comprehensive categorization-based evaluation framework in the style of what Stajano et al. have established for evaluating user authentication [5].

For attack resistance, our minimax-based analysis of optimal attackers provides a new angle into this kind of evaluation in comparison to the prevalent methods in the field. We have also summarized how we have applied the method in practice; the analysis demonstrates that making impact information (minor and major positive and negative outcomes) and credibility evaluation available for the automation policies improves the attack resistance of the system [3].

5 Conclusion

We have identified benefits and limitations of the state of the art in simulation-driven experimentation on trust and reputation systems, and gauged the potential of different methods for a set of behaviour-related measurement purposes. The two major directions we identify are building benchmarks for the inter-enterprise collaboration setting, and robustness analysis, which is by nature more specialized for each system and its purpose. General classification tools can help with this analysis as well.

Benchmarks can be applied to simplify comparisons between systems. One notable extension to the idea are competitions within a given system; we believe the potential for this approach has not yet been exhausted in the state of the art, although the task of designing a high-quality marketplace abstraction is quite demanding. Attack resistance analysis, on the other hand, does not seem to lend itself to simulation.

Acknowledgments. This research has been performed in the Collaborative and Interoperable Computing (CINCO) group at the University of Helsinki, Department of Computer Science.

References

1. Gollmann, D.: From Access Control to Trust Management, and Back – A Petition. In: Wakeman, I., Gudes, E., Jensen, C.D., Crampton, J. (eds.) IFIPTM 2011. IFIP AICT, vol. 358, pp. 1–8. Springer, Heidelberg (2011)
2. Marsh, S., Basu, A., Dwyer, N.: Rendering unto Cæsar the Things That Are Cæsar's: Complex Trust Models and Human Understanding. In: Dimitrakos, T., Moona, R., Patel, D., McKnight, D.H. (eds.) IFIPTM 2012. IFIP AICT, vol. 374, pp. 191–200. Springer, Heidelberg (2012)
3. Ruohomaa, S.: The effect of reputation on trust decisions in inter-enterprise collaborations. PhD thesis, University of Helsinki, Department of Computer Science (May 2012)
4. Zibuschka, J., Roßnagel, H.: On some conjectures in IT security: the case for viable security solution. In: Sicherheit, Schutz und Zuverlässigkeit (SICHERHEIT 2012), Bonn, Germany. Lecture Notes in Informatics, vol. P-195. Gesellschaft für Informatik (2012)
5. Bonneau, J., Herley, C., van Oorschot, P.C., Stajano, F.: The quest to replace passwords: A framework for comparative evaluation of web authentication schemes. In: IEEE Symposium on Security and Privacy, San Francisco, California, USA, pp. 553–567 (May 2012)
6. Ruohomaa, S., Kutvonen, L.: Trust and distrust in adaptive inter-enterprise collaboration management. Journal of Theoretical and Applied Electronic Commerce Research 5(2), 118–136 (2010)
7. Kerr, R., Cohen, R.: Smart cheaters do prosper: Defeating trust and reputation systems. In: Proceedings of the 8th International Conference on Autonomous Agents and Multiagent Systems (AAMAS 2009), Budapest, Hungary, vol. 2, pp. 993–1000. ACM (May 2009)

8. Schlosser, A., Voss, M., Brückner, L.: On the simulation of global reputation systems. Journal of Artificial Societies and Social Simulation 9(1) (January 2006)
9. Farmer, F.R., Glass, B.: Building Web Reputation Systems. O'Reilly (2010)
10. Yao, Y., Ruohomaa, S., Xu, F.: Addressing common vulnerabilities of reputation systems for electronic commerce. Journal of Theoretical and Applied Electronic Commerce Research 7(1), 1–15 (2012)
11. Douceur, J.R.: The Sybil Attack. In: Druschel, P., Kaashoek, M.F., Rowstron, A. (eds.) IPTPS 2002. LNCS, vol. 2429, pp. 251–260. Springer, Heidelberg (2002)
12. Russell, S., Norvig, P.: 6: Adversarial search. In: Artificial Intelligence — A Modern Approach, 2nd edn. Prentice Hall (2003)
13. Ruohomaa, S., Hankalahti, A., Kutvonen, L.: Detecting and Reacting to Changes in Reputation Flows. In: Wakeman, I., Gudes, E., Jensen, C.D., Crampton, J. (eds.) IFIPTM 2011. IFIP AICT, vol. 358, pp. 19–34. Springer, Heidelberg (2011)
14. Nurmi, P.: Perseus – a personalized reputation system. In: Proceedings of the IEEE/WIC/ACM International Conference on Web Intelligence, pp. 798–804. IEEE Computer Society (2007)
15. Jøsang, A., Hird, S., Faccer, E.: Simulating the Effect of Reputation Systems on E-markets. In: Nixon, P., Terzis, S. (eds.) iTrust 2003. LNCS, vol. 2692, pp. 179–194. Springer, Heidelberg (2003)
16. Margolin, N.B., Levine, B.N.: Quantifying Resistance to the Sybil Attack. In: Tsudik, G. (ed.) FC 2008. LNCS, vol. 5143, pp. 1–15. Springer, Heidelberg (2008)
17. Srivatsa, M., Xiong, L., Liu, L.: TrustGuard: countering vulnerabilities in reputation management for decentralized overlay networks. In: WWW 2005: Proceedings of the 14th International Conference on the World Wide Web, pp. 422–431. ACM Press, New York (2005)
18. Fullam, K.K., Klos, T.B., Muller, G., Sabater, J., Schlosser, A., Topol, Z., Barber, K.S., Rosenschein, J.S., Vercouter, L., Voss, M.: A specification of the Agent Reputation and Trust (ART) testbed: experimentation and competition for trust in agent societies. In: Proceedings of the Fourth International Joint Conference on Autonomous Agents and Multiagent Systems, pp. 512–518 (2005)
19. Kerr, R., Cohen, R.: TREET: the Trust and Reputation Experimentation and Evaluation Testbed. Electronic Commerce Research 10, 217–290 (2010)
20. Teacy, W.L., Huynh, T.D., Dash, R.K., Jennings, N.R., Luck, M., Patel, J.: The ART of IAM: The winning strategy for the 2006 competition. In: Proceedings of the AAMAS Workshop on Trust in Agent Societies, Hawaii, USA (2007)
21. Fehr, E., Fischbacher, U.: The nature of human altruism. Nature 425 (October 2003)
22. Akerlof, G.A.: The market for "lemons": Quality uncertainty and the market mechanism. The Quarterly Journal of Economics 84(3), 488–500 (1970)
23. Kaur, P., Ruohomaa, S., Kutvonen, L.: Enabling user involvement in trust decision making for inter-enterprise collaborations. International Journal on Advances In Intelligent Systems 5(3&4), 533–552 (2012)

Mass Customization Oriented and Cost-Effective Service Network

Zhongjie Wang, Xiaofei Xu, and Xianzhi Wang

School of Computer Science and Technology, Harbin Institute of Technology
No.92 West Dazhi Street, Harbin, China 150001
{rainy,xiaofei,xianzhi.wang}@hit.edu.cn

Abstract. Traditional service composition approaches face the significant challenge of how to deal with massive individualized requirements. Such challenges include how to reach a tradeoff between one generalized solution and multiple customized ones and how to balance the costs and benefits of a composition solution(s). Service network is a feasible method to cope with these challenges by interconnecting distributed services to form a dynamic network that operates as a persistent infrastructure, and satisfies the massive individualized requirements of many customers. When a requirement arrives, the service network is dynamically customized and transformed into a specific composite solution. In such way, mass requirements are fulfilled cost-effectively. The conceptual architecture and the mechanisms of facilitating mass customization are presented in this paper, and a competency assessment framework is proposed to evaluate its mass customization and cost-effectiveness capacities.

Keywords: service network, service composition, mass customization, cost-effectiveness, competency assessment.

1 Introduction

The emergence of service-oriented technologies and trends, e.g., cloud computing, SoLoMo (Social, Local and Mobile), virtualization, and Internet of Things, have promoted an increasing number of software services on the Internet. In addition, there are now various offline physical and human services that are virtualized and connected to the Internet and collaborate with online software services. Such a proliferation of available services has led to a situation where it is time-consuming and costly to select the appropriate service from an extensive range of candidates when building a coarse-grained composite solution to satisfy individualized customer requirements.

Within the service computing domain, this issue is both a traditional and popular research topic termed *service composition*. Although there has been much research in recent years, it has been insufficient in the face of *mass customization*. To lower service composition and delivery costs, it is better to build a standard solution and provide it to all customers. However, due to the divergence of requirements of different customers, such standardization-based strategies consequentially lead to lower degrees of customer satisfaction. In contrast, if multiple fully personalized solutions are constructed based on each customer's preferences, then the cost is bound to significantly increase. Therefore, it is critical to look for a tradeoff between a fully generalized solution and multiple individualized ones, and to balance the costs and benefits of a composition solution(s). In addition, the solutions generated by current approaches are usually temporary, i.e., after the corresponding requirements have been fulfilled, they are released and no longer exist. This action further increases costs.

Let us take a referential idea from the Internet: consider the scenario that users make end-to-end communications via the Internet. It is not necessary to establish a direct connection between their computers but a virtual link is dynamically established by a routing mechanism based on the infrastructure. After the communication finishes, this link is disconnected. The persistent Internet infrastructure could satisfy any type of individualized communication demands and end users do not necessarily know the details of the complex protocols.

Using this basic philosophy as a reference, we propose the concept of a "Service Network" (SN). It could be considered as business-level persistent infrastructure in the form of interconnections between distributed services, and able to satisfy a large number of customers with customized requirements. The nodes in a SN would include various services (e.g., e-services, human services, information, and resources), and the interconnections between them are information exchanges and functional invocations following interoperability protocols such as SOAP and REST. As shown in Fig. 1, services are deployed on different servers and they are logically connected under the support of Internet.

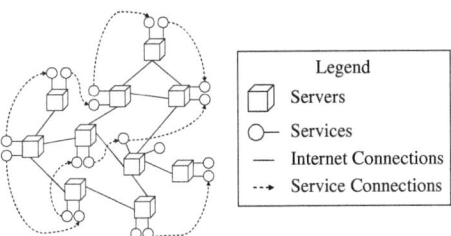

Fig. 1. Service Network: Interconnections between Distributed Services

The SN concept is not a novel idea. Below are two cases from the real world:

(1) *ifttt* (If-This-Then-That, http://ifttt.com). This is a website that aims to connect services from different websites (e.g., APIs of *twitter*, *facebook*, and *instagram*) using an event triggering mechanism to realize cross-domain service invocation. Users set up an "*IF…THEN…*" task on ifttt.com, and when the condition after *IF* is satisfied, the service after *THEN* is triggered. In this way distributed services on the Internet are interconnected as a virtual service network.

(2) *Alibaba* service eco-system. *Alibaba* is a full-scale e-Business provider, whose services include alibaba.com (a B2B platform), tmall.com (a B2C platform), taobao.com (a C2C platform), ju.taobao.com (a Groupon-like platform), alipay.com (a 3rd-party payment service), e56.taobao.com (a $3^{rd}/4^{th}$-party logistics service), and

etao.com (product search service). They are connected as a large service network to jointly fulfill the individualized requirements of millions of buyers and sellers.

Just as the objective of the Internet is more than just the fulfillment of a single demand by two specific users, the purpose of an SN is not to fulfill just one requirement raised by one specific customer. On the contrary, any customers could utilize it for their own purposes. Of course, requirements can vary greatly, so an SN should adapt itself to the requirements (on QoS and function) of mass customers by dynamic "transformations". The more individualized and diverse the requirements an SN can satisfy, the higher its competency to facilitate mass customization. In economic terms, an SN should be "cost-effective", i.e., the sum of construction, maintenance, and customization costs should be below the total benefit gained from mass customization.

This paper is organized as follows. In section 2 related works are introduced, and the similarities and differences between the philosophies of traditional service composition, SaaS, and SN are clarified. In section 3, the conceptual architecture of an SN is described and formally defined. Section 4 explains how an SN facilitates mass customization, and section 5 shows a competency assessment framework and corresponding metrics. Finally is the conclusion.

2   Related Work

Mass Customization (MC) [1] originated in the production domain. Similarly, in the software engineering domain, methods such as software product line and reuse-based software engineering (RBSE) emphasize the philosophy of utilizing standard and reusable fine-grained software components to rapidly build applications in one domain, essentially realizing the mass production and customization of software products [2]. Later, ideas from MC and RBSE were imported into the services computing domain and became a key analysis and design approach in pursuing the mass customization of service-oriented systems using techniques like loosely-coupled architecture, autonomic agent, dynamic workflow, and service family [3][4].

Service discovery, selection, and composition [5][6] play critical roles in constructing coarse-grained service solutions that meet individualized requirements. Applicable services are selected from candidates, then potential composite solutions are generated and evaluated, and the most appropriate one is delivered to the customers [7]. In addition to IOPE (Input-Output-Preconditions-Effects) and QoS [8], the customer's preferences and context are addressed to look for an exact match between composite solutions and customer requirements [9][10]. At present, research on this issue is mainly based on AI planning techniques, i.e., initial and expected states, and the semantics of candidate services are formally described. A planner with reasoning capacity is then employed to look for a composite path that transforms the initial state into the expected one by back-chaining or forward-chaining policies [11]. Semantic querying and reasoning are the pivotal techniques used in the process.

Another popular approach is to look for the underlying pattern of each customer from his/her historical service usage records using data mining techniques.

Personalized solutions are then built following the identified patterns [12][13]. This method is suited to a scenario where customers do not explicitly state their preferences.

Software as a Service (SaaS) is another successful practice in boosting service mass customization [14]. In SaaS, a meta-data model is used to define variability in the data layer, business logic layer, and user interface layer, and each tenant makes personalized configurations on these variability points [15]. In this way, many personalized requirements can be facilitated by one software instance, and the personalized performance of different tenants is ensured by the scalable architecture [16]. However, the services in a SaaS are largely designed, developed, deployed, and run-time provisioned by the SaaS operator itself, and many services distributed on the Internet are seldom used due to reliability considerations.

It would appear that the distinctions of SN are twofold:

(1) It transforms the "centralized service development, maintenance, and evolution" policy adopted in SaaS into "the utilization and aggregation of massive distributed services on the Internet to form a dynamic network structure" policy, thereby extending the scope and flexibility of mass customization; and

(2) It transforms the "one-requirement-oriented temporary solution" policy adopted in traditional service composition approaches into the "massive-requirement-oriented persistent solution", thereby improving the cost-effectiveness of mass customization.

3   Concept and Architecture of an Service Network

An SN is essentially a combination of multiple composite solutions, each of which is established in terms of one customer requirement. Although superficially it appears to be quite complicated and redundant, it has a higher fitness, i.e., when one requirement arrives, it automatically looks for a sub-network and provides it to the corresponding customer. Each solution is the equivalent of a traditional service composition algorithm.

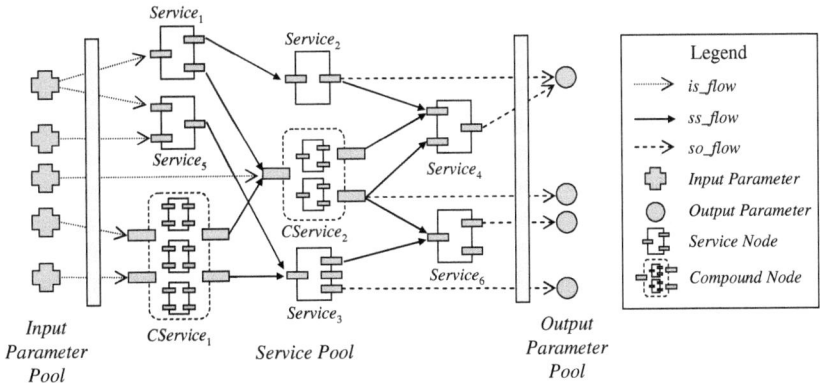

Fig. 2. Conceptual Architecture of a Service Network

As shown in Fig. 2, the structure of an SN looks like an artificial neural network. The left-most part is the input information obtained from three sources: the customers, obtained automatically from the context of customers, or from customers' historical records. The right-most part is the output information expected by customers. In the middle there are multiple layers, with each layer containing multiple services, and the services in the different layers are connected by parameter passing. The input is transformed into the output layer by layer.

An SN is defined by

$$SN=(IN\_Pool, OUT\_Pool, Service\_Pool, IS\_Flow, SS\_Flow, SO\_Flow),$$

where

- *IN_Pool* is the input of an SN and contains a set of parameters. Each parameter $in\_param \in IN\_Pool$ is a term from the domain ontology. For clarity, we suppose that all parameters are atomic and they are mutually independent, i.e., there are no semantics overlaps.
- *OUT_Pool* is the output of an SN and also contains a set of parameters. Different from *in_param*, each parameter $out\_param \in OUT\_Pool$ may be either atomic or compound, and there may be semantic overlaps between different parameters.
- *Service_Pool* is the main body of an SN and contains of a set of service nodes. For each node, $service=\{FD, IN\_slots, OUT\_slots, QoS\_params\}$, where *FD* is the semantic description (in the form of ontology), *IN_slots* is a set of slots, and each slot represents an input parameter of *service*, *OUT_slots* is a set of slots, and each slot represents an output parameter, and *QoS_params* is a set of quality parameters. Further, $\forall in\_slot_i \in IN\_slots$ is defined by $in\_slot_i=(in\_param_i, FD_i)$, where in_param_i is the name of the input parameter and FD_i is the ontology description of semantics. So does $\forall out\_slot_i=(out\_param_i, FD_i) \in OUT\_slots$.

Note that there is a special type of service node called *compound service* (*CS*), denoted by $CS=\{service_1, service_2, ..., service_n\}$. For $\forall service_i, service_j \in CS$, they have the same *FD*, *IN_slots*, and *OUT_slots* but the value of quality indicators in *QoS_params* might be different. For example, the nodes $CService_1$ and $CService_2$ are compound services, shown in dotted rounded rectangles.

- $IS\_Flow=\{is\_flow\}$ is the connections between *IN_Pool* and *Service_Pool*. Further, $is\_flow=in\_param_i \rightarrow service_j.in\_slot_{jl}$ indicates the transferring of the input parameter $in\_param_i \in IN\_Pool$ to the in_slot_{jl} of a $service_j$.
- $SS\_Flow=\{ss\_flow\}$ is the connections between service nodes, and $ss\_flow=service_i.out\_slot_{ik} \rightarrow service_j.in\_slot_{jl}$ indicates the transferring of the output parameter out_slot_{ik} of service $service_i$ to the input parameter in_slot_{jl} of $service_j$.
- $SO\_Flow=\{so\_flow\}$ is the connections between *Service_Pool* and *OUT_Pool*, and $so\_flow=service_j.out\_slot_{jl} \rightarrow out\_param_i$ indicates the transferring of the output parameter out_slot_{jl} of $service_j$ to the output parameter $out\_param_i \in OUT\_Pool$.

For $\forall in\_slot_{ik} \in service_i$, there must be one or multiple flows pointing to one *in_slot* of a service node. Such a flow is either an *is_flow* from *IN_pool* or an *ss_flow* from another service node. When the SN is customized, on most occasions only one flow will be selected and take effect. However, if the customer expects higher reliability, multiple flows may take effect simultaneously, indicating that in_slot_{ik} has multiple data sources (also called *redundancy*). Taking Fig. 2 as an example, the input parameter of $CService_2$ has three distinct sources ($service_1$, in_pool, and $CService_1$). Similarly, with $\forall in\_param \in IN\_pool$, there is at least one is_flow pointing out from it.

For $\forall out\_slot_{jl} \in service_j$, there may be zero, one, or multiple flows pointing out from one out_slot_{jl} of a service node. Such a flow is either a so_flow to OUT_pool or an ss_flow to another service node. When there are no flows pointing out from the out_slot_{jl}, this indicates that this output parameter is trivial and not used by the SN. Similarly with $\forall out\_param \in OUT\_pool$, there is at least one flow so_flow pointing to it. Furthermore, a flow pointing directly out from an $in\_param \in IN\_pool$ to and $out\_param \in OUT\_pool$ is illegal.

4 How Service Network Supports "Mass Customization"

This section describes the SN mechanisms that support "mass customization". Based on the descriptions in section 3, there are two "transformation" mechanisms facilitating mass customization, i.e., (M_1) the dynamic selection of service nodes, and (M_2) the dynamic selection of flows. The variable service nodes and flows are both defined as the *"features"* of an SN, each of which has a limited scope and density of customization. Metaphorically speaking, a feature is like a joint of a human body and its customization scope is the joint's degree of freedom. Table 1 lists a set of customizable features and their customization scope. Focusing on a personalized requirement, the customization of an SN is the process of selecting a specific value for each feature from its customization scope, indicating that a subset of service nodes and a subset of flows are identified, and the SN is transformed into a composite solution.

Table 1. Customizable Features of an SN

Feature		Sub-Feature	Customization Scope
Functionalities	F_1	(M_1) Input parameter in_param_i	{*Selected, Not Selected*}
	F_2	(M_1) Service node $service_i$	{*Selected, Not Selected*}
	F_3	(M_2) The source of an in_slot_{ik} of $service_i$	$\{is\_flow=* \rightarrow service_i.in\_slot_{ik}\} \cup \{ss\_flow=* \rightarrow service_i.in\_slot_{ik}\}$
	F_4	(M_2) The source of an out_param_j in OUT_Pool	$\{so\_flow=* \rightarrow out\_param_j\}$
QoS	Q_1	(M_1) The selected services of a CS_i	$\{service_{i1}, ..., service_{in}\}$
	Q_2	(M_1) The number of selected services of a CS_i	$\{1, 2, ..., |CS_i|\}$
	Q_3	(M_2) The number of sources of an in_slot_{ik} of $service_i$	$\{1, 2, ...,$ $|\{is\_flow=* \rightarrow service_i.in\_slot_{ik}\}$ $\cup$ $\{ss\_flow=* \rightarrow service_i.in\_slot_{ik}\}|\}$
	Q_4	(M_2) The number of sources of an out_param_j in OUT_Pool	$\{1, 2, ...,$ $|\{so\_flow=* \rightarrow out\_param_j\}|\}$

It is easy to imagine that, in terms of a specific requirement, there might be multiple possible results, each of which could fully satisfy the requirement. Therefore, besides the value assignment for each feature, the customization process should also find the "best" solution from these possibilities. We define it as a combinatorial optimization problem following a "*just-enough*" policy [17]. The following is the mathematical model.

Input:

- An SN ;
- Input parameters provided by customer: $\{req\_in\_param\} \subseteq IN\_Pool$;
- Output parameters expected by customer: $\{req\_out\_param\} \subseteq OUT\_Pool$;
- QoS expectations of customer: $\{req\_QoS\_param\}=\{T=TValue, C=CValue, R=RValue\}$, i.e., time, price, and reliability, respectively.

Output: *bp*, a sub-graph of *SN* in which each feature has been assigned a value to.

Decision Variables:

- x_i=0/1 indicates whether *service$_i$* is selected;
- If x_i=1 and *CService$_i$* is a compound node, then y_{ik}=0/1 indicates whether *service$_{ik}$* is selected;
- $z_{ip,jq}$=0/1 indicates whether *out_slot$_{ip}$* of *service$_i$* is connected to *in_slot$_{jq}$* of *service$_j$*;
- $v_{l,jq}$=0/1 indicates whether *in_slot$_{jq}$* of *service$_j$* is connected with *in_param$_l$*;
- $u_{ip,l}$=0/1 indicates whether *out_param$_l$* is connected with *out_slot$_{ip}$* of *service$_i$*;
- $f_T(bp)$, $f_C(bp)$ and $f_R(bp)$ are the calculating functions that compute the global Time, Cost, and Reliability, respectively, of the generated *bp* according to its process structure [18].

Objective Function:

The generated process *bp* satisfies the customer requirement as close as possible, and if no such process can be found, the output is *null*, i.e.,

$$\min y = F(pr, bp) = \left(pr.T - f_T(bp), pr.C - f_C(bp), pr.R - f_R(bp) \right)^T$$

$$s.t.: \ pr.T - f_T(bp) \geq 0, \ pr.C - f_C(bp) \geq 0, \ pr.R - f_R(bp) \leq 0$$

Solving Strategies:

- Phase 1: Pruning

According to $\{req\_in\_param\}$ and $\{req\_out\_param\}$, the initial *SN* is pruned, i.e., (1) $\forall in\_param_i \in IN\_Pool \setminus \{req\_in\_param\}$ and $\forall is\_flow=\{in\_param_i \rightarrow *\}$ are removed from the SN; (2) $\forall out\_param_j \in OUT\_Pool \setminus \{req\_out\_param\}$ and $\forall so\_flow=\{* \rightarrow out\_param_j\}$ are removed from the SN; (3) recursively check each service node from left to right of the SN, examine each *in_slot$_{ip}$* of each *service$_i$*, if there are no flows pointing to *in_slot$_{ip}$*, then *service$_i$* and all related flows are removed from the SN; (4) check the remaining SN, and if it cannot produce any output parameters, then the requirements cannot be fulfilled by the initial SN and *NULL* is returned.

- Phase 2: Optimization

Based on the pruned *SN*, a multi-objective programming approach is employed to solve the combinatorial optimization problem.

5 Competency Assessment of Service Network

In reality, the competency of an SN is limited; in other words, not all individualized requirements can be satisfied by an SN, and only a certain number of requirements can be simultaneously satisfied. Even if a requirement could be satisfied, there are associated costs that must be paid. This section puts forward a set of indicators to assess the competency of an existing SN, with corresponding metrics.

5.1 Competency Assessment Framework (SN-CAF)

The competency of an SN is assessed from two aspects: capacity of mass customization and cost-effectiveness. Figure 3 shows the complete assessment framework containing eight atomic indicators.

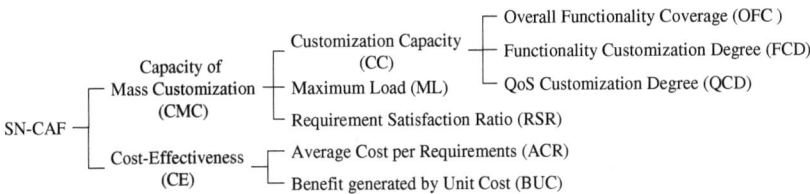

Fig. 3. Competency Assessment Framework of a Service Network

5.2 Assessment of the Capacity of Mass Customization (CMC)

The capacity of mass customization (CMC) is measured by looking at "customization" capacity and "mass" capacity. The former refers to the scope of functionalities and QoS that could be customized in an SN, and the latter refers to the scale or the number of requirements that could be simultaneously fulfilled by one SN. From a statistical point of view, CMC may be indirectly measured by the proportion of satisfied requirements relative to the total arriving requirements.

More specifically, we use five fine-grained indicators, the first three, Overall Functionality Coverage (OFC), Functionality Customization Degree (FCD), and QoS Customization Degree (QCD), measure the "customization" capacity, the fifth (Maximum Load, ML) measures the "mass" capacity, and the final one (Requirement Satisfaction Ratio, RSR) is a statistical measurement.

(1) Overall Functionality Coverage (OFC)

OFC refers to the degree of functionality coverage of an SN relative to the business domain it belongs to. It characterizes the richness of functionality of an SN and is measured by the proportion of the ontology covered by an SN relative to the holistic ontology of the domain. Because the size of the domain ontology is difficult to estimate, we use the number of complete ontology covered by the SN as the metrics, i.e., $OFC(SN) = \bigcup_{service_i} service_i.FD$.

The greater the functionality of an *SN*, the higher the diversity of its functions, and thereby the higher possibility that it might fulfill a varying number of functions, and the broader range of choices a customer may have to customize his/her functional preferences.

(2) Functionality Customization Degree (FCD)

FCD is the metrics indicating the degree by which functionalities could be customized. It may be measured by the percentage of customization relative to the total functionalities, and the customization scope of each functionality feature, using the four functionality features listed in Table 1, i.e., (F_1) the selection of input parameters and (F_2) service nodes, (F_3) the selection of the source of an input parameter of a service node, and (F_4) the selection of the source of an output parameter. The following are detailed metrics to calculate the degree of customization:

For F_1, we check each input parameter whether it is either optional or mandatory. A mandatory input parameter has to be selected when the SN is used, so it cannot be customized, and the opposite is true when it is optional. The pruning strategy (mentioned in section 4) is used to delete in_param_i and all its related service nodes and output parameters from the SN, and if no output parameters remain then in_param_i is mandatory; otherwise it is optional. Fig. 4 schematically illustrates an example pruning process, in which the deletion of the first input parameter leads to the deletion of $Service_1$, $Service_2$ and $Service_5$, but not incurs to the disappearances of the output parameters, so this input parameter is optional. $FCD_1(SN) = \dfrac{|\{in\_param_i : \text{optional}\}|}{|IN\_Pool|}$ is used to measure the percentage of customizable input parameters in *IN_Pool* of SN.

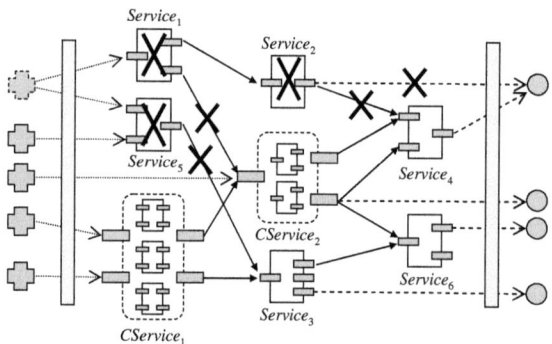

Fig. 4. The Pruning of the SN

For F_2, we check each service node whether it is optional or mandatory. The same pruning strategy is used to prune $service_i$ and all its related service nodes and output parameters to check whether $service_i$ is optional or mandatory. Then $FCD_2(SN) = \dfrac{|\{service_i : optional\}|}{|Service\_Pool|}$ measures the percentage of customizable service nodes in $Service\_Pool$ of the SN.

For F_3, we calculate the number of sources of an in_slot_{ik} of $service_i$ and that the number is larger than 1 implies that this parameter can be customized. Then

$$FCD_3(SN) = \dfrac{\sum\limits_{service_i} |\{in\_slot_{ik} : |\{flow : flow = * \to in\_slot_{ik}\}| > 1\}|}{\sum\limits_{service_i} |IN\_slots_i|}$$ measures the

percentage of customizable input parameters of services in the SN.

For F_4, we calculate the number of sources of an out_param_j and that the number is larger than 1 implies that this parameter can be customized. Then

$$FCD_4(SN) = \dfrac{|\{out\_param_j : |\{flow : flow = * \to out\_param_j\}| > 1\}|}{|OUT\_Pool|}$$ measures the

percentage of customizable output parameters in OUT_Pool of the SN.

Synthesizing the four together is represented by $FCD(SN) = \dfrac{1}{4}(FCD_1(SN) + FCD_2(SN) + FCD_3(SN) + FCD_4(SN))$.

(3) QoS Customization Degree (QCD)

QCD is defined as the overall scope in which the global QoS of the customized solutions can vary. In terms of time, cost, and reliability, the measurements are different.

First we transform the SN into the form of a service process using the following steps:

- Construct a *Start* activity and an *End* activity;
- Construct an *activity* for each simple service node, and for each candidate service in each compound service node;
- For the activities transformed from compound service nodes, add an *or-split* before them and an *or-merge* after them;
- If there is an *ss_flow* pointing from an input parameter in *IN_Pool* to a service node, construct an arrow connecting *Start* and the corresponding *activity*; similarly, place arrows between two activities, and between an *activity* and *End*;
- If there are multiple arrows between two activities, keep one only;
- If multiple flows point to the same *in_slot* of a service node, then label the corresponding arrows *or-merge*;
- If a flow is optional, also label the corresponding arrow *or-merge*.

Figure 5 provides an example process based on the SN shown in Fig. 2.

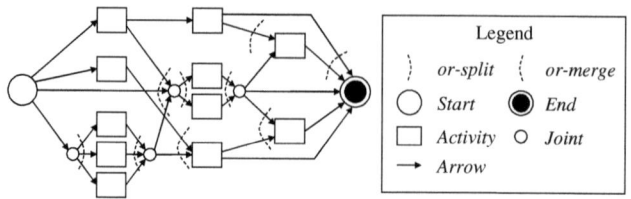

Fig. 5. Service Process based on an SN

Based on the induced process, the following provide accurate measurements of $QCD(SN)$ for time, cost, and reliability:

[*Time*] Identify the paths with the longest time (LT) and shortest time (ST) using the Critical Path Method, and then $QCD_T(SN)=[LT, ST]$.

[*Cost*] To measure the upper bound of cost (UC), keep a branch with a maximal price for each fragment between *or-split* and *or-merge*, delete all other branches, and then sum the prices of the remaining activities; similarly, keep the branch with the minimal price and obtain the lower bound of the cost (LC); then $QCD_C(SN)=[LC, UC]$.

[*Reliability*] To measure the upper bound of reliability (UR), keep the process unchanged and calculate global reliability based on the structure of the process, because the original process retains all the redundancy, and the global reliability is maximized. To measure the lower bound (LR), for multiple arrows grouped by the same *or-merge*, retain one arrow whose source activity has minimal reliability, and delete all other arrows and related activities; then calculate the corresponding global reliability. Such pruning eliminates all redundancy and retains activities with minimal reliability. Thus, $QCD_R(SN)=[LR, UR]$.

(4) Maximum Load (ML)

ML is the maximal concurrency number of requirements that could be simultaneously satisfied by the SN. Different requirements may be allocated to different paths, or share the same path.

Suppose the concurrency number of an atomic $service_i$ is $CN(service_i)$. For a compound service node, namely CS_j, its CN increases to $\prod_{k=1}^{|CS_j|} CN(service_{jk})$ implying all the atomic services contained in CS_j could be concurrently utilized to satisfy requirements.

Essentially, the value of ML lies on the minimal concurrency number of service nodes, which are mandatory and cannot be pruned (this was mentioned in the measurement of FCD). So, $ML(SN)=\min SN(service_i)$ where $service_i \in \{service: \text{mandatory}\}$.

(5) Requirement Satisfaction Ratio (RSR)

RSR is a statistics metric and is not directly related to the structure of SN. It is the ratio that the number of satisfied requirements relative to the total arriving requirements during a period of time. This ratio indirectly reflects the competency of mass customization. If the ratio is low, then there are inevitably deficiencies in the SN and it is necessary to enhance it immediately.

5.3 Assessment of Cost Effectiveness

An SN is cost-effective when the benefit generated by satisfying the individualized requirements of a large number of customers is greater than the sum of the costs incurred during the full lifecycle of the SN, including construction costs, maintenance costs, and customization costs. Otherwise, the SN becomes worthless. Put another way, the more times that an SN is used and the greater the amount and frequency of individualized requirements it could satisfy, therefore the greater significance it has, and the greater benefit it could bring to the operator of the SN.

There are three associated costs:

— Construction Costs (NC): the cost of selecting the appropriate candidate services, negotiating with the providers of these services, and connecting them together to form an initial SN. It is paid for during the initialization of infrastructures and is a "sunk cost" or "fixed investment".
— Maintenance Costs (MC): the cost of provisioning, evaluating, and continuous enhancing (discussed further in section 6) per unit of time (e.g., one month). Such costs are not directly related to the requirements but are seen as similar to daily operation costs.
— Customization Costs (CC): the cost of customizing all of the features of an SN to satisfy a specific requirement.

Suppose there are n possible requirements based on forecasting and historical records, and the "Willing to Pay (WTP)" of the i-th requirement is WTP_i. If they are satisfied by traditional service compositions, i.e., each one is provided with a directly-constructed solution, and the construction cost of the i-th solution is DC_i, then the total benefit is: $DB = \sum_{i=1}^{n}(WTP_i - DC_i)$. If a service network is constructed to satisfy n requirements and they are distributed in m months, then the total benefit is $SNB = \sum_{i=1}^{n}(WTP_i - CC_i) - NC - m \times MC$. Further, the cost-effectiveness of the constructed SN is denoted by $CE(SN) = \dfrac{SNB - DB}{DB}$, indicating the percentage of the increased benefit that the SN produces compared with a traditional approach.

In addition to CE, there are another two meaningful metrics:

(1) Average Cost per Requirement (ACR), i.e.,
$$ACR(SN) = \frac{1}{n}\left(\sum_{i=1}^{n} CC_i + NC + m \times MC\right);$$

(2) Benefit generated by Unit Cost (BUC), i.e.,

$$BUC(SN) = \frac{SNB}{n \times ACR(SN)} = \frac{\sum_{i=1}^{n} WTP_i}{\sum_{i=1}^{n} CC_i + NC + m \times M} - 1.$$

Ideally, if an SN is cost-effective, ACR(*SN*) and BUC(*SN*) will vary, with *ACR(SN)* being extremely high and *BUC(SN)* negative during the stage when an SN is initially constructed; as the number of arriving requirements increases, *ACR(SN)* drops gradually and reaches a stable level, and *BUC(SN)* ascends gradually and becomes positive. As a comparison, *ACR* and *BUC* in a traditional service composition approach remains stable with small fluctuations.

6 Conclusions

By focusing on the mass customization of services, this paper analyzed the deficiencies of traditional SaaS and service composition approaches, and then proposed a "Service Network" as a means to solve the contradictions between "mass-oriented standardization" and "individual-oriented personalization". An SN is constructed and maintained as a persistent existing infrastructure, to be transformed into various concrete solutions to satisfy considerable individualized customer requirements. This is achieved under the support of a set of customized features such as service nodes, flows between services, and varied QoS in compound service nodes. In addition to mass customization competency, this study also highlighted "cost-effectiveness" as an important factor, an aspect that has been ignored in previous research.

Accompanied by the continuing growth in Internet services, customer requirements are becoming increasingly diversified and their granularity tends to large-grained. In such circumstances, cross-organization and cross-regional service collaboration have been the dominant trends in many service industries. Our study provides some perspective references regarding the research and practices in this respect.

Acknowledgment. The work in this paper is supported by the projects funded by the Natural Science Foundation of China (Nos. 61272187 and 61033005).

References

1. Silveiraa, G.D., Borensteinb, D., Fogliattoc, F.S.: Mass customization: literature review and research directions. International Journal of Production Economics 72(1), 1–13 (2001)
2. Hallsteinsen, S., Hinchey, M., Park, S., Schmid, K.: Dynamic software product lines. IEEE Computer 41(4), 93–95 (2008)
3. Karpowitz, D., Cox, J., Humpherys, J., Warnick, S.: A dynamic workflow framework for mass customization using web service and autonomous agent techniques. Journal of Intelligent Manufacturing 19(5), 537–552 (2008)
4. Moon, S.K., Shu, J., Simpson, T.W., Kumara, S.: A module-based service model for mass customization: service family design. IIE Transactions 43(3), 153–163 (2010)

5. Hwang, S.Y., Lim, E.P., Lee, et al.: Dynamic web service selection for reliable web service composition. IEEE Transactions on Services Computing 1(2), 104–116 (2008)
6. Zeng, L., Benatallah, B., Ngu, A.H., Dumas, M., Kalagnanam, J., Chang, H.: QoS-aware middleware for web services composition. IEEE Transactions on Software Engineering 30(5), 311–327 (2004)
7. Ardagna, D., Pernici, B.: Adaptive service composition in flexible processes. IEEE Transactions on Software Engineering 33(6), 369–384 (2007)
8. Cavallo, B., Penta, M.D., Canfora, G.: An empirical comparison of methods to support QoS–aware service selection. In: Proceedings of the 2nd International Workshop on Principles of Engineering Service-Oriented Systems, pp. 64–70 (2010)
9. Li, Y., Huai, J.P., Sun, H., Deng, T., Guo, H.: Pass: An approach to personalized automated service composition. In: Proceedings of IEEE International Conference on Services Computing, pp. 283–290 (2008)
10. Lin, N., Kuter, U., Sirin, E.: Web Service Composition with User Preferences. In: Bechhofer, S., Hauswirth, M., Hoffmann, J., Koubarakis, M. (eds.) ESWC 2008. LNCS, vol. 5021, pp. 629–643. Springer, Heidelberg (2008)
11. Peer, J.: Web service composition as AI planning: a survey. University of St. Gallen, Switzerland (2005)
12. Gaaloul, W., Baïna, K., Godart, C.: Log-based mining techniques applied to Web service composition reengineering. Service Oriented Computing and Applications 2(2-3), 93–110 (2008)
13. Tang, R.: An approach for mining web service composition patterns from execution logs. In: Proceedings of the 12th IEEE International Symposium on Web Systems Evolution, pp. 53–62 (2010)
14. Sun, W., Zhang, X., Guo, C.J., et al.: Software as a Service: configuration and customization perspectives. In: Proceedings of IEEE Congress on Services, pp. 18–25 (2008)
15. Mietzner, R., Metzger, A., Leymann, R., Pohl, K.: Variability modeling to support customization and deployment of multi-tenant-aware Software as a Service applications. In: Proceedings of the 2009 ICSE Workshop on Principles of Engineering Service Oriented Systems, pp. 18–25 (2009)
16. Shim, J., Han, J., Kim, J., et al.: Patterns for configuration requirements of Software-as-a-Service. In: Proceedings of ACM Symposium on Applied Computing, pp. 155–161 (2011)
17. Ni, W., He, L., Liu, L., Wu, C.: Commodity-market based services selection in dynamic web service composition. In: Proceedings of the 2nd IEEE Asia-Pacific Service Computing Conference, pp. 218–223 (2007)
18. Jaeger, M.C., Rojec-Goldmann, G., Muhl, G.: QoS Aggregation for Web Service Composition using Workflow Patterns. In: Proceedings of the 8th IEEE Intl Enterprise Distributed Object Computing Conference, pp.149–159 (2004)

Toward a Methodology to Control Interoperability Improvement Projects Execution

Abderrahim Taoudi, Bouchaib Bounabat, and Badr Elmir

Al-Qualsadi Research & Development Team, Ecole Nationale Supérieure d'Informatique et d'Analyses des Systèmes (ENSIAS), Mohamed V – Souissi University, Avenue Mohammed Ben Abdallah Regragui, Madinat Al Irfane, BP 713, Agdal Rabat, Morocco
`abderrahim.taoudi@um5s.net.ma`, `bounabat@ensias.ma`,
`b.elmir@daag.finances.gov.ma`

Abstract. In front of the increasing complexity of information systems, improving enterprise interoperability has become a crucial element for better management. To address this issue, several research projects have been launched during the last decade and have resulted in a set of frameworks which help organizing and performing enterprise interoperability projects efficiently. In addition to these frameworks, many metrics have been also developed to measure the interoperability degree between systems. However, these frameworks and metrics are not sufficient to better control execution of these projects. Indeed, they don't take into account resource management and unanticipated events or situations that can be encountered during execution. Moreover, there is a real lack in methodologies to deal with this situation. The aim of this paper is to introduce a new approach to control interoperability improvement projects execution by using control theory, project planning theory and a specific quantitative interoperability metric RatIop.

Keywords: RatIop; Control theory, Enterprise Interoperability, Project planning theory, Interoperability improvement, Automated Business Processes.

1 Introduction

According to IEEE definition [1], Interoperability can be defined as the ability for two (or more) systems or components to exchange information and to use the information that has been exchanged. To allow companies to be more competitive, they should share information and competencies internally between departments and employees, and externally with partners. A successful implementation of interoperability helps also the companies to optimize their business processes, reduce their costs, and maximize service quality. In the enterprise interoperability area, many research projects have been launched in the last decades i.e. ATHENA [2], INTEROP [3]. Today, there is a number of mature frameworks that were developed and validated and are available to use i.e. Chen et al. [4], ATHENA [2], LISI [5], IDEAS [6], EIF [7]. In relation to enterprise interoperability measurement, many approaches and measures are available. Ford et al. [8] listed already a number of them. Other new measures also exist like Chen et al [9] and RatIop [10].

Managing and controlling the execution of interoperability improvement projects raise many challenges. Given the current and targeted interoperability degrees as well as the available resources (i.e. Budget Allocation, Human Resources), the first challenge consists in finding the optimal plan for an efficient management of these projects. The second challenge is the ability to handle unexpected events that can be encountered during project execution, so that the managers can know exactly how many additional resources has to be allocated to correct the deviation from the project optimal plan. The available frameworks and metrics are not currently sufficient to handle the aforementioned challenges.

The aim of this paper is to propose a new approach to control the execution of interoperability improvement projects. The proposed approach will be based on mature and proven tools: the framework of chen et al [4] (currently under CEN/ISO standardization process) as the interoperability framework, RatIop[10] as the interoperability quantitative metric, Project Planning theory to define the optimal plan and Control theory to control projects execution.

2   Overview of RatIop

Several dimensions of interoperability have been defined in [1], [11] and [12]:

- Interoperability barriers: Conceptual, technological and Organizational.
- Interoperability concerns: Business, Process, Service and Data.
- Interoperability approaches: Integrated, Unified and Federated.
- Interoperability engineering: Requirements, Design and Implementation.
- Interoperability scopes of application: Within the same organization and Cross independent organization.
- Interoperability transactional aspects of cooperation: Synchronous collaboration and Asynchronous collaboration.

In terms of measurability, three kinds of interoperability measurement have been defined in [9]:

- Interoperability potentiality: it's used to measure the potential of a system to accommodate dynamically to overcome possible barriers when interacting with a partner.
- Interoperability compatibility: it's used to measure the ability of two systems to interact with each other.
- Interoperability performance: it's used to measure the operational performance of interoperability.

RatIop is a new quantitative ratio metric to measure interoperability between automated business processes that was developed in [10]. With this ratio, an organisation can evaluate, at any time and in a quantitative way, the degree of interoperability of its automated business processes.

RatIop takes into account three kinds of interoperability measurement as so as:

1. to quantify the first kind of interoperability, Interoperability potentiality, by using the five levels of IMML (Interoperation Maturity Model Level) [10] calculated as bellow:

$$PI = 0.2 * IMML, \text{ where } IMML = 1,2,3,4 \text{ or } 5 \quad (1)$$

2. to quantify the second kind of interoperability, Interoperability compatibility, by using a modified matrix of Chen et al [10], see Table 1.

Table 1. Interoperability compatibility

	Conceptual		Organizational		Technology	
	syntactic	Semantic	Authorities resposabilities	organisation	platform	communication
Business	0/1	0/1	0/1	0/1	0/1	0/1
Process	0/1	0/1	0/1	0/1	0/1	0/1
Service	0/1	0/1	0/1	0/1	0/1	0/1
Data	0/1	0/1	0/1	0/1	0/1	0/1

By noting dc_{ij} the elements of this matrix, this potential is calculated as bellow:

$$DC = 1 - ((\sum dc_{ij})/24), \text{ where } dc_{ij} = 0 \text{ or } 1 \quad (2)$$

dc_{ij} is given the value 0 if the criteria in an area marked satisfaction; otherwise, if a lot of incompatibilities are met, the value 1 is assigned to dc_{ij}.

3. to quantify the third kind of interoperability, Interoperability performance, by using these three elements:

   — DS: the overall availability rate of application servers.
   — QoS: the service quality of different networks used for interacting component communication.
   — TS: the end users satisfaction level about interoperation.

This potential is:

$$PO = \sqrt[3]{(DS * Qos * TS)} \quad (3)$$

Using these three previous indicators, RatIop is calculated as bellow:

$$RatIop = \frac{(PI+DC+PO)}{3} \quad (4)$$

Using this ratio, [13] introduces a tool, Interoperability Monitoring Tool (IMT), which has three modules:

- Module 1: To assess interoperability at a specific period.
- Module 2: To propose a scenario to reach a planned degree of interoperability.
- Module 3: To give the prerequisites of going from a maturity level to the next one.

3 Defining the Optimal Plan of the Interoperability Improvement Projects

Project planning has different meanings in project management. In this paper, Project Planning is the act of building the task by task schedule which we will call the "Project Plan". The optimal plan is the project plan that minimizes one or more optimization criteria: Cost, Resources and Time. The high level objective of the interoperability improvement projects is to improve interoperability by passing from an initial RatIop R_i, which is the actual state of interoperability, to a targeted RatIop R_t. To define the optimal plan of these projects, we propose to follow these steps:

1. Definition of the project objectives
2. Definition of the optimal plan using project planning theory.

3.1 Project Objectives Definition

The high level objective of the interoperability improvement project defined above must be decomposed to clear, concise and measurable objectives which will be used to plan the project properly. In this vein, the Periodic Interoperability Monitoring Tool (IMT) [13] can be used to define a clear scenario to reach the desired RatIop Rt. the proposed scenario will define:

- The target Maturity Level.
- The prerequisites to reach this target Maturity Level.
- The incompatibilities to remove.
- The target operational performance ratios: Availability rate of application servers, The QoS of different networks and end users satisfaction level.

3.2 Optimal Plan Definition

Using the objectives as defined above, there are many planning methods and tools to define the optimal plan taking into account resources, costs and time. The paper [14] lists many deterministic and non deterministic mathematical models used to define optimal plans. Most of these models are already automated. Bellow some examples of these models:

- The standard Project Management model, PMBOK [15].
- Critical Path Method, CPM, and PERT.
- Non-resource-constrained NPV maximization.
- The Resource-Constrained Project Scheduling Problem, RCPSP.
- The Multi-mode Resource-Constrained Project Scheduling Problem, MRCPSP.

The project planning theory will help us define the optimal plan to satisfy the project objectives listed in the section 3.1.

4 Controlling Execution of Interoperability Improvement Projects

Without careful monitoring and control, many projects fail to achieve the expected results. The aim of this phase is to measure actual execution, compare it with the optimal plan, analyze it and correct the deviations. To achieve this goal, we will use a proven and mature mathematical tool: the feedback control theory.

4.1 Feedback Control Theory

Feedback control theory is widely used in many domains i.e. manufacturing, electronics and physics. It's used also in computer science i.e. apache [16], web servers [17], lotus notes [18], internet [19] and networks [20]. A feedback control system, also known as closed loop control system, is a control mechanism that maintains a desired system output close to a reference using information from measurements of outputs. The feedback control diagram adopted by this paper is illustrated in Figure 1.

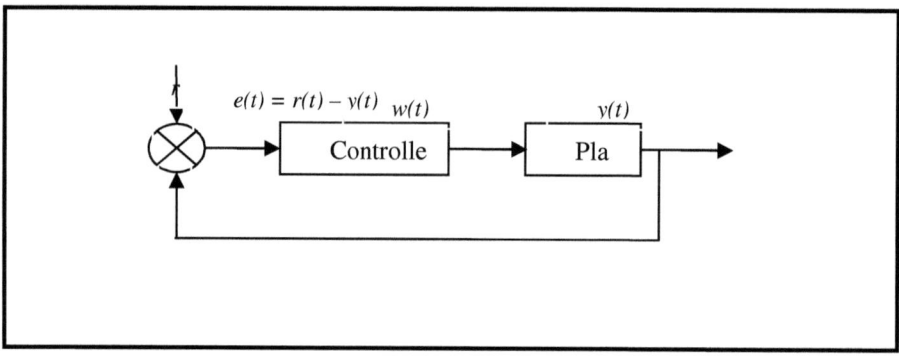

Fig. 1. Feedback control diagram

    The plant is the system to be controlled. In our case, it's the interoperability improvement project. It has a controlled input (denoted by *w(t)*), and a measured output (denoted by *y(t)*). The controller takes as input the control error (denoted by *e(t)*, which is the difference between the observed value and the reference value), and it adjust the input of the plant system to minimize this error. Because of the discrete nature of the system, we will adopt a discrete time approach with uniform interval sizes (Day, Week, two Weeks, or Month).

4.2 RatIop Reference Definition

The reference is the RatIop of the system. Its curve will be derived from the optimal plan. We will take into account the finished tasks to calculate the projected RatIop at a time t. The objective of the control system is to minimize the deviations between the desired RatIop based on the optimal plan and the measured RatIop.

4.3 Modeling the Plant System

The plant system is the interoperability improvement project. The input of the plant system, at a time t, is the effort consumption at this time to release the project. It can be the resources of the project or budget allocation. The output of the plant system, at a time *t*, is the RatIop at this time. Bellow is the definition of the characteristics of the plant system illustrated in Figure 2:

$w(t)$ = the effort consumption at time t to release the project (resources of the project, budget allocation).
$y(t)$ = measured RatIop of the system at time t
$r(t)$ = the desired RatIop of the system at time t based on the optimal plan.

We will model the plant system as a black-box. We will focus on the behavior of the system not on the internal system construction details which are considered complex. To do so, we will use a statistical approach. The model adopted is the statistical model ARMA. To keep things simple, we will adopt ARMA Model of first order.

$$y(t) = a*y(t-1) + b*w(t) \qquad (5)$$

a and *b* are constants which will be estimated statistically. These constants can be estimated by varying inputs (*w(t)*), and calculating the resulting RatIop (*y(t)*). For each value of the effort *w* (resources, budget allocation), an automated project planning software can be used to calculate the optimal plan and derive the values for the RatIop (*y(t)*). Using these experiments, we can estimate the constants *a* and *b* statistically. The use of an ARMA model with greater order will give a more precise approximation of the plant system.

4.4 Modeling the Controller

According to [21], there are four properties of feedback control systems to verify:

- Stability: a system is said to be stable if for any bounded input the output is also bounded.
- Accuracy: a system is accurate if the measured output converges to the reference input.
- Settling time: a system has short settling time if it converges quickly to its steady state value.
- Overshooting: a system that achieves its objectives without overshoot, that is without exceeding an upper limit.

There are three basic controller models:

- Proportional Controller: *w(t) = K*e(t)*
- Integral Controller: *w(t) = w(t-1) + K*e(t)*
- Differential Controller: *w(t) = K*(e(t)-e(t-1))*

The constant *K* is called the gain. To achieve the four properties of our studied feedback control system, the model that we will adopt is the Proportional-Integral model (PI Model) :

$$w(t) = w(t-1) + (Kp + Ki)*e(t) - Kp*e(t-1) \qquad (6)$$

The transfer function of this PI controller is:

$$Kp + (Ki*z/(z-1)) \qquad (7)$$

Thus, we can define the following objectives for our design:

- The system is stable.
- The steady state error is minimized
- The settling time does not exceed a constant value Ks.
- Maximum overshoot does not exceed a constant value Mp.

Using these objectives, [21] discusses in detail the procedure to calculate the appropriate Kp and Ki of the model. With the plant and controller modelled, the control system of interoperability improvement projects is totally defined.

5 Case Study

To illustrate the approach, we will use a real world example which is the e-government example used in [13]. This case consists of an online payment for health care services in a public hospital. It was used in [13] to illustrate RatIop assessment and the usage of the IMT Tool. This system is described in Figure 2.

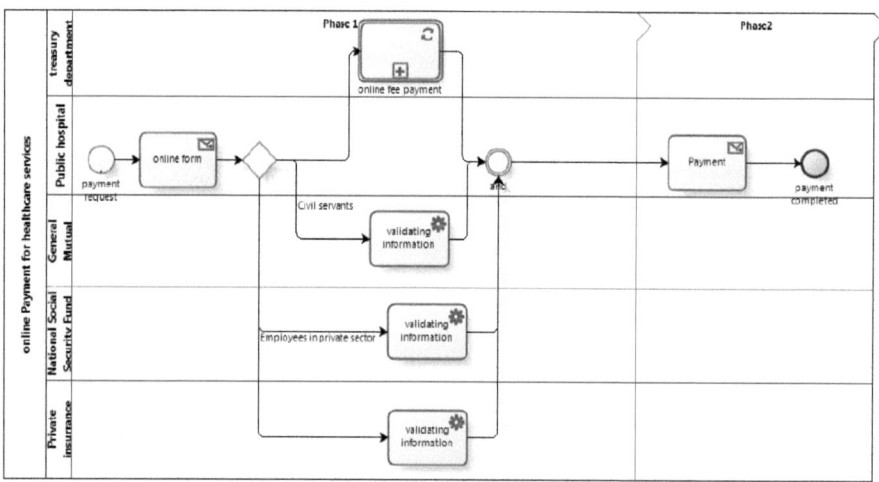

Fig. 2. Online payment business process

The main objective of this case study is to illustrate the details of steps and calculations used by the approach presented in this paper.

5.1 Initial RatIop Assessment

During the implementation phase, three incompatibilities were detected:

- Exchange with mutual servants: Infrastructures are not compatible. It's a Business/Technology platform and communication incompatibility.
- Exchange with National social security fund: Periods for data up-dating not-synchronized. It's a Data/Organizational incompatibility.
- Exchange with private insurance: Process description models can't exchange information. It's a Process/Conceptual syntactic and semantic incompatibility.

Using the framework defined in [10] and section 2 of this paper, the initial interoperability compatibility matrix for the incompatibilities described above is listed in Table 2:

Table 2. Initial Interoperability compatibility

	Conceptual		Organizational		Technology	
	syntactic	semantic	Authorities responsibilities	organisation	platform	communication
Business	0	0	0	0	1	1
Process	1	1	0	0	0	0
Service	0	0	0	0	0	0
Data	0	0	0	1	0	0

Using the framework defined in [10] and section 2 of this paper, the initial interoperability assessment is described in Table 3:

Table 3. Initial RatIop value

Metric	Description	Value
Maturity Level	IMML	0,4
Interoperability compatibility	DC	0,79
Overall application servers availability	DS	0,9
Network quality of service	QoS	1
End user satisfaction	TS	0,8
RatIop metric	**RatIop**	**0,69**

5.2 Project Objectives Definition

The aim of the project is to acheive 80% degree of interoperability instead of the current interoperability degree of 69%. So, the targeted RatIop is 0,8. Using the IMT Tool [13], the proposed scenario to reach this targeted RatIop is:

- Remove the tree incompatibilities of the system.
- Improve the Overall application servers' availability to be 1.
- Improve the end user satisfaction level to be 1.

5.3 Optimal Plan Definition

Using these objectives, the project tasks are defined in Table 4. The duration unit is the week:

Table 4. Tasks description

Tasks	Duration (in weeks)	Resources need
Task1: removing exchange with mutual servants incompatibilities	3	5
Task2: removing exchange with National social security fund incompatibilities	5	6
Task3: removing exchange with private insurance incompatibilities	5	6
Task4: Improving the Overall application servers' availability	2	2
Task5: Improving the end user satisfaction level	3	5

All these tasks are independent. A task cannot begin if the needed resources are not affected to it. The total resources for the project are 6. Using project theory, the optimal plan is described in figure 3.

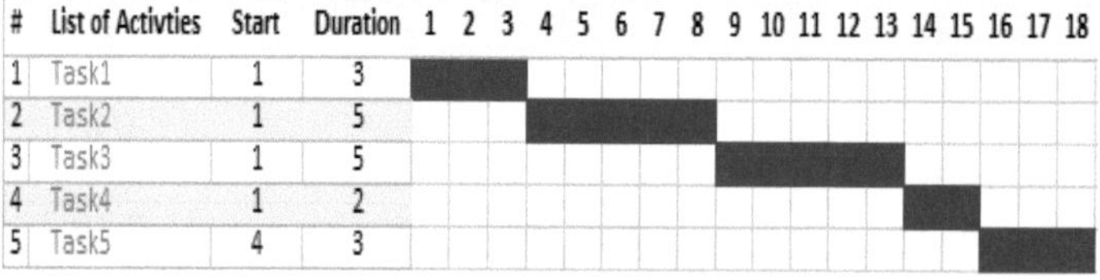

#	List of Activties	Start	Duration
1	Task1	1	3
2	Task2	1	5
3	Task3	1	5
4	Task4	1	2
5	Task5	4	3

Fig. 3. Optimal plan

5.4 RatIop Reference Definition

Using this optimal plan, the RatIop reference is described in figure 4:

Time	1	2	3	4	5	6	7	8	9	10	11	12	13	14	15	16	17	18	19
RatIop	0,69	0,69	0,69	0,72	0,72	0,72	0,72	0,72	0,74	0,74	0,74	0,74	0,74	0,76	0,76	0,77	0,77	0,77	0,80

Fig. 4. RatIop Reference

5.5 Modeling the Plant System

Figure 5 illustrate the evolution or RatIop depending on available resources.

Ressources	Time	1	2	3	4	5	6	7	8	9	10	11	12	13	14	15	16	17	18	19
5	RatIop*100	69	69	69	72	72	72	72	72	74	74	74	74	74	76	76	77	77	77	80
6	RatIop*100	69	69	69	72	72	72	72	72	74	74	74	74	74	76	76	77	77	77	80
7	RatIop*100	69	69	71	73	73	73	73	73	76	76	76	76	76	77	77	77	80	80	80
8	RatIop*100	69	69	71	73	73	73	73	73	76	76	76	76	76	77	77	77	80	80	80
9	RatIop*100	69	69	71	73	73	73	73	73	76	76	76	76	76	77	77	77	80	80	80
10	RatIop*100	69	69	71	73	73	76	76	76	76	76	77	77	77	77	77	80	80	80	80
11	RatIop*100	69	69	71	73	73	76	76	76	77	77	77	77	77	80	80	80	80	80	80
12	RatIop*100	69	69	71	76	76	76	76	76	80	80	80	80	80	80	80	80	80	80	80
13	RatIop*100	69	69	71	76	76	76	76	76	80	80	80	80	80	80	80	80	80	80	80
14	RatIop*100	69	69	71	76	76	76	76	76	80	80	80	80	80	80	80	80	80	80	80
15	RatIop*100	69	69	71	76	76	76	76	76	80	80	80	80	80	80	80	80	80	80	80
16	RatIop*100	69	69	71	76	76	76	76	77	80	80	80	80	80	80	80	80	80	80	80

Fig. 5. RatIop over time and resources

Using the least square regression method, the plant system parameters estimation is:

$$y(t) = y(t-1) + 0.1*w(t) \qquad (8)$$

5.6 Modeling the Controller

The objectives of our design are:

- The system is stable
- The steady state error is minimized
- The settling time does not exceed a constant value 10
- Maximum overshoot does not exceed a constant value 20%.

Using these objectives, [21] discusses in detail the procedure to calculate the appropriate *Kp* and *Ki* of the model. In our case: Kp=2.75 and Ki=1.65.
So, our controller is modelled as:

$$w(t) = w(t-1) + 4.4*e(t) - 2.75*e(t-1) \qquad (9)$$

We can see that the value "4.4" is approximately the mean value of task resources. If the RatIop is less than the reference, the controller will suggest adding this quantity of resources to begin a pending task. This will accelerate the advancement of the project. The proposed approach will be more efficient if these conditions are met:

- Projects are medium to large (more than 50 tasks).
- Choosing the unit of time the largest possible.
- In the plant model, choosing an ARMA model with greater order.

6 Conclusion and Future Work

This paper has proposed a complete approach, which helps controlling the execution of interoperability improvement projects, based on proved mathematical models (feedback control theory and statistics) in addition to the framework of chen et al and the quantitative metric RatIop. This methodology can be easily generalized to use another framework or metric because it does not depends heavily on them.

The interoperability improvement project has been modelled as a black box system without detailing deeply into the relationship between input (i.e. work effort) and output (RatIop). In future work, our objective is to model the system in more details. On the other hand, the applicability of other branches of control theory, like optimal control, will be studied.

References

1. IEEE: IEEE standard computer dictionary: a compilation of IEEE standard computer glossaries (1990)
2. ATHENA: Advanced Technologies for Interoperability of Heterogeneous Enterprise Networks and their Applications, FP6-2002-IST-1, Integrated Project (2003)
3. INTEROP: Interoperability Research for Networked Enterprises Applications and Software, network of excellence (2003)
4. Chen, D., Daclin, N.: Framework for enterprise interoperability. In: IFAC TC5.3 Workshop EI2N, Bordeaux, France (2006)
5. C4ISR: Architecture Working Group (AWG), Levels of Information Systems Interoperability (LISI) (1998)
6. IDEAS: IDEAS Project Deliverables (WP1-WP7), Public reports (2003), http://www.ideas-roadmap.net (retrieved)
7. EIF: European Interoperability Framework, White Paper, Brussels (2004), http://www.comptia.org
8. Ford, T.C., Colomb, J., Grahamr, S.R., Jacques, D.R.: A survey on interoperability measurement. In: Proceedings of 12th International Command and Control Research and Technology Symposium, Newport, RI (2007)
9. Chen, D., Vallespir, B., Daclin, N.: An approach for enterprise interoperability measurement. In: Proceedings of MoDISE-EUS, France (2008)
10. Elmir, B., Bounabat, B.: A Novel Approach for Periodic Assessment of Business Process Interoperability. IJCSI International Journal of Computer Science Issues 8(4) (2011), ISSN (Online): 1694-0814, http://www.IJCSI.org
11. Guédria, W., Naudet, Y., Chen, D.: Interoperability Maturity Models – Survey and Comparison. In: Meersman, R., Tari, Z., Herrero, P. (eds.) OTM 2008 Workshop. LNCS, vol. 5333, pp. 273–282. Springer, Heidelberg (2008)

12. Michelson, B.: Event-Driven Architecture Overview. Technical Report. Patricia Seybold Group, Boston, USA (2006)
13. Elmir, B., Alrajeh, N.A., Bounabat, B.: Interoperability monitoring for e-government service delivery based on enterprise architecture. In: International Conference on Information Management and Evaluation (ICIME), Toronto, Canada (2011)
14. Williams, T.M.: The contribution of mathematical modelling to the practice of project management. IMA Journal of Management Mathematics 14, 3–30 (2003)
15. Project Management Institute: A Guide to the Project Management Body of Knowledge (PMBOK). Project Management Institute, Upper Darby, PA, US (2000)
16. Gandhi, N., Tilbury, D.M., Diao, Y., Hellerstein, J., Parekh, S.: Mimo control of an apache web server: Modeling and controller design. In: Proceedings of the American Control Conference (2002)
17. Lu, C., Abdelzaher, T., Stankovic, J., Son, S.: A Feedback Control Approach for Guaranteeing Relative Delays in Web Servers. In: IEEE Real-Time Technology and Applications Symposium, Taipei, Taiwan (2001)
18. Gandhi, N., Parekh, S., Hellerstein, J., Tilbury, D.M.: Feedback Control of a Lotus Notes Server: Modeling and Control Design. In: American Control Conference, Arlington, VA, USA (2001)
19. Mascolo, S.: Classical Control Theory for Congestion Avoidance in High-speed Internet. In: Proceedings of the 38th Conference on Decision & Control, Phoenix, Arizona, US (1999)
20. Chiu, D., Jain, R.: Analysis of the Increase and Decrease Algorithms for Congestion Avoidance in Computer Networks. Computer Networks and ISDN Systems 17(1) (1989)
21. Hellerstein, J.L., Diao, Y., Parekh, S., Tilbury, D.M.: Feedback Control of Computing Systems. John Wiley & Sons (2004) ISBN 0-471-26637-X

A Panorama of the Semantic EAI Initiatives and the Adoption of Ontologies by these Initiatives

Julio Cesar Nardi[1, 2], Ricardo de Almeida Falbo[2], and João Paulo A. Almeida[2]

[1] Research Group in Applied Informatics, Informatics Department,
Federal Institute of Espírito Santo, Campus Colatina, Colatina, ES, Brazil
[2] Ontology & Conceptual Modeling Research Group (NEMO), Computer Science Department,
Federal University of Espírito Santo, Campus Goiabeiras, Vitória, ES, Brazil
julionardi@ifes.edu.br, {falbo,jpalmeida}@inf.ufes.br

Abstract. Enterprise Application Integration (EAI) plays an important role by linking heterogeneous applications in order to support business processes within and across organizations. In this context, semantic conflicts often arise and have to be dealt with to ensure successful interoperation. In recent years, many EAI initiatives have aimed at addressing semantic interoperability challenges by employing ontologies in various ways. This paper aims to reveal, through a systematic review method, some aspects associated with semantic EAI initiatives and the adoption of ontologies by them, namely: (i) the business application domains in which these initiatives have been conducted; (ii) the focus of the initiatives regarding integration layers (data, message/service, and process); (iii) the adoption of ontologies by EAI research along the years; and (iv) the characteristics of these ontologies. We provide a panorama of these aspects and identify gaps and trends that may guide further research.

Keywords: enterprise application integration, semantics, ontology, systematic mapping.

1 Introduction

In order to be competitive and face changing economic conditions, enterprises need to be flexible and dynamic, which requires the use of information systems that can work together supporting business processes [1]. In this context, Enterprise Application Integration (EAI) plays an important role for linking separate applications into an integrated system driven by business models and the goals they implement [2].

Challenges in EAI arise, among others, from the fact that heterogeneous enterprise applications employ different data and behavioral models [3], leading to semantic conflicts. These conflicts occur whenever applications are built with different conceptualizations, which can impact the integration of data, messages/services, and processes. Despite many advances in EAI, semantic integration of enterprise applications remains a hard problem [4]. In this context, several approaches for semantic integration have been applied, using a variety of instruments, including domain vocabularies, taxonomies, ontologies, logical formalisms, and rules that specify policies, governance, etc. [3]. Among these approaches, ontologies have been acknowledged as an important means to address semantic EAI [4] [3], namely through promoting integration of different information system layers (data, message/service, and process). In the context of semantic EAI, ontologies have been employed with the purpose of contributing to the establishment of common understanding.

This paper aims to reveal, through a systematic mapping [5], some aspects associated with semantic EAI initiatives and the adoption of ontologies by these initiatives, namely: (i) the business application domains in which the initiatives have been conducted; (ii) the focus of these initiatives regarding integration layers (data, message/service, and process); (iii) the adoption of ontologies by EAI research initiatives along the years; and (iv) the characteristics of the ontologies employed. These aspects are structured in six research questions that are investigated using 128 studies selected and analyzed according to a systematic review method.

This paper is organized as follows: Section 2 presents the main concepts used in this paper and clarify some important terminology regarding integration approaches; Section 3 presents the systematic review method adopted, and describes the main parts of the mapping protocol developed during the planning phase; Section 4 presents the results of the mapping, including the selection process, the classification schemas, and data synthesis; Section 5 discusses the findings and the mapping limitations; Section 6 presents concluding remarks and outlines further investigation.

2 Background

The various works in the literature refer to many aspects of enterprise application integration. In this section, we discuss some of the most salient concepts and terms in this broad area of research, in order to characterize the scope of our investigation and support the definition of the research questions that will be the subject of this work.

First of all, we should note that there are several definitions for the terms "integration" and "interoperability" referring to different or interrelated concepts, and these are often used indistinctively. Since we are interested in "application integration" as well as "application interoperability", we considered both terms in the searching string presented in Section 3, and throughout this paper, we use the term "integration" in a broad sense, involving both integration and interoperability.

Secondly, in the investigated literature, the distinction between intra- and inter-enterprise application integration is often present. Intra-EAI aims at integrating applications in the context of a single enterprise, while inter-EAI (also referred to as B2B integration) supports integration of applications of more than one enterprise, linked, in many cases, by a collaborative process [6]. Considering that most techniques and technologies that make up intra-EAI are also applicable to inter-EAI [6], we are interested in both intra- and inter-enterprise application integration and use "enterprise application integration" to refer to both.

Integration can concern one or several information system layers [3], such as: data layer, message/service layer, the process layer. Data layer integration concerns with moving or federating data between multiple databases, bypassing the application logic and manipulating data directly in the databases. Message/service layer integration addresses message exchange between information systems, which can occur in any tier, such as user interface, application logic or even in the data tier. Process layer integration, commonly referred to as Business Process Integration, views the enterprise as a set of interrelated processes, being responsible for handling message flows, implementing rules and defining the overall coordination of the execution.

Ontologies have been acknowledged as an important means for achieving semantic EAI [4] [3], since they aim at providing formal specifications of shared conceptualizations. Considering their level of generality, ontologies continuously range from top-level ontologies, through domain ontologies to application ontologies. Top-level ontologies (so-called foundational ontologies) describe very general concepts like space, time, object, event, etc., and are independent of particular domains or problems [7]. Domain ontologies describe concepts related to a generic domain, sometimes specializing concepts of a top-level ontology. Application ontologies, in turn, describe concepts related to a particular application [7]. Since these kinds of ontologies form a continuum, the borderline between them is not clearly defined. Thus, in this paper, we distinguish only between top-level ontologies - those developed considering theories of Formal Ontology and related areas, e.g. DOLCE (Descriptive Ontology for Linguistic and Cognitive Engineering) and SUMO (Suggested Upper Merged Ontology) - and the rest (including various levels of generality usually referred as domain or application ontologies).

Finally, due to the potential of ontologies as a means to address semantic aspects, in last decades, many ontology implementation languages have been developed and many knowledge representation languages have been used for building ontologies, even they were not initially developed for this purpose [8]. So, it is important to know how ontologies have been designed and implemented in order to understand how appropriate these representations are for semantic EAI. In this context, we can cite knowledge representation languages such as first-order logic, frames and description logic. Based on them, there are some ontology languages, such as [8]: FLogic (Frame Logic), RDF (Resource Description Framework), and OWL (Web Ontology Language). Beyond these languages, ontologies are also developed using technologies associated to service description, such as OWL-S (OWL-based web service ontology) and WSMO (Web Service Modeling Ontology).

3   The Review Method and the Mapping Protocol (Planning)

This *systematic mapping* was conducted taking as basis the method for systematic literature reviews given in [5]. This method is known for its suitability for PhD studies, which is the context of this research, and the research group has expertise on it, although some limitations are known [5].

According to [5], a systematic mapping is a kind of secondary study, which offers a broad view of primary studies in a specific topic in order to identify available evidences. Thus, a *secondary study* is a study that reviews primary studies related to a set of specific research questions with the aim of integrating/synthesizing the evidences related to these research questions. The *primary study* is an empirical study investigating a specific research question.

A systematic mapping involves three phases [5]: Planning, Conducting and Reporting the mapping. *Planning* involves the pre-mapping activities, and encompasses the definition of the following items: research questions, inclusion and exclusion criteria, sources of studies, search string, and mapping procedures. These items compose the mapping protocol. *Conducting* the mapping is concerned with searching and selecting the studies, and extracting and synthesizing data from them. *Reporting* is the final phase and involves writing up the results and circulating them to potentially interested parties.

The mapping protocol is an important artifact in the review process. It is produced during the Planning phase and consumed during the other phases. The main parts of the mapping protocol used by this work are described as follows.

Research Questions. This mapping aims at answering the following research questions, considering the context of semantic EAI initiatives:

RQ1. What are the business application domains addressed?

RQ2. What is the distribution of studies according to the integration layers (data, message/service, and process layers)?

RQ3. Over the years, how wide has been the adoption of ontologies?

RQ4. What is the distribution of studies that use ontologies per integration layer?

RQ5. What kinds of ontologies (considering their generality level) have been used?

RQ6. Which languages/formalisms have been used to create the ontologies?

Inclusion and Exclusion Criteria. The primary studies selection was based on the following criteria, which were organized in one inclusion criterion (IC) and four exclusion criteria (EC). The inclusion criterion is: (IC1) The study addresses enterprise application integration under a semantic perspective. The exclusion criteria are: (EC1) The study is not written in English; (EC2) The study is an older version (less updated) of another study already considered; (EC3) The study is not a primary study (which excludes short papers, editorials, and summaries of keynotes, workshops, and tutorials); (EC4) The study is just published as an abstract.

Sources. We used automatic search to collect the studies. The search was applied in seven electronic databases that were defined based on systematic reviews in the Software Engineering area. The sources are: IEEE Xplore (http://ieeexplore.ieee.org), ACM Digital Library (http://dl.acm.org), SpringerLink (http://www.springerlink.com), Thomson Reuters Web of Knowledge (http://www.isiknowledge.com), Scopus (http://www.scopus.com), Science Direct (http://www.sciencedirect.com), Compendex (http://www.engineeringvillage2.org).

Search String. In order to define the search string, we used two groups of terms that were joined in a conjunction with the "AND" operator. The first group includes terms that aim to capture studies related to "integration" or "interoperability" of enterprise software applications. The second group aims at capturing studies that deal with semantic aspects. Within each of the groups, the "OR" operator was used to allow for synonyms. The search string, as follows, was applied in three metadata fields (title, keywords and abstract) and suffered syntactical adaptations according to particularities of each source:

("application integration" OR "application interoperability" OR "enterprise system integration" OR "enterprise system interoperability" OR "integration of information system"

OR *"interoperability of information system"* OR *"integration of application"* OR *"interoperability of application"* OR *"interoperability of enterprise application"* OR *"interoperability of enterprise system"* OR *"integration of enterprise application"* OR *"integration of enterprise system"* OR *"interoperability of business application"* OR *"interoperability of business system"* OR *"integration of business application"* OR *"integration of business system"* OR *"integration of heterogeneous system"* OR *"integration of heterogeneous application"* OR *"interoperability of heterogeneous system"* OR *"interoperability of heterogeneous application"* OR *"interoperability of information system"* OR *"integrated application"* OR *"interoperable application"* OR *"integrated enterprise system"* OR *"interoperable enterprise system"* OR *"information system integration"* OR *"information system interoperability"* OR *"enterprise system integration"* OR *"enterprise system interoperability"* OR *"business system integration"* OR *"business system interoperability"*) AND (*semantic* OR *semantics* OR *semantically*)

Mapping Procedures (Assessments). Before conducting the mapping, we performed a pilot test of the mapping protocol over a sample consisting of 35% of the studies, which was used to evolve the components of the protocol. Considering that the review process was conducted by one of the authors, an activity of validation was carried out by a second author using a different sample of 35% of the studies. Possible biases were discussed in periodic meetings.

4 Conducting the Mapping

This section describes the main steps that were performed in the mapping, including: search and selection, data extraction and data synthesis.

4.1 Search and Selection

The search process was conducted in the beginning of 2012, and, therefore, we looked for studies published until December 31th 2011. As a result, a total of 702 records were retrieved: 107 from IEEE Xplore, 16 from Science Direct, 17 from ACM Digital Library, 56 from Thomson Reuters Web of Knowledge, 232 from Scopus, 218 from Compendex, and 56 from SpringerLink.

After the search process, the selection process was conducted progressively in five stages. In the first stage, we have eliminated duplicated studies by examining titles and abstracts. In this stage, we had the highest reduction (almost 60%), since many studies are available in more than one source. In the second stage, we have applied the inclusion and exclusion criteria considering title and abstract only (resulting in a reduction of 15.5%). Although we have used language filter mechanisms on the source's search engines, some studies not written in English have been retrieved. Thus, we have also applied EC1 criteria in this stage. The resulting set of studies was refined in a third stage, which also considered the whole text (resulting in a reduction of 44.8%). After preliminary analysis, we noticed that only three studies published before 2001 remained in the end of the third stage (one published in 1993 and two published in 1995). Indeed, they did not characterized representative points of our sample, thus, in the fourth stage, we have eliminated these three studies and defined the lower boundary date as January 1st 2001. In the fifth stage we eliminated the fours studies for which we had no access to the full text.

Table 1 summarizes the stages and their results, showing the progressive reduction of the number of studies throughout the selection process (from 702 to 128 studies, with a reduction rate of about 81.7%).

Table 1. Results of the selection process stages

Stage	Criteria	Analyzed Content	Initial N. of Studies	Final N. of Studies	Reduction per stage (%)
1st Stage	Eliminating duplications	Title and abstract	702	290	58.6%
2nd Stage	IC1, EC1, EC2, EC3 and EC4	Title and abstract	290	245	15.5%
3rd Stage	IC1, EC2, EC3 and EC4	Whole text	245	135	44.8%
4th Stage	Studies published before 2001	---	135	132	2.2%
5th Stage	Studies not accessed	---	132	128	3.0%

4.2 Classification Schema and Data Extraction

Before data extraction, we defined categories for classifying the studies according to the research questions, as follows.

Classification Schema Concerning Integration Focus. This schema is based on [3] and encompasses three categories: Integration at data layer, Integration at message/service layer, and Integration at process layer. So, depending on the focus of the integration approach, the study is classified as one of these layers or any combination of them.

Classification Schema for Kinds of Ontology. This schema encompasses two categories: Top-level ontology and Low-level ontology. According to the generality level of the ontologies, discussed in Section 2, a study is classified as using a Top-level ontology if a foundational ontology is used. On other hand, a study is classified as using a Low-level ontology, if a domain or application ontology is used. A study can be classified in both categories if it employs both top- and low-level ontologies.

Other Classification Schemes. Concerning the categories for business application domains and ontology languages, we collected unstructured data without a pre-defined classification (the categories were only defined during data analysis), in order to deal with the large variety of possibilities. In order to collect data about business application domains, we looked for use cases, examples used for describing the proposed solutions, domains that motivated research initiatives, and so on. Regarding ontology languages, we looked for the formalisms used to represent ontologies, such as OWL, OWL-S, first-order logic, among others. After that, during data synthesis, we analyzed the content and defined the categories. This process was iterative, and the resulting categories were evaluated in periodic meetings. This process involved five steps: (1) analyzing content; (2) defining categories; (3) evaluating categories; (4) classifying studies; and (5) evaluating the classification schema.

The data extraction process consisted in analyzing and collecting data of each selected study, and organizing them in a data collection form, shown in Table 2.

Table 2. Data collection form

Field	Description	Classification schema
ID	Unique identifier	Not applicable
Bibliographic reference	Authors, title, conference or journal, and publication year	Not applicable
Business application domain(s)	Business application domains where study was applied	Not defined a priori
Integration focus	The integration layer(s) which is(are) the focus of the study	[Integration at data layer, Integration at message/service layer, or Integration at process layer]
Kind(s) of ontologies	Kind(s) of ontologies used in the study	[Top-level ontologies, or Low-level ontologies]
Ontology language(s)	Languages/formalisms used to implement/create ontologies	Not defined a priori

4.3 Data Synthesis and Results

Semantic EAI Efforts over the Years. In order to offer a general view about the efforts in semantic EAI area, we present in Fig. 1, a distribution of the selected studies (128) per published year. We can note a growth in the number of published studies from 2001 to 2008, which is characterized by two moments of relative stabilization: from 2001 to 2003, and from 2004 to 2006. After 2008, when we have observed the largest number of published studies, the number of studies decreased until 2010 and remained stable in 2011.

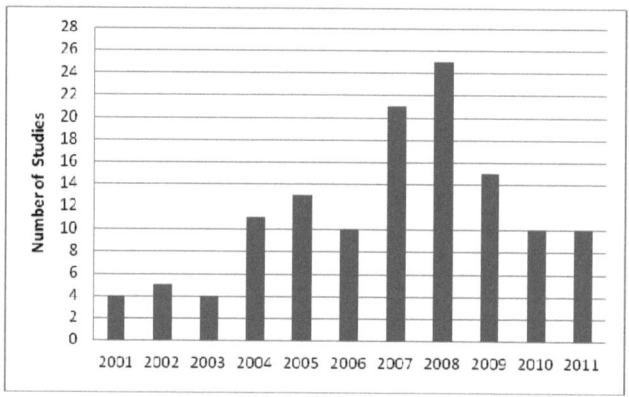

Fig. 1. Distribution of the selected studies over the years

Business Application Domains in Semantic EAI (RQ1). Considering the business application domains in which semantic EAI initiatives were applied, we identified that about 76.6% of the studies presented their solution approaches in the context of specific business application domains. The other 23.4% of the studies were classified as "General", since they just make reference to generic scenarios like "business-to-business", "e-commerce", "business", etc. Considering the approaches that were developed in the context of specific application domains, we have identified 19 categories of business application domains, which are presented in Fig. 2 together with the percentage of studies per category. The "Other" category was introduced to group business application domains that had no representative occurrence (only one paper), such as: Aerospace, Importing and Exporting, Content Publishing, Video Mail System and Software Engineering.

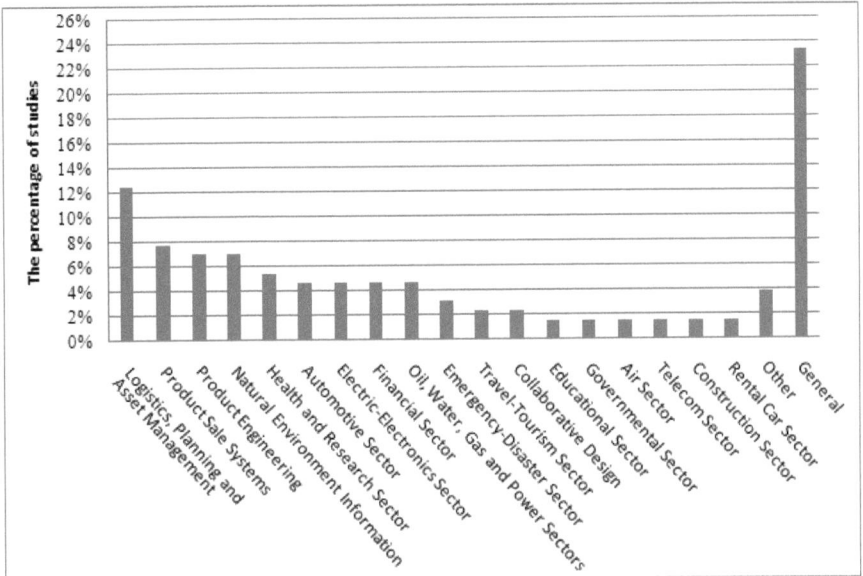

Fig. 2. The percentage of the selected studies per business application domains

Considering the distribution of studies per specific business application domain, we can notice that the "Logistics, Planning and Asset Management" domain has the largest representativeness (12.5%). It stands out, mainly because it involves supply chain initiatives, being characterized by intensive interaction between suppliers and consumers. Besides that, business application domains with representativeness between 7.8% to 5.5% include: "Product Sale Systems" (purchase order in general, and online shopping), "Product Engineering" (industrial automation technology, which requires integration and management of product life-cycle), "Natural Environment Information" (initiatives about geographic location, geographic information systems, meteorological and oceanographic information), and "Health and Research Sector" (pharmaceutical industry, health care, bio-informatics and research organizations). The other categories, although with smaller percentage of studies, still represent important numbers, if we consider that almost 23.4% of the selected studies do not make reference to any specific application domain (General).

Focus on the Integration Layers (RQ2). The studies were classified as promoting semantic EAI on data layer, message/service layer, process layer, or any combination of them. The Fig. 3 presents the percentage of studies per integration layer.

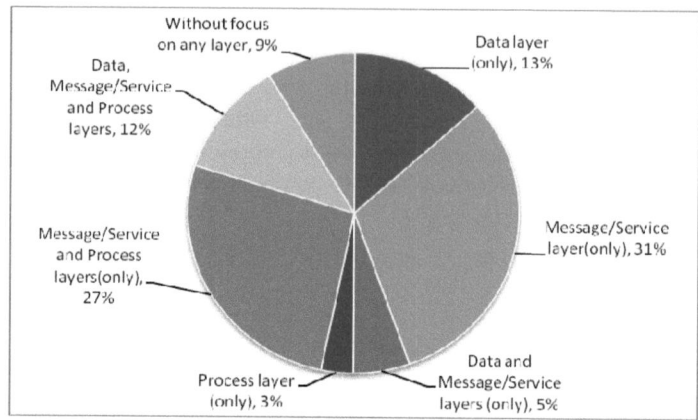

Fig. 3. Distribution of the selected studies per the focus on the integration layers

Some studies focus only on one layer: data layer (13%), message/service layer (31%), and process layer (3%). Others propose integration solutions by addressing two integration layers: data and message/service layers (5%), and message/service and process layers (27%). And, finally, there are studies that address the three layers: data, message/service and process layers (12%). Finally, when considered in isolation or when considered in tandem with other layers, the data layer is addressed by 30% of the studies, the message/service layer is addressed by 75% of studies, and process layer by 42% of them (again either solely or in tandem with other layers).

The studies that address data and message/service layers together are characterized by approaches that define data source integration solutions besides considering direct interactions (by message, service, etc.) among applications. The studies that address message/service layer together with process layer presents initiatives related to service orchestration, workflow definition, as well as business process-driven enterprise application integration initiatives. In this way, the studies that establish integration on data, message/service, and process layers together are characterized by proposing architectures, frameworks and integration approaches related to business process-driven enterprise application integration. The proposed solutions range from data source integration to application interaction driven by business processes. In this context, it is important to remark that no study focused on data and process layers without considering the message/service layer, which reflects the mediation role that the message/service layer plays.

During data extraction phase, we noted that some studies presented generic approaches, which did not make commitments to any integration layer, being classified as "Without focus on any layer" (9%). These studies are characterized by proposing conceptual or generic solutions, like reference models, standards, and metamodels, as well as technical guidance and recommendations, methodologies and life-cycle models, without focusing on any specific integration layer.

Ontologies in Semantic EAI: Adoption over the years (RQ3, RQ4), Kinds (RQ5), and Languages/Formalisms (RQ6). The adoption of ontologies in order to promote semantic EAI has grown over the years, as we can see in Fig. 4. The period from 2001

to 2003 reflects the initial phase of adoption, when the number of studies that did not use ontologies was greater or equal than the number of studies that used ontologies. From 2004, on the other hand, and, mainly, from 2007, the use of ontology became the principal means to promote semantic EAI, achieving more than 70% of the studies. Also, the set of all studies that use ontology represents about 71.8% of all the selected studies, indicating a high level of adoption. Petri nets, UML (Unified Modeling Language) models, standards for data exchange, formal languages for event composition, concept hierarchy, etc., were some of the other techniques used for addressing semantics in EAI. These techniques were used in the 28.2% studies that did not use ontologies, although some have appeared in studies that used ontologies.

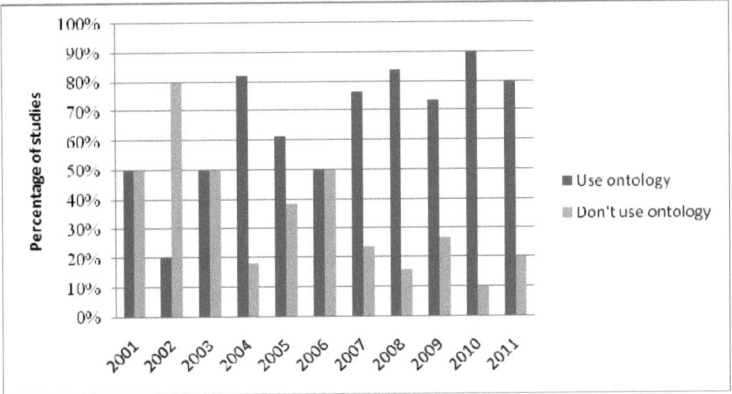

Fig. 4. Adoption of ontologies in semantic EAI along the years

Table 3 presents the percentage of studies that use ontologies per integration layer, and the numbers reflect some equivalence. However, we have two exceptions: (i) none (0%) of the studies that focus only on Process layer uses ontology; and (ii) there is a balance regarding the use of ontologies in studies that do not focus on any layer.

Table 3. Percentage of studies that use ontology per integration layers

Integration layer	Studies that use ontology (%)
Data layer (only)	71%
Message/Service layer (only)	75%
Process layer (only)	0%
Data and Message/Service layers	86%
Message/Service and Process layers	76%
Data, Message/Service, and Process layers	87%
Without focus on any layer	45%

Besides analyzing the adoption of ontologies along the years, we aimed at identifying the kinds of ontologies that have been used. We identified 5 studies that use Top-level ontologies, which represent 5.4% of the studies that use ontologies. Table 4 presents these studies and the respective top-level ontologies they use.

Table 4. Studies that use top-level ontologies

Study	Publication year	Top-layer ontology
[9]	2006	PSL (Process Specification Language) Ontology
[10]	2007	DOLCE – SUMO alignment
[11]	2007	DOLCE – SUMO alignment
[12]	2010	DOLCE
[13]	2011	DOLCE

The various studies claim to represent ontologies using a variety of formalisms and techniques, ranging from Semantic Web languages to more simplistic data representation techniques. Based on this aspect, we identified ten categories: "OWL", "RDF and RDFS", "XML", "OIL, DAML and DAML+OIL", "OWL-S", "WSMO", "Knowledge Representation", "Own language", "Other", and "None".

The first six categories refer directly to a specific technology. The "Knowledge Representation" category represents languages or formalisms associated to knowledge representation languages (Description logic, First-order logic, Frames, etc.) and graphical representations such as UML and Conceptual Maps, among others. The "Own language" category represents languages or formalisms that were proposed in the context of the corresponding work itself. The "Other" category groups technologies that did not appear in a representative number (three studies or less), including KIF, F-Logic, OCML, Common Lisp, Relational database schema and RDF4S. The "None" category groups studies that only propose the use of ontologies, but do not make commitment to any specific language/formalism. The Fig. 5 presents the percentage of studies per category (a study can fit in more than one category).

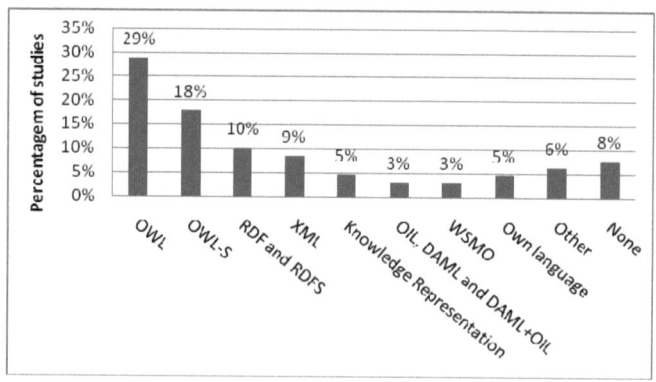

Fig. 5. The percentage of studies per category of ontology languages

We can notice a trend in using Semantic Web technologies, mainly OWL (29%), OWL-S (18%), and RDF/RDF-S (10%). Concerning ontology-based languages for service description, OWL-S (18%) and WSMO (3%) stand out. Despite that WSMO can be used in association with OWL, the largest number of studies used OWL-S instead of WSMO due to a closer relation between OWL and OWL-S.

The other categories do not represent, individually, a high number of studies. However they reflect a diversity of ontology representation languages used in the semantic EAI initiatives. It is worthwhile to point out that 8% of the studies do not address any aspect of formalization/implementation, i.e., they just suggest the use of ontologies by proposing general architectures, life-cycle models, guidelines, etc.

5 Discussion

Based on results presented in the previous section, in this section, we discuss some important findings and limitations of this mapping.

Semantic EAI Efforts over the Years. We consider that the distribution of studies along the years reflects the research efforts in semantic EAI, which suffer influence of the adoption of semantic technologies, mainly ontologies. In our view, the chart shown in Fig. 1 can be analyzed roughly according to the Gartner Hype Cycles [14]. The period between 2001 and 2003 corresponds to the "Technology Trigger" phase. The year of 2008 corresponds to the "Peak of Inflated Expectations". The years of 2009 and 2010 correspond to the "Trough of Disillusionment". The lack of change from 2010 to 2011 suggests that we are aimed towards the remaining phases: "Slope of Enlightenment" and "Plateau of Productivity".

Business Application Domains in Semantic EAI. The identified diversity of business application domains reflects the coverage of the EAI research area, and, therefore, its relevance. Moreover, we notice that, although traditional business application domains are still the most exploited, EAI initiatives span several niche application domains although in lower rate, characterizing a Long Tail-like [15] distribution (cf. Fig. 2). The domain of "Logistics, Planning and Asset Management" has had the largest representativeness, possibly due to the focus on integration that drives this kind of business, which is founded on interoperation in supply chains.

Focus on the Integration Layers. We have observed a predominant number of studies addressing the message/service layer. We believe that this can be justified by the role that functionalities (represented by the message/service layer) play in order to promote the link between data sources and business processes, and the increasing interest in service-oriented architectures in the past decade. We have observed that many of the integration solutions at the message/service layer also consider process technology, which has been seen as a clear trend in EAI. Furthermore, we have observed a low number of studies that focus only on the process layer (3%), suggesting that process layer integration depends on message/service layer integration. Moreover, a considerable number of studies (44%) focus on more than one layer, indicating that integration initiatives have established relations between integration layers to achieve interoperability.

Ontologies in Semantic EAI. We have observed that, in the past decade ontologies have become predominant in the semantic approaches to EAI. Ontologies have been used by the solution approaches in order to achieve integration through the various integration layers (data, message/service and process). Regarding the languages and formalisms used to build ontologies in the context of EAI initiatives, we have observed a predominance of Semantic Web languages, leading to ontologies which should be characterized as lightweight ontologies [16]. We have also noted that a number of *data representation techniques* have been referred to by the studies as ontology representation techniques, indicating a rather permissive use of the term ontology in the literature and a wide variation in what is considered an ontology. Considering the kinds ontologies employed, we can conclude that the use of top-level ontologies in EAI initiatives is relatively underexplored. Nevertheless, these ontologies have gained some attention in the latest years (see Table 4).

Limitations of This Mapping. Due to the fact that some stages were performed by only one of the authors, some subjectivity may have been introduced. To reduce this subjectivity, a second author was responsible for defining a random sample (about 35% of the studies) and performing the same stages. The results of each reviewer were then compared in order to detect possible bias. Moreover, terminological problems in the search strings may have led to missing some primary studies. Thus, we performed simulations in the selected databases and included a large number of synonyms in the search string. We decided not to search specific (non-indexed) conference proceedings, journals, or the grey literature (technical reports and works in progress), having worked with studies indexed by the selected electronic databases only. The exclusion of these other sources makes the mapping more repeatable, but with the consequence that we cannot rule out that some valuable studies may have been excluded from our analysis. Finally, the classification of studies regarding their focus on data, message/service and process layers is not straightforward, due to variety of possible approaches and irregularity of use of terminology in the literature. For achieving a more consistent analysis, some studies classifications were discussed in meetings. Thus, we cannot ensure that the results concerning the layers are fully repeatable, due to some level of subjectivity in this classification.

6 Conclusions

This paper presented a systematic mapping in the context of semantic EAI. Six research questions were defined and addressed investigating the following aspects: (i) business application domains in semantic EAI initiatives; (ii) focus on the various integration layers; and (iii) the adoption of ontologies in semantic EAI.

The contributions of this work are on making evident some aspects associated to semantic EAI research efforts that can drive future research. In this context, we highlight the following conclusions: (i) Most studies in semantic EAI (75%) address message/service layer integration; (ii) Ontologies have became predominant in semantic approaches to EAI; (iii) Semantic Web technologies have been widely adopted by semantic EAI efforts (with OWL being the most common language for ontology representation in the sampled studies); and (iv) The use of top-level (foundational) ontologies, although not expressive yet, has emerged as a new trend in the second half of the period investigated.

As future work, we plan to perform deepen our analysis on the use of ontologies in semantic EAI. In particular, we intend to explore how ontologies have been used in semantic EAI, focusing on the role of ontologies in the integration approach. Further, we intend to investigate how the languages/formalisms used to represent ontologies influence the integration solutions.

Acknowledgments. This research is funded by the Brazilian Research Funding Agencies FAPES (Grant 52272362/11), CNPq (Grants 483383/2010-4 and 310634/2011-3) and PRONEX (Grant 52272362/2011).

References

1. Vernadat, F.B.: Interoperable enterprise systems: Principles, concepts, and methods. Annual Reviews in Control 31, 137–145 (2007)
2. Gacitua-Decar, V., Pahl, C.: Ontology-based Patterns for the Integration of Business Processes and Enterprise Application Architectures. In: Mentzas, G., et al. (eds.) Semantic Enterprise Application Integration for Business Processes: Service-Oriented Frameworks. IGI Pub. (2009)
3. Izza, S.: Integration of industrial information systems: from syntactic to semantic integration approaches. Enterprise Information Systems 3, 1–57 (2009)
4. Bussler, C.: The Role of Semantic Web Technology in Enterprise Application Integration. IEEE Bulletin of the Technical Committee on Data Engineering 26, 62–68 (2003)
5. Kitchenham, B., Charters, S.: Guidelines for performing Systematic Literature Reviews in Software Engineering (Version 2.3) - EBSE Technical Report. EBSE-2007-01 (2007)
6. Endrei, M., Alari, G., Ambati, A., Krogdahl, P., Martin, C.: Patterns: Serial Process Flows for Intra- and Inter-enterprise. IBM Redbooks (2004)
7. Guarino, N.: Formal Ontology and Information Systems. Formal Ontology and Information Systems, 3 (1998)
8. Gòmez-Pérez, A., Fernández-López, M., Corcho, O.: Ontological Engineering: with examples from the areas of Knowledge Management, e-Commerce and the Semantic Web. Springer (2004)
9. Martín-Recuerda, F.: Application Integration Using Conceptual Spaces (CSpaces). In: Mizoguchi, R., Shi, Z.-Z., Giunchiglia, F. (eds.) ASWC 2006. LNCS, vol. 4185, pp. 234–248. Springer, Heidelberg (2006)
10. Alazeib, A., Balogh, A., Bauer, M., Bouras, A., Friesen, A., Gouvas, P., Mentzas, G., Pace, A.: Towards semantically-assisted design of collaborative business processes in EAI scenarios. In: 5th IEEE International Conference on Industrial Informatics, Vienna-Austria, pp. 779–784 (2007)
11. Bouras, A., Gouvas, P., Kourtesis, D., Mentzas, G.: Semantic Integration of Business Applications Across Collaborative Value Networks. In: Camarinha-Matos, L.M., Afsarmanesh, H., Novais, P., Analide, C. (eds.) Establishing the Foundation of Collaborative Networks. IFIP, vol. 243, pp. 539–546. Springer, Boston (2007)
12. Paulheim, H., Probst, F.: Application integration on the user interface level: An ontology-based approach. Data & Knowledge Engineering 69, 1103–1116 (2010)
13. Treiblmayr, M., Scheider, S., Krüger, A., Von der Linden, M.: Integrating GI with non-GI services – showcasing interoperability in a heterogeneous service-oriented architecture. GeoInformatica 16, 207–220 (2011)
14. Gartner Hype Cycles, http://www.gartner.com/technology/research/methodologies/hype-cycle.jsp
15. Levine, D.M., Stephan, D., Krehbiel, T.C., Berenson, M.L.: Statistics for Managers using Microsoft Excel. Prentice Hall (2002)
16. Guizzardi, G.: On Ontology, ontologies, Conceptualizations, Modeling Languages, and (Meta)Models. In: Vasilecas, O., Edler, J., Caplinskas, A. (eds.) Frontiers in Artificial Intelligence and Applications, Databases and Information Systems IV, pp. 18–39. IOS Press, Amsterdã (2007)

Using Metamodels and Ontologies for Enterprise Model Reconciliation

Sabina El Haoum and Axel Hahn

University of Oldenburg, Germany
{elhaoum,hahn}@wi-ol.de

Abstract. Modeling the enterprise from different views, at different levels of abstraction, and in different modeling languages yields a variety of models. Oftentimes the models referring to the same subject exist independently of each other and their semantic relations are hard to discover or to analyze. This fact hinders the effective exploitation of enterprise models for the purpose of integration and interoperability. The method proposed in this paper is based on semantic annotations and aims for the externalization and machine readability of the model contained information. This assures the accessibility for further automatic processing and facilitates the discovery and analysis of inter-model relations.

Keywords: enterprise modeling, semantic annotation, model reconciliation, inter-model relations.

1 Introduction

In today's economy enterprises operate in a fast changing environment and their competitiveness heavily depends on their ability to quickly respond to these changes in an adequate manner.

In this context, decision makers use enterprise models as a means to master this complexity. Depending on the focus in a particular case, models allow to take a certain view and abstraction on the enterprise and concentrate on the goals, processes, structures, competencies, etc. Further, particular models can be broken down into more detailed sub-models. Overall, this yields a "collection of more or less interrelated, special-purpose models" [1]. In contrast to modeling activities known from the field of operations research, business process (re-)engineering, organizational design etc., enterprise modeling accounts for the "need to focus on enterprises as a whole, or at least on a larger set of interacting components, within organization – taking a more 'total systems' approach" [2]. According to [3] the main motivations for enterprise modeling are:

- The possibility to analyze the enterprise, in order to gain a better understanding and to enable the management of system complexity.
- Explicit documentation of enterprise knowledge (know-what, know-how, and know-why).

- Improved change management and the possibility to apply enterprise engineering methods.
- Enterprise integration and interoperability.

Specifically the integration potential lying in enterprise modeling is examined in several works including [3],[4],[5]. Fig. 1 illustrates possible axes of model-based system integration within enterprises:

- *Enterprise Hierarchy*: From management to production. This integration direction is sometimes referred to as "vertical integration" [1].
- *Value Chain*: From procurement to distribution. This integration direction is sometimes denoted "horizontal integration" [1].
- *Product Life Cycle*: From product development to support.

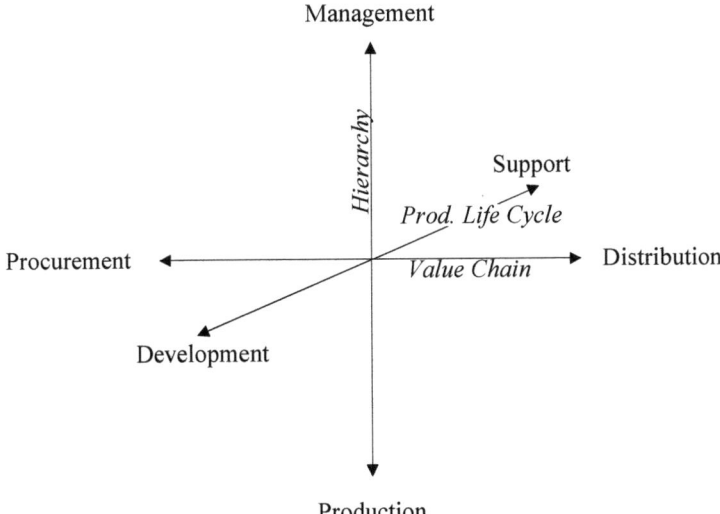

Fig. 1. Possible axes of integration within enterprises, adapted from [5]

The labeled endpoints of each axis denote just the two extremes of the integration dimension. E.g. in the case of integration along the product life cycle axis, models from the product development, design, production and support are involved.

Further, enterprise models play an important role with respect to achieving interoperability in and between enterprises. Interoperability problems are concerned with different dimensions (data, service, process, business [6], [7]) and have to be addressed at different levels of the enterprise (business, knowledge, ICT systems [8]). Considering these characteristics of interoperability problems, Ralyté et al. emphasize that they cannot be isolated to a particular level. Rather, it is required to take a holistic perspective and handle all aspects [9]. In this context, enterprise models are an important enabler.

The remainder of the paper is organized as follows: Section 2 is dedicated to the problem statement. It sheds light on some factors limiting the exploitation of the integration and interoperability potential of enterprise models. Section 3 describes the related work. The proposed solution is presented in section 4, where first high level requirements are formulated, followed by the proposed line of action and the benefits which the authors expect from its implementation. Section 5 contains a conclusion and an outlook.

2 Problem Statement

In practice, the potential of enterprise modeling oftentimes cannot be fully exploited. Some limiting factors are:

- **Different Views:** Enterprise models come in a variety of models. E.g. *product models* specifying the characteristics of products, *organizational diagrams* dealing with the organizational structure of the enterprise, *process models* dedicated to the activities carried out in the enterprise, to list just a few. Each of these models takes a specific view on the enterprise or some part of it focusing on a certain aspect (e.g. products, organizational structure, processes). As the views reflect the same system from a different angle a certain degree of overlap is unavoidable. In order to maintain a coherent view of the whole system it is crucial to reveal the relations between the overlapping models [10].
- **Different Levels of Abstraction:** Enterprise modeling can take place in a top-down manner. The starting point then is some high-level perspective on the whole system, which by means of decomposition gradually is broken down to more detailed information about parts of the system. Alternatively, it is possible to proceed in a bottom-up mode, where "isolated and limited data are collected and then their relationships are mined before the whole system structure can be formed" [5].
- **Different Project Stages:** Enterprise models are used in different project stages to represent: (a) analysis, (b) design, and (c) implementation. Accordingly, on can distinguish (a) as-is models, (b) to-be models, and (c) implementation models [11].
- **Different Modeling Languages:** Enterprise models can be expressed in terms of various modeling languages. Some modeling languages are specific to a certain view, in the context of enterprises e.g. Petri Nets can be used to represent business processes, but are rather unsuitable for modeling the structure of the organization. Other modeling languages offer different diagram types to enable the modeling of different aspects (e.g. UML activity diagrams, class diagrams[1] etc. or the various IDEF diagram types[2]). The existing relations between models referring to the same subject of modeling but expressed by means of different modeling languages oftentimes remain unrevealed.

---

[1] http://www.omg.org/spec/UML/
[2] http://www.idef.com/

- **Informal Modeling Languages:** Studies of the modeling practice in Australian enterprises found Entity Relationship (ER) diagrams, flowcharts and UML based models to be the most frequently used modeling techniques [12]. A similar picture emerges in German enterprises, where ER diagrams, UML, and Event-driven Process Chains are most widely used [13]. These modeling techniques are popular as they come with graphical notations but their downside is that they are not suited for the application of formal analysis methods. This shortcoming has been described in the literature [10], [14].
- **Differences in Terminology:** The enterprise models make use of natural language to label model elements. Different modelers may use different terms in their models even when they describe the same (part of a) system. Depending on the modeler, his background, his position in the enterprise etc. different terminology flows into enterprise models and results in terminological mismatches.

All above mentioned aspects cause a situation of poor model integration and limited interoperability. In an ideal setting, a unified enterprise modeling approach would constitute the solution to this problem. There exist various Enterprise Architecture frameworks supporting unified enterprise modeling (see [10] for a survey). However, in practice greenfield projects are seldom and enterprises facing reorganization projects or undergoing mergers and acquisitions have to deal with legacy systems [15]. What is required is a means to externalize the inter-model relations in order to overcome the modeling islands built around specific modeling languages, views etc. The authors argue that the approach presented in the paper at hand helps in this situation as it offers a method to deal with diverse models. It allows establishing semantic annotations and therefore facilitates the application of advanced analysis methods.

3 Related Work

In recent years Semantic Web methods as a means to achieve model-based integration have been discussed in various works. Liao et al. [16], [17] describe semantic annotation of models for the purpose of information systems interoperability. Bräuer and Lochmann [18], [19] investigate the use of semantic technologies in model-driven software development with multiple domain-specific languages. In their work, Agt et al. [20] consider the semantic conflict analysis of different models at different abstraction levels of the Model Driven Architecture approach.

Several works are dedicated specifically to the semantic enrichment of business process models. The work of Fellmann et al. [21] examines the semantic constraint checking in process models. Missikoff et al. also focus on business process models. They use the BPAL (Business Process Abstract Language) to achieve a formal representation of the business semantics in a Business Process Knowledge Base. Born et al. [22] consider in their approach the semantic enrichment of Business Process Modeling Notation (BPMN) models. Lin et al. [23] propose a Process Semantic Annotation

Model, which based on a metamodel annotation links content and goal annotation to the represented process.

The authors of [24] and [25] turn their attention to interoperability of enterprise models for the purpose of model exchange. They formulate the need for effective support of the semantic annotation process. The Astar (respectively A*) annotation tool [26] represents one prototype tool for semantic annotation. In the work of Fill [27] a semantic model annotation language is proposed.

Integration of enterprise models can also be based upon their metamodels [28]. In [29] an object oriented metamodel is used as integration foundation for heterogeneous modeling languages. However, the domain semantics aspect is not included in this type of work.

A further line of related research is the field of model comparison. E.g. in the work of Gerke et al. [30] the compliance of process models with reference models is examined. They identify the difficulty to overcome different levels of detail in the models to be compared.

4 Combining Metamodels and Ontologies for Model Reconciliation

The proposed solution aims for a comprehensive externalization of the information contained in enterprise models. To realize this, a combination of metamodeling and domain ontologies is used. The metamodel is the model of the modeling language itself, it defines a set of modeling artifacts and the valid usage of these artifacts [31]. Domain ontologies are machine readable representations of the concepts in the application domain and the relations among those concepts [32]. In order to externalize the information of a particular model:

- The model is expressed in terms of an ontological representation of the related metamodel.
- The model is semantically annotated [25], i.e. linked to concepts in a domain ontology.

In the literature the combination of metamodel information and semantic annotation linking the model to concepts of domain ontology has been presented as a method to cope with the various kinds of information contained in a conceptual model [28].

1. Modeling artifacts: Which modeling artifacts are used?
2. Model structure: How are the artifacts arranged?
3. Domain semantics: Which application domain terms are used to label the artifacts?

Fig. 2 illustrates the idea by means of a simple example. The model under consideration may be a fragment of an Entity Relationship (ER) model belonging to a campus management system in the university domain. In the graphical representation of the ontology the solid arrows symbolize a subclass relation whereas the dashed lines indicate an object property. The arcs pointing from the ER diagram to the Metamodel Ontology on the left hand side and to the Domain Ontology on the right hand side indicate the semantic links (i.e. annotations) being established to explicitly record the information contained in the model.

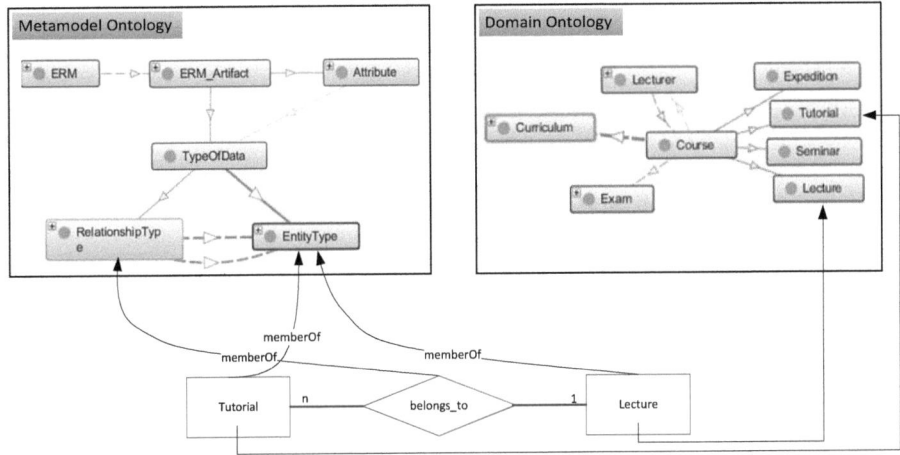

Fig. 2. Comprehensive model externalization using metamodel and domain ontology

In the example in the figure, the Metamodel Ontology holds a description of the main concepts in the ER metamodel. Describing the model in terms of this Metamodel Ontology makes it possible to store the information about *modeling artifacts* being used (namely EntityType and RelationshipType). These annotations are shown in the figure as arrows pointing from the modeling artifacts to corresponding concepts in the Metamodel Ontology. Further, the appropriate properties (e.g. from_entity and to_entity) allow expressing the *model structure*.

On the other hand, the Domain Ontology provides for the explication of the semantic of the *domain terms* used as labels in the model (*domain semantics*). In Fig. 2 these annotations appear as arrows pointing from the labels "Tutorial" and "Lecture" to the corresponding concepts in the Domain Ontology.

Overall the result is a semantically annotated model holding all the information about modeling artifacts, model structure and domain semantics of a particular model instance. Accordingly a substantial part[3] of the model contained information is available in a machine readable form allowing further automatic processing.

---

[3] Obviously, in the given example a complete representation of the model contained information is not reached. On the one hand, the cardinality information is not (yet) handled in the Metamodel Ontology and therefore no annotation of the cardinality of the "belongs_to" relation is recorded. On the other hand, the label "belongs_to" also bears no annotation (yet). However, even with this incomplete coverage of all model details, it is possible to process the annotations and harness the externalized information.

4.1 Requirements

A solution using metamodel and domain ontology for the purpose of comprehensive model externalization has to fulfill certain requirements. These requirements are derived from the problem description presented in section 2 and formulated as follows:

- R1: The solution facilitates the reconciliation of different views on the enterprise. It is not specific to a certain view, e.g. to process models only.
- R2: The solution offers a means to overcome different levels of abstraction and to express that some (part of a) model is semantically related to some other more general or more specific (part of a) model.
- R3: Enterprise models are described in terms of different modeling languages. Therefore, the solution must consider multiple modeling languages and their metamodels and be extensible with respect to additional modeling languages respectively metamodels.
- R4: The system represents the model contained information in a machine readable manner and enables the application of formal analysis methods (like reasoning). In order to assure the applicability of available state of the art technology, the system processes ontologies in some standard ontology language (e.g. OWL[4]).
- R5: The system enables the user to create new semantic annotations, and to view and/or edit existing ones.
- R6: The semantic annotation is not an end in itself. Based on the provided annotation the system discovers inter-model relations and supports their adequate visualization.

4.2 Enterprise Model Reconciliation Methodology

The proposed method works on models represented as individuals of an ontology describing the concepts of its metamodel (*metamodel ontology*). According to Requirement R3 for each modeling language under consideration the systems holds the corresponding metamodel ontology. Then the line of action is the following:

1. The enterprise models to be analyzed are stored as individuals of the respective metamodel ontology.
4. The semantic annotation of the models is performed. Based on the state of the art methods ([33] presents a survey) annotation candidates are presented to the user, who can accept, modify or reject the proposed annotations. He can also add further annotations manually. The annotations are stored according to a predefined syntax, the so called annotation scheme [24],[25] or annotation (structure) model [16].
5. The analysis process is executed. The result is presented in a Matrix Browser [34] (see Fig. 6), where for a pair of models their relations are visualized in a user-friendly way.

---

[4] See http://www.w3.org/TR/owl2-overview/

5 Method Demonstration

We tested the method in the context of the evaluation of the Campus Management Software of the University of Oldenburg. The aim was to reconcile the process models (business perspective) with the data model (technical perspective) of the application. We use this case to explain the proposed method.

Suppose one of the processes to be supported by the Campus Management Software concerns the preparation of a teaching activity report. According to the university's administration policies every lecturer has to provide such a report at the end of the term. To collect the data the lecture has to determine the courses he has taught and the theses he has supervised in the term under report. Fig. 3 holds the description of this simple process represented as Event-driven Process Chain (EPC) [35].

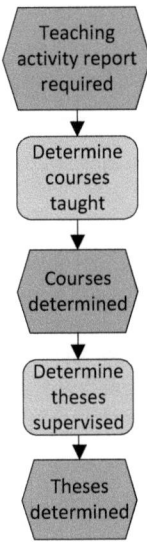

Fig. 3. EPC of the teaching activity report preparation

The question is whether the Campus Management Software holds all the data required to prepare the teaching activity report. In order to find the answer the data model of the system is considered. Fig. 4 shows the relevant (in this case minimal) fragment of the data model.

Fig. 4. ER representing a fragment of the campus management software data model

Now consider Fig. 5 which illustrates some basic semantic annotations of the two models relating the terminology to a domain ontology. In this use case demonstration it suffices to concentrate on the domain semantics of the model labels. The annotation

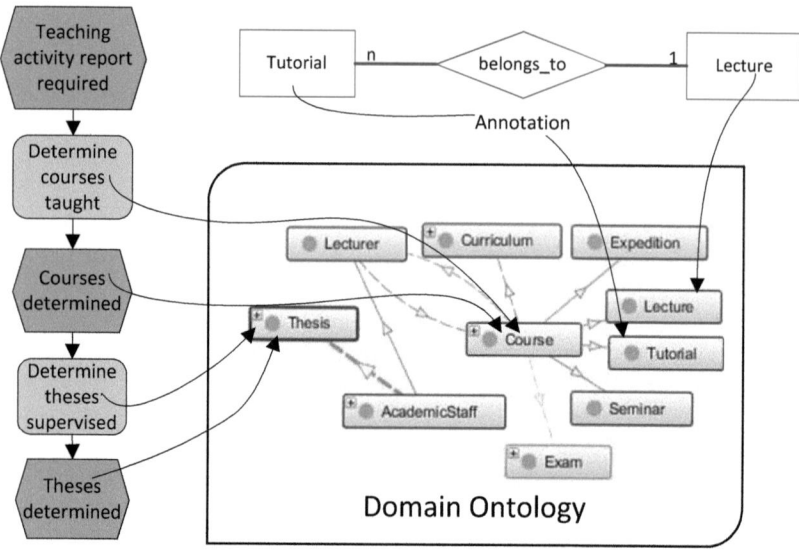

Fig. 5. Semantic annotations of the EPC and ER models

of modeling constructs with respect to a metamodel ontology is therefore neglected in the example.

In Fig. 5 the following annotations are symbolized by an arrow pointing from a term in a modeling artifact label to a term in the domain ontology. There are four annotations from the EPC model (on the left hand side) connecting the terms "courses" and "theses" to the equivalent terms in the ontology and two annotations from the ER diagram (at the top) externalizing the relation between the entity labels "Tutorial" and "Lecture" and the corresponding concepts in the ontology.

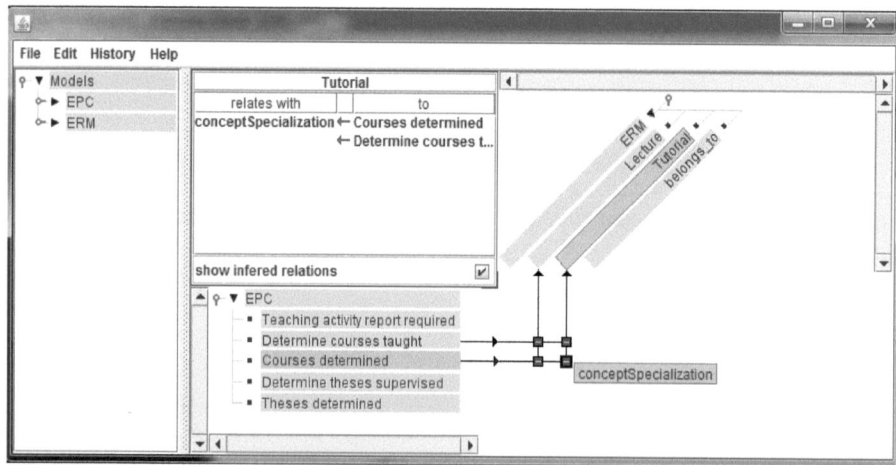

Fig. 6. Inter-model relations visualized in the Matrix Browser

Based on the provided annotations it is possible to relate the two models. The result of this analysis can be visualized as depicted in Fig. 6 in the Matrix Browser [34]. There, the ER model appears horizontally in a tree form with the root node ERM, while the process model is shown in the tree with the root node (EPC). According to the domain ontology "Lecture" and "Tutorial" are two specializations of the concept "Course". Hence the system reveals the semantic relation between the function "Determine courses taught" and the event "Courses determined" of the EPC and the entities "Lecture" and "Tutorial" of the ERM fragment. From the result of the analysis the user can extract two relevant facts:

1. As for the courses taught by some lecturer, the relevant information is covered in the data schema fragment of the Campus Management Software.
2. The data schema fragment does not provide the required information about supervision of theses.

With this result at hand it is now possible to answer the initial question whether the Campus Management Software holds all the data required to prepare the teaching activity report.

Clearly, in the case of two simple and limited models, such an analysis can be done manually without any problem. However in more realistic settings, where we have to deal with a bundle of complex models, the possibility of automatic analysis of inter-model obviously is favorable.

6 Discussion and Outlook

The approach proposed in this paper is based upon a combination of metamodel information and semantic annotation linking enterprise models to domain ontologies. The result is the explicit and machine readable representation of the models under consideration. Therefore, from the implementation of the proposed method the authors expect:

- A better model documentation and improved readability for the human user.
- Enhanced automatic model analysis possibility with respect to different criteria, e.g. consistency of the models.
- Qualitative and quantitative model comparison possibility. E.g. the question: Which percentage of one model is covered by another model?
- Inter-model navigation possibility based on the discovered inter-model links.

While the method demonstration in section 5 highlights the annotations between models and the domain ontology, the metamodel related information remains unused. As the instantiation of the metamodel ontology explicates the modeling artifacts and model structure, also this kind of information facilitates further examination.

The work presented here is ongoing, therefore advanced case studies have to be conducted and the evaluation performed yet. Next steps include the implementation of a prototype and experiments with realistic model instances. One critical point which needs special attention in this context is the user interaction in the semi-automatic annotation process. On the one hand, it is desirable to limit the user involvement to the minimum. On the other hand, the quality of the annotation can be expected to increase with stronger user involvement.

Another critical question is the availability of appropriate ontologies. While the elaboration of the metamodel ontologies appears a minor issue and partially is covered by the existing research in this field, it is clear that the required domain ontologies are possibly not yet been developed. This aspect is insofar crucial as it can be expected that the quality (i.e. correctness, sufficient level of detail, coverage etc.) of the domain ontologies has a direct impact on the result of the analysis.

References

1. Vernadat, F.: Enterprise Modeling and Integration: Principles and Applications. Springer (1996)
2. Fraser, J.: Managing Change through Enterprise Models. In: Milne, R., Montgomery, A. (eds.) Applications and Innovations in Expert Systems II. SGES Publications (1994)
3. Molina, A., Chen, D., Panetto, H., Vernadat, F., Whitman, L.: Enterprise Integration and Networking: Issues, Trends and Vision. In: Bernus, P., Fox, M.S. (eds.) Knowledge Sharing in the Integrated Enterprise. IFIP, vol. 183, pp. 303–313. Springer, Boston (2005)
4. Weston, R.H.: Steps towards enterprise-wide integration: a definition of need and first-generation open solutions. Int. J. Prod. Res. 31, 2235–2254 (1993)
5. Li, Q., Chen, Y.-L.: Introduction to Enterprise and System Modeling. In: Modeling and Analysis of Enterprise and Information Systems, pp. 3–17. Springer, Heidelberg (2009)
6. Chen, D.: Enterprise Interoperability Framework. In: Missikoff, M., De Nicola, A., D'Antonio, F. (eds.) Proceedings of the Open Interop Workshop on Enterprise Modelling and Ontologies for Interoperability. CEUR-WS.org, Luxembourg (2006)
7. Chen, D., Doumeingts, G., Vernadat, F.: Architectures for enterprise integration and interoperability: Past, present and future. Computers in Industry 59, 647–659 (2008)
8. Chen, D., Doumeingts, G.: European initiatives to develop interoperability of enterprise applications—basic concepts, framework and roadmap. Annual Reviews in Control 27, 153–162 (2003)
9. Ralyté, J., Jeusfeld, M.A., Backlund, P., Kühn, H., Arni-Bloch, N.: A knowledge-based approach to manage information systems interoperability. Information Systems 33, 754–784 (2008)
10. Li, Q., Chen, Y.-L.: Enterprise and Information System Architectures. In: Modeling and Analysis of Enterprise and Information Systems, pp. 18–65. Springer, Heidelberg (2009)
11. Chapurlat, V., Braesch, C.: Verification, validation, qualification and certification of enterprise models: Statements and opportunities. Computers in Industry 59, 711–721 (2008)
12. Davies, I., Green, P., Rosemann, M., Indulska, M., Gallo, S.: How do practitioners use conceptual modeling in practice? Data & Knowledge Engineering 58, 358–380 (2006)
13. Fettke, P.: Ansätze der Informationsmodellierung und ihre betriebswirtschaftliche Bedeutung: Eine Untersuchung der Modellierungspraxis in Deutschland. Schmalenbachs Zeitschrift für betriebswirtschaftliche Forschung (ZFBF) 61, 550–580 (2009)
14. Panetto, H., Molina, A.: Enterprise integration and interoperability in manufacturing systems: Trends and issues. Computers in Industry 59, 641–646 (2008)

15. Bailey, I.: Enterprise Ontologies – Better Models of Business. In: Tolk, A., Jain, L.C. (eds.) Intelligence-Based Systems Engineering. ISRL, vol. 10, pp. 327–342. Springer, Heidelberg (2011)
16. Liao, Y., Lezoche, M., Panetto, H., Boudjlida, N.: Semantic Annotation Model Definition for Systems Interoperability. In: Meersman, R., Dillon, T., Herrero, P. (eds.) OTM 2011 Workshops. LNCS, vol. 7046, pp. 61–70. Springer, Heidelberg (2011)
17. Liao, Y., Lezoche, M., Loures, E., Panetto, H., Boudjlida, N.: Formalization of Semantic Annotation for Systems Interoperability in a PLM Environment. In: Herrero, P., Panetto, H., Meersman, R., Dillon, T. (eds.) OTM 2012 Workshops. LNCS, vol. 7567, pp. 207–218. Springer, Heidelberg (2012)
18. Bräuer, M., Lochmann, H.: An Ontology for Software Models and Its Practical Implications for Semantic Web Reasoning. In: Bechhofer, S., Hauswirth, M., Hoffmann, J., Koubarakis, M. (eds.) ESWC 2008. LNCS, vol. 5021, pp. 34–48. Springer, Heidelberg (2008)
19. Lochmann, H.: HybridMDSD: Multi-Domain Engineering with Model-Driven Software Development using Ontological Foundations (2010), http://nbn-resolving.de/urn:nbn:de:bsz:14-qucosa-27380
20. Agt, H., Bauhoff, G., Kutsche, R.-D., Milanovic, N., Widiker, J.: Semantic Annotation and Conflict Analysis for Information System Integration. In: Hein, C., Wagner, M., Mader, R., Kreis, A., Armengaud, E. (eds.) Proceedings of the third Workshop on Model-Driven Tool and Process Integration (MDTPI), Paris, France, June 16, 2010, pp. 7–18. Fraunhofer FOKUS, Berlin (2011)
21. Fellmann, M., Thomas, O., Busch, B.: A Query-Driven Approach for Checking the Semantic Correctness of Ontology-Based Process Representations. In: Abramowicz, W. (ed.) BIS 2011. LNBIP, vol. 87, pp. 62–73. Springer, Heidelberg (2011)
22. Born, M., Dörr, F., Weber, I.: User-Friendly Semantic Annotation in Business Process Modeling. In: Weske, M., Hacid, M.-S., Godart, C. (eds.) WISE Workshops 2007. LNCS, vol. 4832, pp. 260–271. Springer, Heidelberg (2007)
23. Lin, Y., Strasunskas, D., Hakkarainen, S., Krogstie, J., Solvberg, A.: Semantic Annotation Framework to Manage Semantic Heterogeneity of Process Models. In: Martinez, F.H., Pohl, K. (eds.) CAiSE 2006. LNCS, vol. 4001, pp. 433–446. Springer, Heidelberg (2006)
24. Boudjlida, N., Panetto, H.: Enterprise Semantic Modelling for Interoperability. In: IEEE (ed.) 12th IEEE Conference on Emerging Technologies and Factory Automation, ETFA 2007, pp. 847–854. IEEE, Patras (2007)
25. Boudjlida, N., Panetto, H.: Annotation of Enterprise Models for Interoperability Purposes. In: International Workshop on Advanced Information Systems for Enterprises, pp. 11–17 (2008)
26. Vujasinovic, M., Ivezic, N., Kulvatunyou, B., Barkmeyer, E., Missikoff, M., Taglino, F., Marjanovic, Z., Miletic, I.: Semantic Mediation for Standard-Based B2B Interoperability (2010)
27. Fill, H.-G.: On the Conceptualization of a Modeling Language for Semantic Model Annotations. In: Salinesi, C., Pastor, O. (eds.) CAiSE Workshops 2011. LNBIP, vol. 83, pp. 134–148. Springer, Heidelberg (2011)
28. Karagiannis, D., Höfferer, P.: Metamodeling as an Integration Concept. In: Filipe, J., Shishkov, B., Helfert, M. (eds.) ICSOFT 2006. CCIS, vol. 10, pp. 37–50. Springer, Heidelberg (2008)
29. Kühn, H., Bayer, F., Junginger, S., Karagiannis, D.: Enterprise Model Integration. In: Bauknecht, K., Min Tjoa, A., Quirchmayr, G. (eds.) EC-Web 2003. LNCS, vol. 2738, pp. 379–392. Springer, Heidelberg (2003)

30. Gerke, K., Cardoso, J., Claus, A.: Measuring the Compliance of Processes with Reference Models. In: Meersman, R., Dillon, T., Herrero, P. (eds.) OTM 2009, Part I. LNCS, vol. 5870, pp. 76–93. Springer, Heidelberg (2009)
31. Favre, J.-M.: Megamodelling and Etymology. Transformation Techniques in Software Engineering. Internationales Begegnungs- und Forschungszentrum f. Informatik (IBFI), Dagstuhl, Germany (2006)
32. Guarino, N., Oberle, D., Staab, S.: What is an Ontology? In: Staab, S., Studer, R. (eds.) Handbook on Ontologies. Springer (2009)
33. Kalfoglou, Y., Schorlemmer, M.: Ontology Mapping: The State of the Art. In: Kalfoglou, Y., Schorlemmer, M., Sheth, A., Staab, S., Uschold, M. (eds.) Semantic Interoperability and Integration, Internationales Begegnungs- und Forschungszentrum fuer Informatik (IBFI), Schloss Dagstuhl, Germany (2005)
34. Ziegler, J., Kunz, C., Botsch, V.: Matrix browser: visualizing and exploring large networked information spaces. In: CHI 2002 Extended Abstracts on Human Factors in Computing Systems, pp. 602–603. ACM, New York (2002)
35. Scheer, A.-W.: Aris - Business Process Modeling. Springer (2000)

Author Index

Allen, M. David   91
Almeida, João Paulo A.   198
Antonescu, Alexandru-Florian   131

Bounabat, Bouchaib   186
Braun, Torsten   131
Bui, Duc Viet   50
Buschle, Markus   104

Chapman, Adriane   91

Da Silva, Catarina Ferreira   77

El Haoum, Sabina   212
Elmir, Badr   186

Falbo, Ricardo de Almeida   198
Figay, Nicolas   77
Frank, Ulrik   104

Ghodous, Parisa   77

Hahn, Axel   212
Han, Yanyan   22

Iacob, Maria Eugenia   50, 118

Johnson, Pontus   104, 118

Khalfallah, Malik   77
Kutvonen, Lea   6, 158

Ladhe, Tobias   118
Lartigau, Jorick   36
Liu, Shijun   22

Magnusson, Christer   118
Meng, Xiangxu   22
Mintsi, Theano   131

Nardi, Julio Cesar   198
Nie, Lanshun   36

Reichert, Manfred   4
Rosenthal, Arnon   91
Ruohomaa, Sini   158

Seligman, Len   91
Shahzad, Khurram   104
Soley, Richard Mark   1

Taoudi, Abderrahim   186
Thoma, Matthias   131
Trajanović, Miroslav   65

Ullberg, Johan   104

Välja, Margus   118
van Sinderen, Marten   50, 118
Versendaal, Johan   145

Wang, Xianzhi   172
Wang, Zhongjie   172
Wu, Lei   22

Xu, Xiaofei   36, 172

Zarghami, Alireza   50
Zdravković, Milan   65
Zhan, Dechen   36
Zoet, Martijn   145

MIX
Papier aus verantwortungsvollen Quellen
Paper from responsible sources
FSC® C105338

If you have any concerns about our products,
you can contact us on
ProductSafety@springernature.com

In case Publisher is established outside the EU,
the EU authorized representative is:
Springer Nature Customer Service Center GmbH
Europaplatz 3, 69115 Heidelberg, Germany

Printed by Libri Plureos GmbH
in Hamburg, Germany